THE RISE OF SOCIALISM IN BRITAIN

c. 1881–1951

SUTTON STUDIES IN MODERN BRITISH HISTORY

General Editor: Keith Laybourn
Professor of History, University of Huddersfield

1. The Rise of Socialism in Britain, *c.* 1881–1951
   Keith Laybourn

2. Workhouse Children: Infant and Child Paupers under the Worcestershire Poor Law, 1780–1871
   Frank Crompton

3. Social Conditions, Status and Community, *c.* 1860–1920
   edited by *Keith Laybourn*

Forthcoming Titles

The National Union of Mineworkers and British Politics, 1944–1995
Andrew J. Taylor

The Age of Unease: Government and Reform in Britain, 1782–1832
Michael Turner

SUTTON STUDIES IN MODERN BRITISH HISTORY

THE RISE OF SOCIALISM IN BRITAIN
c. 1881–1951

KEITH LAYBOURN

First published in 1997 by
Sutton Publishing Limited · Phoenix Mill
Thrupp · Stroud · Gloucestershire · GL5 2BU

British Library Cataloguing in Publication Data
A catalogue record for this book is available from the British Library

ISBN 0 7509 1340 1 (hardback)
ISBN 0 7509 1341 X (paperback)

*Cover illustration: Clement Attlee speaking at a peace demonstration,
Cathays Park, Cardiff, August 1936 (The Hulton Getty Picture
Collection Limited)*

To my wife, Julia Mary Laybourn

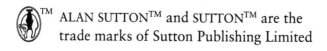 ALAN SUTTON™ and SUTTON™ are the
trade marks of Sutton Publishing Limited

Typeset in 11/14pt Sabon.
Typesetting and origination by
Sutton Publishing Limited.
Printed in Great Britain by
Hartnolls, Bodmin, Cornwall.

CONTENTS

ACKNOWLEDGEMENTS

Many people have helped me in the development of the research and reading which led to the publication of this book. Pride of place must go to Jack Reynolds (1915–88) who first taught me about the history of the Independent Labour Party. In addition, there have been many academics, librarians and archivists to whom I owe a great debt. In particular, I must recognise the late David James, the Bradford Archivist, for his help in locating ILP, Labour Party and trade union records and Martin Crick, with whom I have had many constructive debates on socialism ever since he enrolled as an MA student at Huddersfield Polytechnic, now the University of Huddersfield, in January 1977. I would also like to thank Steven Bird, Archivist at the National Museum of Labour History, Manchester, who allowed me access to the Labour Party records and the records of the Communist Party of Great Britain; the staff of the British Library of Political and Economic Science who have provided me with access to the Francis Johnson Collection and many other collections of records; and the staff of the archives section of the Library of the University of Liverpool for access to the J.B. Glasier papers.

ABBREVIATIONS

ASE	Amalgamated Society of Engineers
ASRS	Amalgamated Society of Railway Servants
BAIU	British Advocates of Industrial Unionism
BSP	British Socialist Party
BUF	British Union of Fascists
CLPD	Campaign for Labour Party Democracy
CPGB	Communist Party of Great Britain
GMWU	General and Municipal Workers' Union
ILP	Independent Labour Party
IWW	Industrial Workers of the World
LEA	Labour Electoral Association
LRC	Labour Representation Committee
NAC	National Administrative Council (of the ILP)
NATO	North Atlantic Treaty Organization
NEC	National Executive Committee (of the Labour Party)
NFRB	New Fabian Research Bureau
NHS	National Health Service
NGL	National Guilds' League
NSSWCM	National Shop Stewards' and Workers' Committee Movement
NUR	National Union of Railwaymen
NUWCM	National Unemployed Workers' Committee Movement
PLP	Parliamentary Labour Party
SDF	Social Democratic Federation
SDP	Social Democratic Party
SLL	Socialist Labour League
SLP	Socialist Labour Party
SPGB	Socialist Party of Great Britain
TGWU	Transport and General Workers' Union
TUC	Trades Union Congress
UDC	Union of Democratic Control
WEC	War Emergency Committee

INTRODUCTION

The collapse of the Soviet Union, the consequent decline of the Communist Party of Great Britain (CPGB) and the Labour Party's recent retreat from Clause Four as the new leadership attempts to attract the voters, have meant that traditional British socialism, although not necessarily Labour politics, is now in decline as the credibility of any socialist alternative to capitalism has disappeared. This situation is in sharp contrast to the emergence of socialism in the years between 1881 and 1951. Although socialism, of all forms, remained a minority interest throughout these seventy years there was growing confidence that it would be established, in some form, in Britain. In the 1880s and 1890s most socialists believed in its imminence. By the end of the First World War socialism's success was not immediately apparent but, through the growth of the Labour Party, which adopted Clause Four in its constitution in 1918 committing it to the control of the means of production, and the activities of the CPGB, many socialists came to believe that it was only a matter of time before socialism would be achieved. By the late 1940s there seemed to be tangible proof that it had arrived with the creation of the modern welfare state under Attlee's Labour government. Although this was more illusion than reality, it appeared that a socialist Britain was at hand. It is this vital growth and development of socialism, over a period of seventy years, that is the focus of this study. Above all, it stresses that the parliamentary or social democratic approach to socialism in Britain became predominant because of the association of the Labour Party with the trade union movement which partly restricted its vision and made it incapable of breaking away from political orthodoxy and becoming truly innovative. While the Labour Party felt that its public ownership programme of the late 1940s, and its social welfare measures, gave the impression of 'mission accomplished' it is clear that its socialism in many respects strengthened capitalism by alleviating some of its major features. The weakness of socialist alternatives explains why many members of the Labour Party felt that they had reached the new Jerusalem in the late 1940s.

From the outset, however, one must recognise that the study of labour history has changed rapidly over recent years and that socialism is itself being challenged as a distinctive and meaningful term. While historians have written about the various types of socialist alternatives – the gradual and reformist parliamentary approaches, 'the making of socialists' and the Marxist alternative which will be examined in detail in this book – it is clear that even that assumption of socialism as a distinctive political philosophy and tradition is now being questioned. The challenge has mainly come from the broadly-based works of both G. Stedman Jones and Patrick Joyce, even if they do not agree with each other on points of detail and interpretation.[1] These post-modernist and post-structuralist works have challenged the primacy of class unity (with the emphasis upon shared experiences and patterns of consciousness) as being of central importance in working-class life and have emphasised the importance of language in creating the illusion of social reality, along with decentring and deconstruction – with their emphasis upon differences, diversity, fragmentation of thoughts and actions, complexity and nuance. To them it is power, political power, that creates its own reality. As Stedman Jones suggests 'it was not consciousness (or ideology) that produced politics, but politics which produced consciousness.'[2] To Joyce, such consciousness does not necessarily have to produce class antagonism for he believes that 'the term "proletarian" does not do justice to the range of experiences involved.' Indeed he argues that 'The vested interest workers and employers have in co-operation is at least as great as any tendency towards conflict.'[3]

These views have been greatly influenced by the closely-related theories of Jean-François Lyotard, Ferdinand de Saussure and Michel Foucault. Lyotard has written about the 'death of centres' and the 'growing incredulity of metanarratives'.[4] In other words, he rejects the imposition of the Eurocentric view of history as being something that could be applied to the rest of the world. Uniformity of experience should not be expected. Saussure suggested that there was no intrinsic link between the signifier (the word) and the signified (what it means). Therefore, meaning could only be derived from the entire system of language and thus from the power structure of society. Foucault, in examining theories of power, suggested that power is omnipresent and de-centred, dispersed through all social relations.[5] Indeed, he maintains that the less educated in society will be subject to the dominant forces of society, that knowledge brings power and that the author, in particular, has power for languge is a very precise weapon which can impose a new reality, even though there is no certainty that everyone will interpret language in the same way as the author.

Out of these related theories emerge the main differences between the modernist attitudes and those of the post-modernist and post-structuralists. The modernist schema of things suggests that knowledge creates power and the post-modernist approach argues that it is power that creates language and knowledge. Critics of post-modernism would suggest that the crude economic determinism of Marxism has now been replaced by 'linguistic determinism'.

More specifically for this study, the supporters of the post-modernist approach stress the populist notion of nineteenth-century politics and the sense of continuity in the language of radicalism and radical liberalism which permitted no sudden changing point in the development of the working classes and socialism. To them, the language may have changed but the forces and meaning are the same.

The recent works of Eugenio Biagini and Alistair Reid have tended to develop this reinterpretation of the relationship between class and modern British political developments from the early nineteenth century.[6] The fact is that they have attempted to establish continuities between Chartism and a long political tradition emphasised by Gareth Stedman Jones, and to extend it through the mid-Victorian period to the formation of Gladstonian Liberalism and to the rise of Labour and class politics. The suggestion is that class had its part to play but that there were continuities from the past and that populism, gender and other factors were also at work. In effect, what they aim to establish is the importance and continuity of 'plebeian liberalism'. They further maintain that these developments had a coherence and rationality in outlook and this was an 'authentic' representation of the personal interest of the working-class groups. In this respect it is Labour, which embraced 'state socialism', that deviated from the radical tradition of popular democracy and limited government.[7]

None the less, the post-modernists maintain that, as many Labour historians have recognised in the past, there were always overlaps between liberalism, labourism and socialism. Rewording the famous comment of Thomas Duncombe, in 1842, that 'Those who were originally called radicals and afterwards reformers, are called Chartists', Biagini and Reid take as their theme that 'those who were originally called Chartists were afterwards called Liberal and Labour activists'.[8] Indeed, they point out that although Gladstone believed in a minimalist state it was also the case that his radical programme for political and social democracy merged into municipal socialism.[9]

Biagini and Reid in fact challenge many of the explanations offered for the rise of Labour and socialism. They reject the view, allegedly represented by E.P. Thompson, of the sudden emergence of socialist groups and new unionism in the 1880s ushering in a new era and argue that there were no fundamental differences between old unionism and new unionism and emphasise that there was an older radical tradition which flowed into the Labour Party.[10]

Secondly, they dismiss the views of orthodox Marxists who are criticised for being far too deterministic in identifying turning points. They stress that there was far more continuity than Marxists would accept and far more support for Old Liberalism than is supposed. Indeed, they place increasing emphasis upon examining the timing and location of events.[11] Thirdly, they find the argument of right-wing Labour historians that the Labour Party was the latest manifestation of the trade union movement's involvement in politics more convincing, although they feel that this approach underestimates the Labour Party's political pragmatism.

Their viewpoint, then, is that there was moral coherence between the radical ideas of the Liberal Party in the nineteenth century and the Labour Party of the twentieth century. In effect, they see the Labour Party as the major party of twentieth-century radicalism.[12] They argue that because the Labour Party called its policies socialist it alienated many significant groups of middle-class liberals whose radical credentials were not that distinct from what the Labour Party was in fact offering.

This, of course, affects our understanding of the three main strands of socialism developed in Britain in the late nineteenth century. It also challenges the notion of a re-emergence of British socialism in the late nineteenth century and the distinctiveness of socialist ideas in Britain. Nevertheless, one ought to reflect that most historians of the Left have not been as deterministic as Biagini, Reid, Stedman Jones and Joyce would suggest. E.P. Thompson, Stephen Yeo, David Clark and many other historians have noted the varied cultural factors that played upon the creation of British socialism and the political Labour movement. They have accepted the impact of nonconformity and recognised, as did David Martin many years ago, that Labour politicians depended upon the traditions of the past.[13]

Indeed, few historians of the Labour Left would deny that British socialism owed a debt to the past. Parliamentary socialism, the predominant form in Britain, and its representatives such as Ramsay

MacDonald and Philip Snowden, drew from earlier radical, individualistic and nonconformist traditions. Even many Marxists would acknowledge a clear link between the Chartists and the socialists of the 1880s through the O'Brien clubs and similar organisations. Even those who stress the 'making of socialists' are prepared to hark back to an earlier democratic and radical tradition.

The recent work of Joyce, Stedman Jones, Biagini and Reid is offered as an alternative to the work of Labour historians of the Left who have attempted to explain why socialism emerged in Britain in a largely moderate and gradualist parliamentary form. The fact is that it is blind to many of their stated views, thus calling into question the validity of their view of the modernist and structuralist constructs that they attack.

SOCIALIST ALTERNATIVES

Socialism is an immensely variable political and social animal. Auguste Comte's Positivist ideas emphasised the scientific investigation of human societies and influenced the Fabian Society in its social investigations during the late nineteenth century, directing it towards gradual social reform. Sheer frustration at the gross inequalities in society, combined with a sense of radical and nonconformist outrage against authority, served to direct the social policies of the Independent Labour Party (ILP) towards collective controls to ensure that each individual's rights were properly protected and that wealth was redistributed. Trade unions, out to obtain a minimum wage and a forty-eight hour working week for their members, also influenced the type of socialism that the ILP developed. For the Social Democratic Federation (SDF), it was Marx's ideas, particularly relating to the theory of surplus value and the exploitation of the working classes by the employers, that combined with a rather idiosyncratic and radical set of policies to produce the approach to socialism adopted by Henry Mayers Hyndman and his supporters. Within these strands of socialism there were those who also felt that they could lead a socialist life with the egalitarian principles it suggested, even within a capitalist society, and spoke of brotherhood and fellowship. It was partly as a consequence of the amorphous and contradictory nature, that British socialism was fragmented in its policy and methods of securing social change.

How can socialism be achieved in Britain? This is the major question that has occupied the minds of both socialist politicians and historians who have attempted to assess the effectiveness, or ineffectiveness, of the alternative socialist strategies. Three major approaches have emerged: the gradual and reformist parliamentary pathway, the 'making of socialists', and the Marxist avenue in both its 'sit back and wait for the revolution' style and its more positive Leninist 'go out and organise' strategy. In addition, and cutting across some of these approaches, there has been the conflict of style between collectivist or statist socialists and individual socialists, largely over the issue of democratic and individual rights.

The parliamentary route way to socialism is based upon an alliance with the trade union movement and an input of Fabian gradualism which emphasised a type of national socialism and elements of Liberal Radicalism. This approach was advocated by the ILP, formed as a national organisation in 1893, and by the Labour Party which accepted Clause Four, and its commitment to public ownership in 1918.

As Pat Thane suggests, socialist gradualism was something of a recomposition of the variety of values evident within working-class politics, which developed in municipal politics before and while it was developing within parliamentary politics.[14] Duncan Tanner makes much the same claim for the Edwardian years.[15] Indeed, both stress the gradual, holistic and organic approach of many of the leaders of the ILP and the Labour Party. Thane, in fact, notes the importance of MacDonald in reorganising the working-class support for Labour in terms that recognised the past but added increments for the future, noting that there were no sharp discontinuities and conflict but gradual evolutionary change.[16]

It was the parliamentary approach that became the dominant form of British socialism with the emphasis it placed upon the nationalisation of industry and services under the supervision of impartial administrators by the early twentieth century. It combined with the trade union concern to raise wages, redistribute wealth and to protect free collective bargaining.[17] All these elements had come into place by the end of the First World War, and in the socialist planning exercises of the early 1930s, although the nationalising tendency of British parliamentary socialism reached its apogee in the late 1940s with the emergence of Labour's modern welfare state and the nationalisation of several key industries and services. Even then, nationalisation was restricted to only a small number of industries and services such as coal and the railways and was never to deal with much more than one-fifth of the British economy.

Some politicians certainly see the Attlee years as the apotheosis of Labour's planned socialist economy but many on the Left were less convinced by the nationalisation of industry and the creation of the National Health Service (NHS). Marxist historians have suggested that the

Attlee governments appeared vague and uncommitted to anything other than the nationalisation of industries and services and that this was the playing out of previous policies rather than the inauguration of a new period of socialist advance. There was, according to this criticism, little desire by Attlee to use public ownership as an effective weapon to control the economy. Indeed, to Ralph Miliband Labour's nationalisation programme was designed to 'achieve the sole purpose of improving the efficiency of the capitalist system'.[18] John Callaghan is similarly disparaging and argues that 'nothing that Labour introduced under Attlee had not already been advocated by non-socialists, especially Liberals but also Conservatives' and that the Attlee reforms were the 'end of a particular road rather than the first step in the construction of socialism, as the Left of the party believed'.[19] Indeed, Callaghan suggests that the 'Labour government used the colonies to protect Britain from the full cost of post-war reconstruction. This was social imperialism as classically defined.'[20] Yet these, and similar, views are hardly surprising coming as they do from historians and political scientists who perceive the parliamentary system to be an inefficient and ineffective means for achieving socialism. They recognise Labour's radical past but ignore the unique contribution made by Aneurin Bevan in creating the NHS, which reorganised the supply of medical provision rather than simply making the contributory system of demand more comprehensive, as William Beveridge had suggested. These views also contrast sharply with those of Kenneth Morgan who has emphasised the achievements of the Attlee government even if these evaded rather than resolved the 'beguiling vision of socialism in our time'.[21]

Labour historians have clearly played down the importance of the Labour government's nationalisation and welfare programmes and played up its subsequent abandonment of such changes after 1948. They have explored the reasons for Labour's failure to introduce socialism and Miliband, in particular, has pointed to the weakness of the parliamentary Labour Left as an explanation for the failure to implement socialism. They maintain that socialism failed because it cannot be achieved by parliamentary means. To Tony Cliff, the founder and leader of the International Socialists, which became the Socialist Workers' Party, there is no prospect that the parliamentary pathway will bring about the fundamental social and political changes he seeks. Instead he finds more hope in a powerful trade union movement, dominated by revolutionary intent, forcing change.[22] Others would not agree. According to Ralph Miliband socialism was a lost cause by the late 1950s because it could only have been fought for in the immediate wake of the Attlee years when the electorate was still sensitive and sympathetic towards it.[23] Tony Crosland, *The Future of Socialism* (1956) argued that socialism needed to go beyond Clause Four in a democratic society, James Cronin has looked towards pragmatism and a rather vague and amorphous commitment to establishing a more equal society, while Ben Pimlott has referred to the revival of socialist ideas and the development of social policies of equity.[24] To the last three writers, parliamentary socialism is still a viable proposition for socialism if it develops its policies to meet the changing needs of society.

These debates about parliamentary, or British, socialism raise a wide variety of issues, including the impact of Fabian thinking, the importance of the ILP, the influence of the First World War on the Labour Party adopting Clause Four, the limited internationalism of much of British socialism, the long timescale to achieving socialism adopted by the leaders of the ILP which, as David Howell has stressed, rendered them 'subject to conservative influences', the struggles about policy in the 1930s, and the challenge of the Keep Left Group and Bevanism.[25] According to Howell, it was not at all clear that parliamentary socialism, through the vehicle of the Labour Party, would be the British way to socialism until at least 1906.[26]

There is a second distinct line of development to socialism in Britain which contrasts with the progressive and parliamentary method. That alternative is the idea of 'making socialists'. It was most evident in William Morris's Socialist League, which rejected parliamentary means, and also present in the Clarion movement, with their glee unions and orchestras, the Labour churches and the ILP clubs. According to Stephen Yeo, it appears to have been important in 1896 when electoral considerations took over from the business of 'making socialists'.[27] Others would suggest that its roots lay in earlier political forms of radical politics and that it remained meaningful as a force until at least 1914.

Implicit in this approach to socialism was the commitment to a socialist lifestyle and a reluctance to identify with political organisations as such. Unfairly, James Hinton has played down this strand of socialism as a brief episode, or fissure, in British socialism which did little to further the movement.[28] Cultural activities, such as club life, socialist Sunday schools and Labour churches, seem to have consumed energy and direction just as certainly as did electoral activities. Behind this approach was a political commitment to Socialist Unity with the desire to bring into existence a relatively unified, if not united, British socialist movement. The amorphous nature of the Socialist League, of the 1880s, and the Clarion movement, meant that this vision of the mass of people leading the lives of socialists was never achieved.

A third strategy emerged with the SDF. Although the SDF tended to follow the lines set down by Henry Mayers Hyndman there were in fact several groups within it, including the O'Brienites, anarchists and trade unionists, all of whom had different objectives from H.M. Hyndman, whose preoccupation appears to have been to create a British version of the German Social Democratic Party. Quasi-Marxist in approach, acting as a propaganda organisation based in London, the SDF wished to act as a Committee of Public Safety awaiting a spontaneous revolution which it would take charge of, offering palliative measures in the meantime to further the cause of Marxism. This small and relatively ineffective organisation was frequently divided over the issue of trade unionism. Hyndman was ambiguous about trade unionism but generally considered it and strikes to be dead ends as far as socialism and class conflict were concerned, despite the fact that many of the SDF supporters came from a trade union background. From time to time, the SDF membership amended the SDF's official line on trade unionism but, in the end, Hyndman and his immediate supporters remained supreme until the international peace section of the party, by that time known as the British Socialist Party (BSP), forced them out in 1916.

As with British parliamentary socialism, the Marxist alternative was deeply rooted in the past. Recently, Mark Bevir has examined the early years of the SDF and established that some of Bronterre O'Brien's supporters were the dominant force in the London district that provided the silent majority for the SDF.[29] He argues that it is this fact that explains why the majority of the SDF stayed with Hyndman through the constant splits and fragmentation and supported his ambiguous attitudes towards trade unionism and palliatives. Generated in London clubland and the Manhood Suffrage League, the O'Brienite views supported the political approach to change which Hyndman had emphasised.[30] The fact that they were republican in politics did not seem to pose a problem since they had come to accept the need for collectivisation, the eight-hour day and public works for the unemployed. Effectively, they had come to accept Hyndman's views by the mid-1880s.

The SDF, in its various guises, was not the only Marxist alternative in Britain. The Socialist Labour Party (SLP) offered a more trade union approach to socialism while the Socialist Party of Great Britain (SPGB) offered a largely educational and propaganda approach to spread Marxist ideas during the early Edwardian years. Nicknamed the

'Impossibilists', neither of these two organisations was able to secure the support of more than a few hundred members each and the fragmentation of the Marxists reminds one of the *Guardian* article in the late 1970s entitled 'A Trot around the Left', which listed about twenty or so minor Marxist organisations in Britain. It was not these small splinter groups that were to make the pace as far as Marxism was concerned.

The SDF, or the British Socialist Party as it became, was to be the base of the Communist Party of Great Britain when it was formed in London in July/August 1920 and re-formed at Leeds in 1921. It adopted an entirely different approach to creating a communist society. Unlike the SDF's 'wait and see' tactics it adopted the Leninist approach of organising for revolutionary change and eventually targeted the trade union movement as its means of creating a mass socialist party in Britain. Nevertheless, its 'Class Against Class' politics of the late 1920s and early 1930s, which damned the Labour Party as the third capitalist party, did damage its influence within the trade unions and it is debatable how far it recovered its influence with its United Front and Popular Front campaigns against fascism during the 1930s. Most certainly, there is recent evidence to suggest that Communist influence within the trade unions and trades councils was larger than Callaghan and other writers have suggested, even if the number of Communist activists was relatively small and even if the Communist trade union policy of Harry Pollitt and Johnny Campbell emphasised trade union loyalty at the expense of rank-and-filism.[31]

Yet, was the Marxist approach ever a viable alternative to the parliamentary and gradualist route advocated by the Labour Party and the ILP? Inevitably, this raises a number of questions. Why did the SDF develop more powerfully in Lancashire and London than elsewhere? To what extent did the SDF depend upon the London O'Brienite influence? Why was it unable to capture the mass support of the working class? Was the Socialist Unity campaign of 1911–14 the last opportunity for an alternative type of strategy?

On the last question, the Socialist Unity campaign seems to have failed partly because the parliamentary ILP, the 'making of socialists' Clarion movement and the quasi-Marxist SDF found it impossible to subordinate their differences to the common cause but it is uncertain whether this situation was simply a product of the events on the eve of the First World War or whether earlier conflicts had made Socialist Unity impossible.

The history of the CPGB has been written by many writers, including L.J. MacFarlane, Walter Kendall, John Callaghan, Nina Fishman and Francis Beckett.[32] They have focused upon the reasons for its formation and asked whether it was the result of Moscow/Lenin's influence or the product of natural progression? They have also asked why the CPGB failed to make a significant impact upon British politics during the interwar years. Was it because it was a revolutionary party operating in a non-revolutionary situation or because it found it impossible to win substantial trade union support? Many other questions have also arisen. Why, for instance, was the CPGB ostracised by Labour politicians? Was the CPGB dominated by Moscow? What future has Marxism in Britain? How influential was Marxism within the trade union movement? Why did it change from the revolutionary to the constitutional, or 'British Road', to socialism by 1951?[33]

Parliamentary socialism, 'the making of socialists' and Marxism form the three main rival approaches to achieving socialism in Britain, even though they themselves were subject to their own internal variations. One can view these alternatives through their contrasting and competing organisations, which made all attempts to unite them in a Socialist Unity campaign from the 1890s to 1914 ineffective. Nevertheless, cutting across these divides is a broader perspective. W.H. Greenleaf points not to the split between Labour Party hacks and vigorous socialist proselytisers but to that between collective socialists, who were generally statist, and individual socialists, who were generally anti-statist. This conflict was evident within the ILP, syndicalism, guild socialism, and within the Fabian Society and Marxist organisations. Indeed, even the Labour Party was divided upon such lines for both Philip Snowden and Ramsay MacDonald, of 'the class of 1906', were much more committed to an individual approach to socialism than the more collectivist trade unionists.[34] Indeed, Snowden's *The Individual Under Socialism* emphasised that the individual would only enjoy freedom once state socialism was established and that the long hours of work and low pay of capitalism denied them any meaningful freedom.[35] Elsewhere, he argued that there were two salvations, an individual one and a moral one; the Christian religions could deal with the first and socialism, by which he meant public control, could deal with the second.[36] Not all individualists would necessarily have agreed with Snowden's balance of forces and interpretations, although many such as G.D.H. Cole and Harold Laski swung between individualism and collectivism according to the circumstances operating at the particular time.[37]

This conflict between individualism and collectivism became far more exaggerated in the 1950s. The attack upon Clause Four levelled by Hugh Gaitskell and Tony Crosland divided the Left and Right within the Labour Party in a basic and fundamental manner. More recently, Tony Blair's espousal of a more individual and less statist version of socialism for the Labour Party where justice and equity are more important than state control of industries and services has reopened the divisions between individualist and collectivist socialists.

It could be argued that the statist solutions have failed most spectacularly with the limited nationalisation of industry in the late 1940s and the subsequent retreat from this approach by Labour, as well as Conservative, governments. The way forward may be through the less statist approaches favoured not only by guild socialists such as G.D.H. Cole, but also by pluralists like Harold Laski in his pre-Marxist phase.[38] These debates were evident throughout the formative period of socialist growth in Britain and remain so today.

THE HISTORIOGRAPHY OF DEBATE

The socialist alternatives mentioned above have divided politicians and, often, politically committed historians who have been keen to explain how socialism could be brought about or why it failed. The following five chapters return to these themes but also examine the peculiar and more detailed issues of debate that have emerged.

Socialism in Britain re-emerged during the 1880s, albeit out of a deeply-rooted radical tradition. This was a decade when the number of British socialists increased from a few hundred to about 2,000 active members as a result of the development of the SDF, the Socialist League and the Fabian Society. There are many issues here about the reasons for the collapse of the Socialist League and the limited impact of Fabian socialism, which may have much to do with the amorphous nature of the one and the middle-class nature of the other. Yet the major question is: why did the socialist movement as a whole not do better? The answer may have something to do with the dominating nature of Henry Mayers Hyndman's leadership of the SDF. R. Page Arnot, Henry Collins and Eric Hobsbawm have been critical of Hyndman's ability to alienate fellow socialists with his anti-trade union sentiments, his intense nationalism and his narrow dogmatism.[39] Yet, more recently, such views have been challenged by Mark Bevir and Martin Crick who feel that Hyndman was much more a product of his time than is usually acknowledged and that he has been stereotyped into a myth. Apparently, Hyndman was never as dominant, and therefore as destructive, as is often supposed.[40] There is, however, sufficient evidence to suggest that Hyndman's policies, if not omnipotent within the SDF, were vitally important in forcing William Morris and the Socialist League members out and in deflecting trade unionists, such as Tom Mann, to other socialist organisations. The debate goes on.

The major formative period of socialist expansion in Britain occurred between 1890 and 1918, and it is one riddled with arguments. There are five main debates here. Historians have asked the question: why did the Independent Labour Party develop so effectively in the early 1890s and again in the decade before the First World War? Was its growth because of its attachment to the local trade union movements, as many historians such as Jeff Hill, Keith Laybourn, Jack Reynolds, Pat Dawson and others suggest, or because of the club life and cultural activities which sustained the movement as David Clark and David James maintain?[41] In this debate it is interesting to note how all the leading ILP figures who could be were members of local trade unions, even in areas such as David Clark's Colne Valley constituency.

The issue of support for the ILP has also taken on a second dimension in an argument between those, such as Duncan Tanner, who play down the political breakthrough made by the ILP and the Labour Party, and others who suggest that the ILP and Labour were breaking through on a wider political front.[42] David Howell, in a more balanced account, suggests that there were wide regional and local variations in ILP support but that there were some significant areas of success.[43]

The success of the Labour Party, influenced if not dominated by socialists, in these years has also been the subject of much controversy. While Liberal historians, such as Trevor Wilson, P.F. Clarke and Michael Bentley, play down Labour's growth, suggesting that it replaced the Liberal Party because of the division between the Asquith and Lloyd George Liberals during the First World War and the fixity of the Liberal mind, many others, including Ross McKibbin, argue that the Labour Party captured the support of the trade unions and thus the working classes.[44] In other words, class politics was responsible for Labour's growth and success. The fact that in 1909 the Labour Party had well over one million trade union supporters of the three million trade union members affiliated to it, and was gathering pace, suggests that its political breakthrough had occurred just at a time when there was a rising tide of municipal and local political successes.

The fate of both the SDF and the Socialist Unity campaigns has also produced a flurry of publications. Why did the SDF lead such a fitful existence between 1890 and 1914? Why was Socialist Unity not achieved and was it ever a realistic possibility after the formation of the LRC in

1900. The fate of the SDF, and the reason for its fitful existence, has already been mentioned in relation to the character of Hyndman. Yet there is also the question of why Lancashire and London alone remained the strongholds of the SDF. Crick suggests that the SDF's strength reflected its effort and Hill notes that in Lancashire the SDF was influential because it ignored the dictates of the national SDF, operated with the trade unions and the ILP, and because branches often remained within the local LRC despite the departure of the national organisation from the LRC in 1901. The matter of Socialist Unity is more problematic.

Stephen Yeo feels that Socialist Unity became impossible after the mid-1890s, David Howell suggests that it became unlikely after 1900 or 1905, while Martin Crick argues that it remained a viable alternative to the Labour Party and the ILP until the eve of the First World War.[45] Keith Laybourn suggests that given the opposition of the ILP, and allowing for the fact that Hyndman wanted any Socialist Unity party to be an extension of the SDF, it seems unlikely that it could have ever occurred.[46] Indeed, there was strong opposition to Socialist Unity from the ILP in the West Riding of Yorkshire and Jeff Hill has noted that there were problems arising from the dual membership of the ILP and the SDF that occurred in Lancashire which would have made Socialist Unity difficult.

Given that it was the Labour Party that was becoming the mass party of the working classes, that it contained socialists and needed to distinguish itself from the Liberal Party, it is perhaps not surprising that one of the major themes of this book is the way in which the Labour Party came to accept Clause Four during the First World War. There are other debates at play, most obviously those concerned with the impact of the Russian Revolutions upon the growth of Marxism in Britain and the declining fortunes of the ILP, which was far from being the pacifist party it is often made out to be.[47] Yet it is Clause Four that takes the limelight. While J.M. Winter suggests that it was a product of the war which forced the Labour Party to sift through the socialist policies to find and develop a peaceful alternative to Bolshevism, a process which favoured the Webbs collectivist policies, Ross McKibbin feels that Clause Four was almost an irrelevance since the main purpose of Labour Party's 1918 Constitution was to formalise the control of the right-wing trade union movement over the Labour Party.[48] But Clause Four must have meant something to someone and Royden Harrison may well have offered the real explanation when he suggested that it was vague enough to gather around it adherents of different ideologies. In other words, it could both accommodate and conceal many different socialist interests and even be acceptable to non-socialists.[49]

The lack of development in socialism during the interwar years 1918 to 1939 form the basis of Chapter 4. It examines the reasons for the CPGB failure to become the mass party of the working classes and attempts to explain why the Labour Party did little more than specify which industries it would take into public ownership. There are few major historiographical debates here although there are four major areas where differences of opinion and new issues have emerged. First, John Callaghan does suggest that the CPGB's failure to develop in a significant manner owes a great deal to its inability to capture the support of the trade unions. This contrasts with a variety of other explanations of its failure mentioned previously and with Nina Fishman's suggestion that by the end of the 1930s the CPGB was moving to becoming a force within the trade union movement – a view also supported by Richard Stevens in his recent PhD.[50] Secondly, it is clear that the very fact that the trade unions dominated the Labour Party may have imposed limits and controls upon the extent to which its socialism could be developed within its organisation. The nature of this problem has been examined by Lewis Minkin, who suggests that the trade unions and the Labour Party operated in different spheres but within a set of developing ground rules during the interwar years. Thirdly, the collapse of the second Labour government damaged the political potential of the Labour Party just as certainly as it opened the way for the socialist planning exercise of the Labour Party in the early 1930s. Fourthly, new research by Pamela M. Graves suggests that Labour unity was threatened in the 1920s as the women's question came to the fore within the Labour movement, although the political debacle of 1931 subsumed the women's question in the quest for party unity in a period of political adversity.[51]

The Second World War and the immediate post-war years provide the setting for Chapter 5. It is clear that the wartime situation helped to create a sense of unity between socialists in Britain but that soon fell apart in the immediate post-war world when Soviet expansionism in Europe and the formation of the North Atlantic Treaty Organization (NATO) fomented the Cold War. Between 1945 and 1951 Attlee's Labour governments nationalised some industries and services and created the modern welfare state. The extent to which Labour's welfare provisions were the product of the wartime conditions and Beveridge has been hotly disputed, for, as already indicated, there is a conflict between those who see the modern welfare state being an extension of Beveridge and those who feel that it had some distinctive contribution from Nye Bevan and the Labour Party. On a wider front, the Attlee governments have provoked criticism from Ralph Miliband, James Hinton and many others, for their failure to introduce a comprehensive system of socialism and for their almost slavish loyalty to the United States. They feel that Labour's nationalisation was simply designed to improve the efficiency of capitalism.[52] Nick Tiratsoo is also not impressed with the overall performance of Attlee's post-war Labour government, which failed to come to terms with the industrial machine it relied upon for growth.[53] Generally, as already suggested, this is a point with which Kenneth Morgan does not agree.[54] On balance, and given the post-war circumstances which forced a financially desperate post-war Britain into the hands of the United States, there would appear to be some evidence that the Labour government did remarkably well given the immediate post-war difficulties.

The evolving nature of the relationship between the trade unions and the Labour Party has also come under great scrutiny. Lewis Minkin argues that during the Second World War many Labour figures felt that the Labour Party was being held back by the trade unions but that Labour's landslide general election victory of 1945 buried such sentiments for at least another three decades. This, of course, raises the whole issue, currently being addressed, of how to maintain trade union support for Labour and to involve it in the policy-making process without alienating public opinion which is often suspicious of trade unionism. Minkin suggests that the alliance between the trade unions and the Labour Party has never been easy although it has been essential for Labour's growth. Three questions arise from this point. Has trade unionism been a conservative force within the Labour Party, acting as the Achilles heel to Labour's socialist development and retarding socialist advance? How much power has the trade union movement wielded? What have been the objectives of its leaders?

The weakness of the Labour Left, in both its 'hard' and 'soft' forms, has also been blamed for the failure of the Attlee governments to impose socialism. Eric Shaw suggests that the years between 1945 and 1951 were 'relatively strife free' and that the Left was ineffective while Miliband generally feels that the failure of the Labour Left had much to do with the Labour government's failure to introduce socialism.[55] In contrast Jonathan Schneer accepts that the Labour Left was weak and fragmented but suggests that it, Keep Left and the 'hard' Left were not as quiescent as has been suggested.[56] Indeed, Keep Left was to form the basis of the Bevanite group of the 1950s, even if its own influence was limited in the 1940s.

THE ARGUMENT

What, then, is the approach of this book? The gist of the argument presented is that while socialism re-emerged in Britain in the 1880s it drew deeply from the past. As it developed there were three possible alternative routes to socialism before 1900 but by 1906, at the latest, it was clear that the parliamentary route would be supreme and that Socialist Unity campaigns would not be able to change this. Thereafter, the constant strengthening of the progressive and socialist alliance with trade unions both dictated, and limited, the pace of socialist advance in Britain, despite the operation of their influence in different spheres, and, in general, excluded Marxist and Labour Left influence from the wider British Labour movement. There was no dichotomy between trade unionism and the 'making of socialists', for the two movements could clearly be interlinked, but it is obvious that the majority of trade unionists identified with the Labour Party's parliamentary approach rather than with syndicalism, guild socialism or Marxism. There may have been communist influence within some trade unions and behind some strikes, as well as 'entryism' into the Labour Party, but by and large such influences exercised only a marginal impact upon British parliamentary socialism. In any case, any challenge to the Labour Party's policies was usually dealt with firmly by a policy of control and expulsion, which was brought to a fine art in the late 1940s by Morgan Phillips, general secretary of the Labour Party between 1945 and 1964, and best exemplified in his 'Lost Sheep' files. The fact that parliamentary socialism has been in retreat since the early 1950s does not alter the fact that it, with its essentially statist approach, captured the genuine radicalism of the British people in the 1940s. A less statist view will almost certainly emerge under the leadership of Tony Blair although it is not certain that the new Labour Party will be a socialist party in any meaningful sense of the word. Perhaps David Howell was correct in his assumption, made in the mid-1970s, that 'the epoch of social democratic control is drawing to a close in Britain' as the Labour Party emerges in modernising form content to operate a mixed economy.[57]

Thus, the main purpose of this book is to examine the reasons for the rise of British socialism up to about 1951 and to explain why it took the shape and form that it assumed. It will stress the predominance, if not omnipotence, of the parliamentary route throughout the first half of the twentieth century, with its trade union base, whatever its deficiencies.

CHAPTER

1

SOCIALISM IN THE 1880S

Unlike its continental counterpart, British socialism barely existed at the beginning of the 1880s. It was confined to some radicals of Chartist pedigree, in the Soho O'Brienite clubs, to a few people who identified with Karl Marx's International Working Men's Association and to a small number of socialists who were scattered among various clubs and organisations.[1] They numbered several hundred and carried little influence in the trade union movement and the organisations of the working classes which, in a political sense, were most closely associated with the Liberal Party and Liberal Radicalism. As Royden Harrison suggests, there were many reform organisations active in the 1860s and '70s, but most saw themselves as just that and were prepared to work with, or through, the trade unions, the National Reform League and similar bodies and did not identify with socialist groups.[2] Not surprisingly, in 1878 a despairing Marx described the working class in 1878 as 'the tail of the "great Liberal party", that is of the oppressors the capitalists' and Engels denied that there was any 'real labour movement in the Continental sense' in Britain.[3] Nevertheless, the position of British socialism improved markedly in the 1880s, even though the splintering of socialist organisations in the mid and late 1880s meant that the 2,000 or so socialists and anarchists were divided between the Social Democratic Federation, the Socialist League, the Hammersmith Socialist Society, the Fabians, and a number of local societies and individuals who were not attached to the national organisations. The SDF rose from 377 members in 17 branches in 1885 to 674 members in 40 branches in 1889 before plummeting to 453 members in 34 branches in 1890.[4]

Socialists had strengthened their position during the 1880s but it was clear that neither socialism nor Marxism had taken Britain by storm. Even the most prominent socialists were barely known nationally and socialism was deeply divided between personalities and over policy. This was most evident in the personal conflicts between Henry Mayers Hyndman and William Morris and in the rival policies of the SDF, the Socialist League, the Fabians and the anarchists. Neither Hyndman nor Morris could lay claim to a wide parish of support and their organisations were ultimately superseded by the Independent Labour Party, which emphasised the need for socialism to both capture trade unionism and fight for both local and parliamentary representation. The SDF's failure to capitalise on its emergence as the first modern British Socialist Society produced a dispute between historians about the extent to which Hyndman's dominating character was responsible for the fragmentation of socialism. Marx and Engels both disliked the organisation and many leading socialist figures left it in despair. Historians have equally debated the extent to which there were marked differences of policy on the issue of trade unionism, parliamentary politics and the international aspect of socialist activity. More recently, they have examined the reasons why the majority of SDF members stayed with Hyndman rather than joining Morris in the Socialist League.[5]

THE CLIMATE OF CHANGE

The 1880s was a watershed decade in British social history. It was a period when Britain was experiencing economic depression and deflation, unemployment marches in London, social surveys which highlighted the blight of poverty, and when a range of radical and Liberal opinion was asking what could be done to improve the quality of life for the working classes. Andrew Mearns produced *The Bitter Cry of Outcast London* (1883) which examined the conditions of those who lived in the London slums. Charles Booth began his enormous investigation into the *Life and Labour of the People in London*, the first volume of which appeared in 1889, which indicated that about 35 per cent of the 900,000 people in Tower Hamlets were living in poverty or were being driven to want. William Booth, founder of the Salvation Army, wrote *In Darkest England and the Way Out* (1890), which investigated the poor social conditions that existed in the rest of England in the late 1880s. All these revelations encouraged attempts to alleviate the suffering of the poor through a variety of philanthropic activities, such as the provision of cheap homes for the working classes by the Peabody Trust and through Octavia Hill's housing experiments. Joseph Chamberlain launched his 'unauthorised' radical programme in January 1885 to encourage the working classes to vote Liberal and issued the 'Chamberlain Circular' in March 1886, which advised local authorities to provide municipal relief work for the unemployed, thus implicitly accepting that unemployment was not a personal failing. In such a climate of concern and self-doubt in Victorian society is it not surprising that, as Stanley Pierson has suggested, many individuals began to question the society in which they were operating and their own personal position?[6]

Thus socialism began to extend its influence within a climate of social, economic and political criticism. Many new socialist groups began to emerge, although they gradually accreted to three major organisations, the Social Democratic Federation, the Socialist League and the Fabian Society. The first two of these were Marxist in orientation while the third was much more concerned with the scientific study of human society, with gradual reform and with working through the existing political system. Direction was given to some of their work by Henry George's *Progress and Poverty*, published in the USA in 1879 and in Britain in 1881, which advocated the 'single tax' on land rent, and caught the imagination as a result of his two successful lecture tours to Britain in 1882 and 1884. George's ideas drew upon the Radical assumption that land was capable of supporting all and that unemployment was, in effect, labour turned off the land. His ideas combined the idea of natural rights with the ideas on rent advanced by Ricardo and Mill and those of various land schemes. In effect, George's ideas became the basis of the view that land nationalisation would cure unemployment and poverty. George's influence was profound and Max Beer later claimed that four-fifths of the socialist leaders in the 1880s had 'passed through the school of Henry George'.[7] Indeed, while giving some direction to the SDF, his views and his 1884 campaign gave rise to the Scottish Land Restoration League.

THE SOCIAL DEMOCRATIC FEDERATION

The most important of the new socialist societies, the SDF, was formed as the Democratic Federation, following a meeting of London radicals at the Rose Street Club, Soho, on 2 March 1881. It became the Social Democratic Federation in 1884, although it was committed to socialism by 1883. It began as a Radical organisation on the fringes of the Liberal Party, despite Henry Mayers Hyndman's Conservative credentials, and pursued an eclectic body of policies and campaigns ranging from Home Rule for Ireland to land reform and the democratic reorganisation of the Empire. Hyndman gave the organisation a steer towards socialism when he read Marx's *Capital* and converted the theory of surplus value, which explained how workers were robbed by their employer of the value of the work they produced and provided merely with the minimum wage necessary for subsistence, to chapter three of his *England for All* (1881). Nevertheless, the original programme of the Democratic Federation emphasised the need for political reforms such as triennial parliaments, payments for MPs, equal electoral districts, the abolition of the House of Lords and manhood suffrage for all parliamentary and municipal elections. It also favoured the eight-hour day, several years before Tom Mann wrote his famous pamphlet on the subject, and advocated the nationalisation of land and railways, public housing and free education. It aimed to 'unite the great body of people, quite irrespective of party in favour of these principles of justice, freedom, and steady progress, which are now too often set aside to suit the convenience of factions'.[8] Yet its principal aim was to bring about a 'thorough reform of the present Electoral System . . . so that the working classes may be enabled to send their own representatives to Parliament'. It was also concerned to expose the injustices that went on in Ireland and Gladstone's policy of repression in response to the agitations of Davitt's Irish Land League, formed in 1879.

The Democratic Federation soon lost the support of the middle classes who were quickly detached by its hostility towards the British government's actions in Ireland. Thereafter, the movement became increasingly socialist in orientation. Hyndman was influenced by Henry George's tour of Britain in 1882 in which land reform and the 'single tax' became the focus of debate and was joined in the Democratic Federation by H.H. Champion, E. Belfort Bax and William Morris in a demand for land reform. John Burns and Harry Quelch, members of the working classes who were active in labour organisations, were also attracted to the movement and by the second annual conference, in 1883, the Democratic Federation had adopted nationalisation of the means of production and exchange as its central aim. It produced *Socialism Made Plain* (1883) which emphasised the need for land reform and noted that 30,000 persons 'own the land of Great Britain' and that they had got it by robbery and confiscation.[9] This assessment was in fact drawn from the so-called New Domesday Book, *The Return of Owners of Land* (1873) which was later publicised by J. Bateman in *Great Landowners of England and Wales* (1883). By 1883, supported by such evidence, the Democratic Federation had come to accept that these reforms were 'stepping stones' to the ultimate objective of the common ownership of the means of production.

There were numerous factions drawn together within the emerging SDF, most obviously Hyndman's quasi-Marxist section, based partly upon the German Social Democratic Party and a tradition of British conservative paternalism. There were the O'Brienite radicals, trade unionists, anarchists, intellectuals attracted to socialism and Andreas Scheu's Scottish Land and Labour League, which wanted affiliation with the SDF rather than fusion and the central control which Hyndman favoured and was anti-parliamentarian in approach, divisions guaranteeing that there would be constant conflict within the SDF and little semblance of unity. Indeed, there were to be many political breakaways from the parent organisation.

Until recently, the SDF has been ill-served by historians. An official history was written by H.W. Lee and E. Archbold, but this was a blatant apologia which concluded by arguing that the party disappeared because it was successful, its principles having been accepted by the labour movement at large and the Labour Party in particular.[10] Walter Kendall also provided a valuable study of its activities in the early twentieth century and C. Tsuzuki offered some narrative details of its activities through the medium of writing a biography on Hyndman.[11] Yet none of these books provided a comprehensive and balanced view of the SDF's history. Their shortcomings have been overcome largely by Martin Crick's full and detailed account of the SDF's national and local movements which has challenged the accepted views of its development and failures.[12]

It used to be argued that the SDF failed to exert much impact because of the obstacle presented to its growth and unity by Hyndman's dominating and self-publicising character, his nationalism and his anti-semitism. R. Page Arnot referred to Hyndman as 'the evil genius of the Socialist Movement'[13] and Tsuzuki tended to portray him in a similar light.[14] Eric Hobsbawm was less harsh but suggested that 'Hyndman's personality made it difficult for him to collaborate except with inferiors', that he was quirky and drove away many gifted socialists from the SDF. In the end

Especially, he cannot escape blame for the failure of the SDF to exploit its unique position as the pioneer socialist organisation in Britain. Engels' bitterness had good reasons. He saw the SDF throw away opportunity after opportunity in the 1880s when it had the field virtually to itself, he saw Hyndman alienate valuable supporters, and the major advances of the movement left either to Marxists forced to act independently of it, or to theoretically far more confused and undesirable elements. The 'new unionism' of 1889–90 and the triumph of independent working-class candidates in 1892 demonstrate what could have been achieved: but it was not the SDF who achieved it. Rather it hindered these achievements and in turn never fully recovered from its loss of initiative.[15]

Apparently, from Hyndman's domination sprang the SDF's hostility towards trade unionism as a means of bringing about change and the intensely nationalistic, patriotic and imperialistic policies of the SDF. As a result the SDF became immensely sectarian and was effectively a small élite of middle-class and working-class men, out of the mainstream of trade unionism in Britain and incapable of adapting itself to the changing political situation. Indeed, Henry Collins suggested that it was dominated by a narrow dogmatism due to the lack of Marxist literature in Britain and the contaminating influence of the German Social Democratic Party's Gotha programme, inspired by Ferdinand Lassalle, which displayed a distinct dislike of trade unionism.[16]

Stanley Pierson has also made a similar point. He argued that there were three strands (organised religion, the writings of Thomas Carlyle and John Ruskin, and the republicanism of Tom Paine flowing through to the utilitarianism of Jeremy Bentham and J.S. Mill and the secularism of Charles Bradlaugh) that formed the basis of British Marxism and that the problem was that Hyndman was influenced by Lassalle's national socialism which ran counter to the three streams that flowed into British Marxism.[17] Willard Wolfe, in his study of Fabian socialism, has also argued that Hyndman was largely out of step with the rest of the membership of the SDF in his advocacy of Lassallean state socialism.[18]

Such views about Hyndman and the SDF have come under intense scrutiny. Recently, Mark Bevir has suggested that Hyndman was neither a straightforward revolutionary nor an uncomplicated parliamentary reformer but reflected both contemporary Marxism and the sentiments of the old Soho O'Brienite section of the SDF.[19] In his two articles, he rejects the 'three streams' idea of Pierson. In the article focused upon Hyndman, he charts the history of radical conservatism as a distinctive intellectual tradition and the influence it exerted upon Hyndman and the SDF. In his second article, which examines the early years of the SDF, he maps out the influence of Bronterre O'Brien on the Federation. The two articles together help to dispel the impression that Hyndman simply applied the German scheme of socialism. Indeed, Bevir is at pains to present Hyndman's theories not as private ideas but as one facet of an existing political tradition. He represents Hyndman's radical conservatism as a lineal succession of ideas which originated with

Edmund Burke's diatribe against the French Revolution, through the work of Samuel Taylor Coleridge, Robert Southey and the ideas of both Thomas Carlyle and Benjamin Disraeli. He claims that radical conservatism had much in common with its liberal counterpart but, unlike the Liberals, felt that the Industrial Revolution had destroyed the old society without establishing a new direction. He suggests that the rationale of radical conservatism was to renew the paternal position, to alleviate the condition of the working class and to stave off anarchy. To Bevir, Hyndman linked his belief in radical conservatism with his belief in the inevitability of the collapse of capitalism. The continuity emphasised by some post-structuralist writers is thus combined with the distinctive changes put forward by many structuralists.

Bevir also suggests that the O'Brienites were the silent majority within the SDF who supported Hyndman throughout the Socialist League split in the mid-1880s. He notes that James Bronterre O'Brien (1804–64) believed that social problems have political solutions and could be dealt with through parliament. O'Brien also believed that since land was owned by the few, capitalist exploitation was inevitable. He felt that the way to rectify this situation was to introduce the political reforms of the Charter, particularly manhood suffrage, which would get rid of unrepresentative government and enable the people to eradicate poverty through legislation. The first piece of legislation would have to be a Land Nationalisation Act which would free the people from the tyranny of the landlord and the capitalist.

To Bevir, it was these views which dominated London clubland between the 1860s and 1880s. Such views were supported by Charles and James Murray at the Rose Street Club, and by Edward Dunn, secretary of the Marylebone Democratic Association, and James MacDonald, who was a member of the same. These views, in placing their emphasis upon political reform, were supportive of the views that Hyndman was reflecting. Gradually, the O'Brienites began to go one step further and accepted the collectivisation of the means of production, noting that social change also needed social solutions. Indeed, at a special meeting at the Anderton Hotel in January 1884 it was James Murray who proposed the resolution 'that this meeting of Socialists demands universal suffrage, proportional representation and the payment of members as a means of obtaining reduction of the hours of labour, socialisation of the means of production, and the organisation of Society'.[20] This extension into socialism cemented the relationship with Hyndman, and Bevir explains the transition of the O'Brienites from radicals to socialists in terms of the general economic conditions of the time which saw Britain facing deep depression.[21] When it came to the splits then, and most particularly to the one that led to the formation of the Socialist League, it is clear that the majority of SDF members, dominated by the O'Brienites, stayed with Hyndman, and Bevir concludes that 'In my opinion the bulk of the membership stuck by Hyndman because, like them, but unlike the founders of the Socialist League, he wanted political reforms to create a democratic state as a preliminary to ending capitalist exploitation.'[22] In other words, he feels that the split was not one, as Tsuzuki would have it, between those who would or would not support electoral action, or parliamentarianism, but between those who believed in political action as the basis of bringing about social reform and those who did not. The O'Brienites supported Hyndman because his political strategies were like his own. Hyndman was in tune with his movement.

Martin Crick is also critical of the stereotyped images presented of Hyndman and the SDF. He argues that Hyndman was never as dominant as is suggested, that the SDF was far less dogmatic and sectarian than is often supposed, and that it acted as an important training ground for socialists and carried more local influence, particularly in Lancashire, than is usually acknowledged. The 'SDF was not the highly centralised body it is often portrayed to be. Its branches were autonomous, its debates democratic and, as Hobsbawm points out, the party often ignored Hyndman where he conflicted with its fundamental orientation and eventually abandoned him altogether.'[23] Crick also suggests that the SDF was successful in areas where it put resources and that it was often prepared, as in Lancashire, to work with the trade unions and other political organisations.

There is much that rings true in the revisionism offered by Bevir and Crick although much of the assessment still remains open to debate. The debate about the origins of Hyndman's ideas hardly affects the outcome that he espoused the seeking of state socialism through political action and rejected trade unionism, even if there is doubt about the reasons for their approach. There is also no doubt that some of the old charges, of the autocratic and intensely nationalistic Hyndman, are still valid. In addition, Hyndman's character was still fundamental to many of the problems of the SDF.

William Morris said that 'Hyndman can accept only one position in such a body as the SDF – that of master: some may think that position on his part desirable; I don't and I cannot stand it.'[24] Eleanor Marx, writing to Karl Liebknecht in January 1885, stated of the Socialist

League that 'One of our chief points of conflict with Hyndman is that whereas we work to make this a really international movement . . . Mr. Hyndman, whenever he could do so with impunity, has endeavoured to set English workmen against "foreigners".'25 These views were echoed by many other members of the SDF who left to form the Socialist League in December 1884. The fact is that for the majority of the years between 1881 and 1916, Hyndman, supported by Harry Quelch and H.W. Lee, dominated the proceedings and actions of the SDF, even though there were several occasions when his political dominance was challenged and overthrown. It was his attitudes that dominated the actions of the SDF and this was most apparent in the case of trade unionism.

That the SDF failed to become a mass party must be put down partly to the failure to win substantial trade union support and the fact that such a policy was discouraged by Hyndman's hesitancy about trade unionism. From the start, Hyndman saw 'the trade union fetish' as the 'chief drawback to progress'.26 He was willing to support the demands of the trade union leaders for immediate reforms, such as an eight-hour working day, but was formally opposed to the alliance between Social Democrats and the trade unions for political purposes. Hyndman felt that an alliance here would be disastrous because the trade unionists were 'an aristocracy of labour, who in view of the bitter struggle now drawing nearer' represented a 'hindrance to the complete organisation of the workers which can alone obtain for the workers their proper control over their own labour'.27 Not surprisingly, the SDF followed the Hyndman line of reasoning in the manifesto it published in *Justice* on 6 September 1884, accusing the trade unions, not entirely unreasonably, of having concluded an alliance with capitalism, forgetting the existence of the class struggle, and catering to the needs of a few favoured workers rather than the masses who lived in misery. The trade unions were urged to understand that it was revolution, not reform, that was required. Also accepting the 'iron law of wages' Hyndman and the SDF suggested that trade unions could not influence the level of wages in the existing capitalist system. It followed that strikes were ineffective and pointless, 'a lowering of the flag, a departure from active propaganda, and a waste of energy'. SDF members were encouraged to explain to their fellow members that strike pay would be better spent on Socialist propaganda. This was the official line of the SDF throughout the 1880s and was reiterated at the 1889 Birmingham Conference where there was no reference to trade unions in the nine points of the SDF programme that was outlined. The fact that Hyndman and the SDF changed their views on the 'iron law of wages' with the emergence of new unionism did little to change their views, for trade unions still remained good things if they supported socialism and bad things if they focused upon industrial action alone.[28]

This lack of a positive policy towards trade unions was a fatal flaw in the SDF's political programme. Engels recognised this in 1891 when he suggested that the SDF was becoming a 'mere sect because they cannot conceive that living theory of action, of working with the working classes at every possible stage of its development'.[29] Tom Mann was similarly critical: 'I am convinced, however, that Hyndman's bourgeois mentality made it impossible for him to estimate the worth of industrial organisation correctly.'[30] The fact is that the lack of a positive policy towards trade unions and industrial action was to undermine constantly the position of the SDF in relation to other socialist groups, and particularly to the ILP. This issue cropped up throughout the history of the SDF and was evident in the case of the Socialist Unity debate before the First World War, which is dealt with in the next chapter.

The SDF's attitude to trade unionism was partly conditioned by the extracts of Marx's writings that were published by the SDF. *Wages, Labour and Capital*, which was translated by J.L. Joynes and serialised in *Justice* in 1884, the first volume of *Capital* partially translated in *Today* in October 1885 and the *Communist Manifesto*, serialised in *Justice*, were, on the whole, dismissive of trade unionism. The first two suggested that trade unions could have no more than a marginal influence upon wages and working conditions, although the third of these did suggest that trade unions could help to build up organisation. In a period of weak trade unionism when the collapse of capitalism seemed imminent it appeared foolish to assign much importance to trade unionism.

Crick is quite right to suggest that there were many members of the SDF who disagreed with Hyndman. As already suggested, Tom Mann was less than happy about the neglect of trade unionism, there was strong support for trade unionism among provincial members of the SDF and the organisation did campaign for the unemployed and help out in strikes in 1886 and 1887. Hyndman gave his help to the dockers involved in the famous London Dock Strike of 1889 but did not believe that their actions could bring about any permanent improvement. Yet one should not ignore the fact that Harry Quelch led a section of the SDF towards cooperating with the trade unions in the 1890s, to the SDF's first official pronouncement in favour in 1897 and its involvement in the formation of the Labour Representation Committee (LRC), an alliance between trade unionists and socialists, in 1900. This group began to suggest that trade unions embodied socialist principles and therefore supported them.

There was clearly heated debate about trade unions within the SDF. Hyndman was in a clash at the SDF's 1894 Conference, where he fought against allowing trade unions to attend the International Congress to be held in London in 1896.[31] His views were rejected by J. Hunter Watts. Despite Hyndman's victory the 1896 SDF Conference heard Wilhelm Liebknecht praise British trade unionism, and this led to the delegates present at the 1897 Conference advocating that SDF members should join trade unions and demand their political support. In any case, there was much trade union support for the SDF in important industrial areas such as Lancashire, where there were many more political opportunities.

Nevertheless, the SDF, in all its political guises, retained the image that it was dubious about the value of trade unionism. Indeed, the issue of trade unionism, syndicalism and industrial action was to later divide the BSP (dominated by the old SDF/SDP) on the eve of the First World War.

The dominance of Hyndman and the political and industrial attitudes which the SDF projected meant that in the 1880s it carried little political support. The SDF's main stronghold was London where it had significant influence upon the London Trades Council, in the Gasworkers' Union through Will Thorne and on the local democratic institutions such as boards of guardians and school boards. There was even a joint council of the ILP and the SDF to deal with unemployment.[32] Yet even here its impact was limited. The London Radicals reorganised as the Metropolitan Radical Federation in 1885–6 and many of them gravitated towards offspring organisations, most notably the Socialist League.

Outside London, it was Lancashire that dominated SDF activities. However, in the 1880s, the Lancashire branches struggled to survive. The Blackburn branch was, at one stage, reduced to six members and the Oldham branch collapsed. Otherwise, only Nottingham, where John Burns obtained 598 votes in the Nottingham West constituency at the 1885 general election (5.4 per cent of the vote), provided any evidence of significant support for the SDF.

The real problem was that in the 1880s there were tensions among the small group of London activists who dominated the SDF. Hyndman's patriotic concern about General Gordon's problems in Khartoum in 1884 worried many who had noted Hyndman's nationalistic tendencies. Others were alarmed that Hyndman, with the support of H.H. Champion and John Burns, was anxious to put forward parliamentary candidates to allow the SDF to benefit from the popular agitation that was occurring in the mid-1880s. Some felt that the SDF would look ridiculous if its candidates were humiliated in such elections while William Morris, and some, although not all, of his supporters, objected to the whole idea of parliamentary politics which they saw as corrupt and a threat to social change.

Faced with these concerns the majority of the SDF's Executive Committee left to form the Socialist League on 30 December 1884. The leaders of the new organisation were William Morris, Dr Aveling, Eleanor Marx, Ernest Belfort Bax and Andreas Scheu. They were joined by some anarchist groups. However, Joseph Lane's working-class Labour Emancipation League (formed in 1881 and committed to the belief that Labour was the foundation of all wealth and to nationalisation) remained a separate organisation.

These departures left the SDF very much under Hyndman's control and allowed him to pursue his 'step by step' approach to Socialism and his acceptance of palliatives, which involved the obtaining of £340 from the Conservative agent Maltman Barry, the infamous 'Tory Gold', to support the three SDF candidates in the 1885 General Election.[33] Not only did the incident bring the SDF into ridicule but it also produced no political advantage, for while Burns received 598 votes in Nottingham, John E. Williams received a mere 27 in Hampstead and John Fielding only 32 in Kensington. Morris, and the Socialist League, were appalled at this action and the SDF's political failures led to a decline in its already paltry support. As Lee wrote later: 'The effect of the disagreement arising out of the candidature was, in my opinion, worse than that of the split which led to the formation of the Socialist League, for added to the loss of members was the feeling of depression among those who remained.'[34]

The SDF recovered some ground in the winter of 1886/7 as a result of the demonstrations of the unemployed, its espousal of the 'right to work' campaign and the subsequent campaign to establish popular control of the Metropolitan Police which culminated in the Trafalgar Square Meeting of 13 November 1887, the famous 'Bloody Sunday' when two demonstrators were killed by the police and soldiers. This produced a temporary alliance between the SDF, the Radical Federation, the Socialist League and the Fabians within the compass of the Law and Liberty League. They held a mass demonstration of 40,000 people at Hyde Park on Sunday 20 November during which the mounted police charged the crowd and Alfred Linnell, a passer-by, was crushed by the police horses and died of his wounds twelve days later.

His funeral cortège was followed by 120,000 people, including William Morris, John Burns and Cunninghame Graham.

Popular agitation was a useful platform upon which to build support for the SDF but that renewed interest soon slipped away. There were several reasons for this. In particular, the antipathy of Hyndman towards trade unions meant that the SDF lost out to other socialist organisations in the North who worked with the unions before joining with the Independent Labour Party in January 1893. The international socialist credentials of the SDF were further undermined by its attitudes towards international conferences in 1888. In September 1887 the Trades Union Congress (TUC) had called for a meeting on the eight-hour day legislation. Two meetings were held on the same day in 1889, one dominated by the trade unionists and Paul Brusse, the French possibilist leader, and the other which favoured the formation of the Socialist International, supported by Engels and the French Marxists, led by Jules Guesde. The SDF went to the former, associating with the trade unionists it so much ignored, rather than to the latter to which the SDF ought to have been attracted.

By 1890 the membership of the SDF was in decline. Hyndman was largely discredited, other socialist organisations were emerging, the SDF's policy of palliatives alienated many would-be supporters and the northern parts of Britain were seeing the emergence of new trade unions and numerous small socialist groups which were not attached to the SDF. Despite the corrective work of both Bevir and Crick, it is still clear that the SDF was hamstrung by a leader with a domineering attitude, quirky views and an indolence towards organising for change, due partly to his assumption that the SDF would act as some type of Committee of Public Safety when the revolutionary moment arrived. The fact that Hyndman favoured political reforms as a means of bringing about social revolution might have endeared him to the O'Brienites but it must be remembered that this group represented only a small proportion of socialist opinion by the mid and late 1880s. Other socialist groups had emerged and, for a short time, the Socialist League looked likely to challenge the SDF for primacy within the British socialist movement.

WILLIAM MORRIS AND THE SOCIALIST LEAGUE

William Morris was, like Hyndman, a vital figure in the emergence of socialism in Britain in the late nineteenth century. Yet since his death in 1896 many books and commentaries have asked why he joined the socialist movement and have enquired about the precise nature of his contribution. Historians have speculated about whether or not he was a romantic, a utopian socialist or a revolutionary socialist in the true Marxist tradition. Early writers often dismissed his socialism as an aberration but E.P. Thompson, in his seminal work *William Morris: Romantic to Revolutionary*, raised Morris to being one of the finest socialist and Marxist theorists of his day.[35] Apparently, Morris's commitment to socialism was not an aberration but owed much to his youthful revolt and was reflected in his 'How I became a Socialist' article in 1894, where he described his hatred of modern industry, the destruction of art and the loss of hope for his socialist connections.[36] Thompson presents Morris as a Marxist, much as Robin Page Arnot did in the 1930s,[37] and an inspirational figure for many who wished to become involved in the 'making of socialists' and the promotion of Socialist Unity in the 1890s. The fact that he left the Socialist League in 1890 and that his anti-parliamentary and anti-state socialist ideas were rejected by the majority of British socialists does not seem to have diminished his importance.

Fiona MacCarthy's more recent contribution is less forceful about Morris's socialist commitment but, by examining the forces that shaped his life, comes to the conclusion that his commitment to socialism was not a temporary madness.[38] In attempting to uncover Morris as a whole, MacCarthy lays great emphasis on his background and the importance of his family and childhood. Apparently his socialism emerged, like that of Hyndman, out of Tory morality, and particularly through Charles Kingsley and Christian Socialism.[39] She argues that the balance of evidence suggests that Morris's life led him to socialism and that he was committed to revolutionary socialism of a Marxist kind.

These modern assessments seem fair and balanced in the light of the recent evidence. Morris, like Hyndman, came from the middle classes and drew partly upon the influences of conservative paternalism but the similarities ended there since Hyndman's policies and opportunism contrasted sharply with those which Morris developed during the mid-1880s. During Morris's early years he ranted against capitalism and 'Gradgrindism'. He particularly objected to the exploitation of the workmen and the loss of skill represented by the development of machine production. Influenced by John Ruskin, he also became involved in medievalism. He had been interested in medieval poetry but became increasingly concerned to support concepts of medieval art in architecture. In the 1850s, as a young architect, he became involved in the medieval revival and Gothic architecture. Heroism, beauty, high endeavour and love were now combined with a sense of nostalgia and loss at the removal of Gothic architecture and by their replacement with bogus or mock-Gothic machine-cut buildings. Leading the anti-scrape movement, against Victorian rebuilding, Morris focused upon the revival of skill and design. The 'savageness and rudeness' of Gothic architecture particularly appealed to Morris. He felt that every man had within him a slumbering creative power and maintained that labour must be creative labour, demanding intellectual, moral, physical and mechanical powers. This was required in the medieval world, but not in the nineteenth century. Where was their joy in making a cog?

From this background and interest Morris, the poet, craftsman and designer set up the Red House at Bexley Heath in Kent where he became involved with Rossetti, Philip Webb and Madox Brown. The last three formed the Pre-Raphaelite Brotherhood in 1848, a small group of artists who were determined to raise the banner against the art of their times. (The title represented a rejection of early Italian Renaissance art and a return to an earlier period.) Morris joined them in the mid-1850s and experimented with chivalrous designs and romantic medieval poetry, such as *The Defence of Guinevere*. A visit to Iceland in the 1870s sparked off his interest in Icelandic literature and produced *Journals of Travels to Iceland*.

Morris's political education began in the late 1870s when, convinced of the need for freedom and democracy, he helped form the Eastern Question Association when it became known that Disraeli had formed an alliance with the Turks, a sensitive decision since the Turks had committed atrocities against Christian Bulgarians. This was the first political commitment from a man who was a successful businessman, had set up Kelmscott Press at Kelmscott Manor, his Oxfordshire retreat before moving to Kelmscott House in London, and had established the Merton Abbey Works of Morris & Co., on the river Wandle in Surrey, where tapestries, chintzes, wallpapers and stained-glass windows were made. His financial successes became a constant source of embarrassment to him. None the less, Morris joined the Democratic Federation in January 1883 and remained an active socialist until his death in 1896. He carried many of his ideas into the SDF, the Socialist League and the Hammersmith Socialist Society.

Morris was a moral socialist. He believed, in utopian form, in the need to revive medieval architecture and work practices. He was also committed to genuine democracy and involvement which he felt would be best represented through cooperation and brotherhood rather than state socialism. Above all, he did not believe in parliamentary socialism, which to him was both undemocratic and reactionary, and maintained that it was essential to support workers when they were on strike.

Although he worked with anarchists he himself was more a believer in cooperation rather than individual anarchism, which he felt had no responsibilities to the community as a whole. His poetry and writings began to combine both ideas on medieval literature, society and craftsmanship with his new-found socialist ideas. This was evident in his *A Dream of John Ball* (1886), which took the form of a speech and discussion in prison by this medieval advocate of democratic rights.

Morris joined the Democratic Federation in 1883, and the SDF when it was formed in 1884, but left it and helped form the rival Socialist League, which was committed to the 'religion of socialism', in December 1884. By late 1884 tensions had been building up within the SDF, particularly between Andreas Scheu's Scottish Land League and Hyndman and his supporters. Others became contemptuous of the activities of the SDF and, in Morris's words, it was felt by many that 'the old organisation was not worth having'.[40] As a result the dissidents met and announced, on 30 December 1884, the formation of the Socialist League. They explained, in their manifesto, that there had been 'a tendency towards political opportunism . . . towards national assertion . . . to attempts at arbitrary rule'.[41] The new organisation took the Merton Abbey, Hammersmith, Woolwich and Leeds branches of the SDF, the Labour Emancipation League and the Scottish Land and Labour League with it and established a new branch at Norwich.

Morris became editor and the financial benefactor of *Commonweal*, where some of his writings such as *A Dream of John Ball, News from Nowhere, Chants for the Socialists* and *The Pilgrim of Hope* first appeared. These works provided the inspiration for many socialists who did not want to see the development of state socialism, although Morris's anti-state and anti-parliamentary attitudes became even more evident in *News from Nowhere*. This was published as a book in 1890 and offered a vision of a cooperative type of socialism in contrast to the state socialism offered by some socialists, including Edward Bellamy in *Looking Backwards*. Typically utopian, it envisaged life in London a century into the future where life and work were enjoyable, based upon good fellowship and cooperation, and where money was no longer required and medieval beauty was appreciated. As Guest travels around London he finds that he is not embarrassed because 'here I could enjoy everything without an afterthought of the injustice and miserable toil which made my leisure; the ignorance and dullness of life which went to make my keen appreciation of history; the tyranny and the struggle full of fear and mishap which went to make my romance.'[42] He found that the transition from capitalism to socialism came through industrial conflict and factionalism, and for this he drew heavily upon the disturbances in London in November 1887.

The Socialist League was a small organisation which peaked at about 700 members at the end of 1886. It lacked unity for it had gathered a disparate array of talents. There were anti-Hyndmanites, anti-parliamentarians, parliamentarians, educationalists and anarchists within its ranks. By the late 1880s it had become dominated by the anarchists. Their views went well beyond the collectivist, brotherhood and commonwealth approach that Morris was advocating.[43] Morris soon found that his control of *Commonweal* was being challenged and in 1889 he was forced to reassert that he was a communist and did not wish to qualify the term. He made it clear that the communistic life would be one of equality between men and one of brotherhood and not of 'an individual man doing what he pleases under all circumstances'.[44] Shortly after producing *News from Nowhere* as articles in *Commonweal*, Morris left the Socialist League. Thereafter, he became deeply involved in the work of the Hammersmith Socialist Society, which he helped form in 1891 in the hope that its public lectures would educate the working classes and provide a forum for Socialist Unity. Indeed, he was involved in the earliest attempt to encourage Socialist Unity in 1893 and was always identified with the ethical side of the socialist movement and with the 'religion of socialism'.

Rather like Hyndman, Morris dominated the Socialist League until the late 1880s and offered policies that were distinctively his own. He and his colleagues had formed the Socialist League in order to overthrow the existing system by force and felt that it would be 'a body of able, high-minded competent men, who should act as instructors of the masses, and as their leaders during critical periods of the movement'.[45] The Socialist League might act as a form of Committee of Public Safety, in the way in which the SDF saw itself acting once the revolution came about, but it saw itself as initiating that revolutionary situation and not simply idling and awaiting the spontaneous revolution while in the meantime advocating palliatives and reforms.

This difference between the SDF and the Socialist League was reflected in the conflict over parliamentary action. The SDF, as already noted, put candidates forward to contest parliamentary seats and took 'Tory Gold' to do so in the 1885 general election. Such actions appalled Morris who was most critical of the SDF's 'Tory Gold' scandal. Morris's attitude towards parliamentary action appeared strongly after the third annual conference of the Socialist League. In a letter to John Glasse he wrote that

I believe that the Socialists will certainly send members to Parliament when they are strong enough to do so: in itself I see no harm in this, so long as it is understood that they go there as rebels, not as members of the governing body, prepared by passing palliative measures to keep 'Society' alive. But I fear that many of them will be drawn into that error by the corrupting influence of a body professedly hostile to Socialism; and therefore I dread the parliamentary period (clearly a long way ahead at the present) of the progress of the party; and I think it will be necessary always to keep alive a body of Socialists of principle who will refuse responsibility for the actions of the parliamentary portion of the party . . . I repeat, the non-parliamentary feeling will assuredly not be represented entirely.[46]

Later in the year, Morris formulated his policy of abstention designed to prevent parliament swallowing up all effort and energy and to encourage workers to organise their own industrial activities, as in the case of the strike of the Northumberland miners in 1887. He had already informed John Lincoln Mahon before the third annual conference of the Socialist League that 'Finally, you must not forget that whatever open steps I might take, I personally would have nothing to do with politics properly so-called. The whole business is so revolting to a decent quiet body with an opinion of his own, that if that were the road, I should not be able to help dropping off it.'[47]

This was an attitude most readily understood by many of those who formed Socialist League branches in 1885 and 1886 and was particularly so in the case of the Leeds branch. It had been formed as the Leeds branch of the SDF in 1884 but on 8 February 1885 had decided to form itself into the Leeds Socialist League after a speech in which Mahon stressed to them that 'such a revolution involved the termination of political opportunism and State Socialism of the SDF and a full endorsement of the purely revolutionary propaganda to which the Socialist League was pledged'.[48]

Morris naturally gave support to trade unionists and workers who were involved in strike activity, and this policy seems to have gained wide support within the Socialist League, but he found himself in conflict with Mahon and many others who quickly realised that the success of socialism would have to come through involvement in both parliamentary and municipal politics. There were many members of the Socialist League in the provinces who agreed with this view, including Fred Jowett, later to become the first Labour MP for Bradford in 1906, who was one of the leading members of the Bradford Socialist League between 1885 and 1887. Some of these, including Fred Jowett, George Minty, James Bartley and Leonard Robinson, were to find themselves in the ILP in the 1890s.

As already mentioned, Morris left the Socialist League in 1890 and, with the 120 members of the Hammersmith branch, pursued his vision of socialism and 'the making of socialists' through their activities. He soon found that he had to compromise on his views and contemplate attempts to bring about some form of Socialist Unity with the prospect of some type of accommodation with the SDF. He also had to consider working with the middle-class, bureaucratic, non-class-war and institutional approach to socialism offered by the Fabian Society, the third of the major socialist parties which had emerged in the early and mid-1880s, as his own brand of socialism moved from the particulars of policy to a general commitment of inspiring and making socialists. There is little evidence that he ever approved of what he had always considered to be a rather arid and gentle form of socialism which played down the importance of class conflict.

Despite the obvious failure of Morris's movement, Stephen Yeo has seen his work as vital to the development of the early socialist movement. Yeo has emphasised how Morris was responsible for the Socialist League's 'single-hearted devotion to the religion of Socialism, the only religion which the Socialist League professes'.[49] He maintains that the 'religion of socialism' which Morris generated was not a backwater in the development of socialism but a vital part of the process of the development of British socialism between 1883 and 1896, until the demands of party politics consumed the time, energy and resources of the socialist movement. He records how forty-six people made their conversion to socialism, referring to issues of gender, class, background, geographical location, and other factors[50] and notes that they were free from constraint.

> Socialism in that period [1883–96] had not become the prisoner of a particular elaborate party machine – a machine which would come to associate its own well-being with the prospects for socialism. One of the most important (and unwritten) parts of the history of the mid-1890s is precisely the shaping of the ILP into such a machine against much resistance from below.[51]

Yeo argued that there was a sense of unity between socialist politicians and religion but that this disappeared in the mid-1890s, without Morris's resolute hand, as employers began to strike back at trade unions and as electoral politics became more important.

Yeo's views have been much criticised, not least because some of the agencies of the 'religion of socialism', such as socialist Sunday schools and the Clarion movement, did survive until the First World War. Yet the core of his argument is valid, since there was a rising concern for electoral success within the socialist movement, sparked off by its disastrous performance in the 1895 general election. Guidance in municipal politics electioneering programmes, for the ILP and other groups, was to be supplied by the Fabians, which provided the basis of the gradualist parliamentary approach in the fullness of time.

THE FABIANS

The Fabian Society developed from a group of spiritualists, social reformers and moralists who had set up the Fellowship of the New Life in 1883, under the leadership of Dr Thomas Davidson.[52] It was formed on 4 January 1884, out of a motion put forward by Frank Podmore which was carried by nine votes to two. The aim of the Fabian Society was to help reconstruct society and it reflected the sentiment of a number of lower-middle-class clerks, writers and officials that were adrift from Victorian society since they were neither workers, in the traditional sense, nor employers in business. They were the new middle class who identified with the sentiment expressed by William Clarke to Davidson when he wrote that: 'I am utterly at sea as any human being ever was. . . . This is a miserable condition to have no beliefs and to feel that there is no place for you in the world and that you have nothing to live for.'[53] They were concerned about the increasing evidence that British society was plagued with social problems and felt that they were powerless to determine an improvement. For many the Fellowship of the New Life was not concrete enough and so they found themselves creating the Fabian Society.

The Fabians have been described as 'armchair socialists' but in the 1880s they drew upon many different experiences and did not all sing the same political and social tune. With a membership of between about 150 and 190 in the 1880s, the Fabians attracted the full range of political opinions from Marxist collectivists to anarchists and radicals. Hubert Bland was a Marxist, had joined the SDF because of William Morris's temporary commitment to that organisation and enjoyed the 'exhilarating atmosphere of confidence' which Hyndman brought to socialism for 'The Marxist system, as expounded by Hyndman, with its air of pontifical infallibility, with its prophetic note of fatefulness, with its pose of scientific exactitude, with its confident appeal to history, is of all others best fitted to impose upon and impress the plastic mind of the uninstructed inquirer.'[54] Mrs Charlotte Wilson, one of the five members of the Executive Committee in 1884, was an anarchist. Sidney Olivier and Graham Wallas, both sons of clergymen, had rejected orthodox religions by the early 1880s and felt rootless. Wallas was a teacher and a university extension lecturer while Olivier held a post at the Colonial Office and was 'a pessimist by profession'.[55] George Bernard Shaw, who joined in May 1884, harboured Marxist sentiments before committing himself to land reform and state control. Annie Besant, the freethinker and secularist, joined in 1885 and Sidney Webb, a clerk at the Colonial Office and a firm believer in the impartiality of the bureaucratic state, joined in May 1885.

Shaw, Webb, Olivier and Wallas formed the Hampstead Marx Circle in 1885. It was in the meetings of this group, discussing Marxism, that these leading lights gradually drifted towards Fabianism, although along the lines already outlined in the early Fabian tracts. They discussed Marx's *Capital* and, according to Shaw, 'expected to agree with Marx' but changed their views when Shaw's Marxist inclinations were undermined by the Revd Philip Wicksteed, a disciple of the English economist Stanley Jevons, who in the October 1884 issue of *Today* challenged Marx's Labour Theory of Value on the grounds that labour could not be the sole determinant of value since differences in the fertility of soil and consequent land values could be crucial in determining the value of the commodity. Subsequently, the recognition of rent as a value not reducible to individual human labour began to dominate Fabian thinking and they were encouraged further in that direction by the work on land and rents by Henry George, J.S. Mill and David Ricardo.

Yet the Fabian philosophy emerged only gradually. Their first tract, *Why are the Many Poor?*, suggested that poverty was the inevitable outcome of the competition for wages in a capitalist society and implied that 'socialised property' would solve the problem. The second tract, *A Manifesto*, written by Shaw, emphasised the need for land reform in order to remove the worst excesses of inequality.[56] Shaw also wrote the sixth tract which suggested the need for a 'Radical Programme' based upon the taxation of unearned income, municipalisation of land and local government, the nationalisation of the railways and the provision of state education for all.[57] *Facts for the Socialists*, written by Sidney Webb in 1887, provided statistical evidence of the unearned income gained by property owners and suggested that it caused poverty. This income, it was argued, needed to be restored to the nation.[58]

Notwithstanding such effort and ingenuity, the first serious attempt to offer a comprehensive set of ideas occurred with the publication of *Fabian Essays in Socialism* in December 1889, drawn from eight highly individualistic lectures given by the leading Fabian figures.[59] Shaw's contribution on 'The Economic Basis of Socialism' was to become a central feature of Fabian philosophy defining its attitudes to policy and action. He suggested that there were at least three rents that went to make surplus value and that the most obvious was the rent accruing to different fertility of land. He called this economic rent and suggested that surplus value was also gained from rent of ability, a product of the fertility of the brain, and rent of capital, produced by an employer putting someone to work on the land. The implication of this article is that there were many levels of rent and that there were many individuals of all classes obtaining the surplus value. It was not simply a matter of one class exploiting another, for many people of all classes were involved.

Such an analysis downgraded the importance of class conflict and suggested that all that was needed was a change in the structure of society and that a redistribution of income, which would produce economic growth, could be achieved by state ownership of the land and progressive taxation. Sidney Webb, in his essay on the 'Historic Basis of Socialism', argued that socialism was extending its grip as society became more involved in education and municipal reform. William Clarke took this further by suggesting that as industry developed in size there were moves towards more state controls which were paving the way for the development of state control of industry. Sidney Olivier added, in his 'Moral Basis of Socialism', the view that society was increasingly developing a common morality which linked social progress and the development of society with increased cooperative production. The other essays tended to endorse these views about the general extension of state and municipal control.

The Fabian approach was thus to play down the importance of class conflict and to stress the need to extend gradually the control of the state and municipal authorities in order to redress the economic imbalance. These arguments were later to be developed to suggest that industry and services would be administered by impartial bureaucrats who had no financial stake in the operation they were in charge of. In other words, they would be drawn from the type of clerical and managerial groups represented within Fabian ranks.

There was, however, a note of dissent. The Fabian authors were not decided about what political medium to use to press home their policies.

Shaw felt that Fabian policies would simply occur as a result of the gradual extension of existing practices whereby municipal authorities were extending their influence. Bland, the old Marxist, felt that class interests might figure in the change and that there was a need to develop a distinctively socialist party, while Webb believed in the need to use 'permeation' by working through the Radicals and Liberals. Over the next twenty-five years or so, the Fabians dithered between supporting the ILP, the Labour Party and the Liberals before alighting more firmly on the Labour Party as their political medium for change during the First World War.

The *Fabian Essays in Socialism* projected the Fabians into the public limelight. It sold 25,500 copies between December 1889 and March 1893 and 46,000 copies by 1914. Hundreds of thousands of Fabian tracts were produced and the movement offered its services to inform the working classes of their poor situation and how it could be changed. From 1890 onwards they fought to bring about change all over the country and their peak of influence seems to have occurred in 1892. Their fitful influence over the next two or three decades will be examined in the next chapter. Nevertheless, it is clear that by the end of the 1880s the Fabian approach to socialism had been established. The Fabian tracts had formed the link with the utilitarian through their concern for efficiency, facts and guidance.

Middle-class dominance of the Fabians was also evident. Eric Hobsbawm's analysis of their membership indicates the point. The Fabian Society had 188 members in 1890, 626 in 1892, 767 in 1904 and 1,060 in 1906. Sampling between a third and a quarter of these members for each of the years mentioned, Hobsbawm suggests that about 10 per cent of the male membership were journalists and writers, hence his comment that 'they have never required others to blow their own trumpet', and that at any given time between 20 and 30 per cent of their members were women.[60] The working class rarely exceeded 10 per cent of the membership even in the years of expansion into the provinces. They were, as suggested earlier, representatives of a new social stratum of the middle class who found it difficult 'to find a firm place in the middle- and upper-class structure of late Victorian Britain'.[61]

CONCLUSION

The 1880s had seen the reappearance of socialism in Britain in a viable form, drawing its support from a patchwork of Radical and O'Brienite clubs and small socialist organisations. Although several other bodies emerged, the most important organisations were the SDF, the Socialist League and the Fabians. Yet all three organisations failed to capture much political support and were fragmented and limited in their appeal. The SDF tended to lose its dissident spirits to other socialist groups, the Socialist League was divided and the Fabians represented the conscience of a section of the middle class rather more than they did the workers. Watmough suggests that throughout the 1880s the SDF averaged about 580 members, although Crick feels that this was something of an underestimate.[62] The Socialist League peaked at about 700 in 1887 before losing many members in the 1880s. The Fabians never reached 200 members and normally numbered about 150. By 1890, then, there were possibly 1,300 or 1,400 fee-paying members attached to the three main socialist organisations in Britain with possibly 700 or more people who might have regarded themselves as socialists in an active and lasting sense, many of whom were unattached or belonged to other organisations such as the Hammersmith Socialist Society.

The chief weakness of these organisations is that they had made little political progress among the working classes and their agencies, such as the trade unions. The SDF and the Fabians eschewed such contacts, comforted by the belief that their forms of socialism were not going to emerge through the trade unions. The Socialist League nurtured trade union relations but fragmented and collapsed too quickly to do more than offer some socialist help during the outbreak of provincial gas strikes in 1889 and 1890. William Cockayne and Tom Paylor were active in organising the gasworkers in the textile district of Yorkshire although their actions did not seem to have endeared them to the majority of local trade unionists.[63]

There is no doubt that compared to the 1870s the progress of socialism in the 1880s had been considerable. Yet they lacked significant political support among the working classes and the trade unions. What they failed to achieve, the Independent Labour Party and the Labour Representation Committee (Labour Party) achieved over the next quarter of a century, even if it was only the ILP of these two organisations that was overtly socialist before the First World War.

2

THE CLASH OF SOCIALIST ALTERNATIVES AND THE SOCIALIST UNITY DEBATE, c. 1890–1914

It was the 1890s that saw the most remarkable growth of socialism in Britain with the emergence of the ILP in 1893 and the resurgence of both the SDF and the Fabian Society. Although there was something of a decline in socialist influence towards the end of the 1890s there was a resurgence of activity to such an extent that there was a major attempt to create Socialist Unity in Britain through the British Socialist Party on the eve of the First World War. Yet it became obvious in these years that socialism had to be attached to trade unionism if it was going to make a political impact, and that there was little prospect that there could be unity between those socialist parties which favoured an alliance with the trade unions and those which did not. Indeed, the prospect of Socialist Unity in Britain was a faint hope by 1900. That left a relatively powerful ILP as the dominant socialist conscience in these years with a much less powerful BSP in its wake. The ILP was also distinguished by the fact that it was able to exert a major influence upon the emerging Labour Party. There were two major problems that this imposed. First, there was the need to win trade union support from the Liberal Party in order to create a viable political organisation. Secondly, there was the need to combine the very individualistic type of socialism offered by the ILP and the collectivism implied in an alliance with trade unionism, a problem which was to create major difficulties for the Labour Party, which inherited this equation, from the First World War onwards.[1]

THE INDEPENDENT LABOUR PARTY IN THE 1890S

The demand for independent Labour representation had been voiced by a number of people, most obviously by George Potter in the 1860s, and certainly arose as a result of the Reform Act of 1867. The London Working Men's Association had demanded the presence of working men in parliament in 1867 and Henry Broadhurst had helped form the Labour Representation League in 1869 in order to extend the registration of votes among the working class and to promote the parliamentary candidature of working men. The League contested parliamentary seats in 1874, returning Thomas Burt and Alexander MacDonald to parliament where they were joined by Henry Broadhurst, secretary of the Parliamentary Committee of the TUC, who also secured a parliamentary seat in 1880. Yet efforts to gain parliamentary representation for the working classes produced little reward and there were only three MPs from the working classes in 1880, all of whom were Liberals/Lib.-Labs. The extension of the parliamentary franchise in 1884 to more than four million male voters, increased the vote threefold. This meant that an increased number of working men were obtaining the vote, although even by the First World War only about 60 per cent of working men held the parliamentary franchise.

For many years it seemed as though the Liberal Party was the natural political terrain for the working-class electorate, particularly so after Joseph Chamberlain encouraged the formation of the national Liberal Federation in 1877 in order to promote domestic reforms. But with Chamberlain's departure from the Liberal Party in 1886, following the Home Rule crisis, the pressure for reform within the Liberal Party waned and the votes of the working classes were increasingly divided between both the Liberal and Conservative parties. At this juncture it was clear that the working classes would have to develop their own independent political party.

Frederick Engels raised the standard for independent political action in his articles in the *Labour Standard* between May and August 1881. This idea was taken further by J.L. Mahon who attempted to lead the Socialist League in this direction in 1886 and 1887, until he seceded with the Bloomsbury Socialist Society to form the Labour Emancipation League in 1888. Mahon had already moved in that direction in 1887 when he helped form the North of England Socialist Federation at the time of the Northumberland coal strike. The Federation faded quickly but did hope that the socialist bodies would form both a national and international Socialist Labour Party.[2] This commitment to political independence was also encouraged by H.H. Champion, a Tory who had joined the SDF and produced his own monthly journal, *Common Sense*, which later became known as the *Labour Elector* (1888). He used the Labour Electoral Committee, which the TUC had formed at its Southport Conference in 1886 at the insistence of T.R. Threlfall, and attempted to use it as the central organisation for Labour's demands for political independence when it was re-formed as the Labour Electoral Association (LEA) in 1887. Through this medium, Champion encouraged the demands for an eight-hour working day and other social measures.

The LEA has been the subject of examination in a wider study of Lib.-Lab. MPs.[3] The thrust of this research has been to suggest that the Lib.-Labs. were the first working-class MPs, drawing from nonconformity, temperance and Liberal Radicalism for inspiration, and that they and their tradition influenced the early Labour Party (LRC) MPs. Obviously, the Lib.-Lab. MPs had their limitations. In the first place, there were very few of them – a mere twelve in 1885. Secondly, efforts to develop a more powerful Lib.–Lab. group within the Liberal Party failed. The LEA became a mere appendage of the Liberal Party, supported by only a few prominent members of the working classes in Bradford, Hull, Sheffield and Southport.[4]

The LEA met with little success in attempting to get support for Lib.-Lab. candidates at both municipal and parliamentary elections. The Liberal Party would not respond to the challenge and, after the 1892 general election, T.R. Threlfall reflected that

> Of the thirteen labour MPs in the present House, four ran in opposition or without recognition of the caucus, five represented constituencies where organised miners absolutely demanded the position and where the shop-keeping and employing class are so small in number as to have comparatively little power, and only four either captured or out-generalled it. . . .[5]

The fact is that the LEA got nowhere and the organisation and its members were accused of not being truly representative of the working classes.

It was at this time that a multitude of organisations emerged to demand independent Labour representation. Mahon's demand for political independence for socialists, Champion's 'Tory Socialism', and the success of John Burns in winning a seat on the London County Council in 1889 all conflated with other developments pointing to the need for political independence for the working classes. James Keir Hardie attacked

Broadhurst for his support of the Liberal Party at the Bradford TUC conference of 1887 and repeated the attack in 1889 when, once again, he berated him for being a shareholder in J.T. Brunner's chemical works which operated dangerous working conditions.[6]

Hardie had by this time emerged from his staunchly Liberal background, carrying with him the political baggage of Liberal Radicalism. He had been secretary of the Lanarkshire miners since 1878 and had become committed to the eight-hour movement in 1883. He was still strongly attached to the Liberal Party and worked with it in the 1885 and 1886 general elections. Yet Hardie was dissatisfied, particularly after Henry George's tour in 1884 when the Scottish Land Restoration League was set up and J.L. Mahon and Andreas Scheu set up the Land and Labour League in Edinburgh.[7] Gradually, through a baptism of strikes and riots, connected with the Scottish Miners' Federation decision to take strike action in 1887, and along with the decision to set up a journal entitled the *Miner*, Hardie began to move towards a more overtly socialist stance. He maintained that poverty was caused by capitalism, not drink, and demanded state intervention on such matters as the eight-hour day. In 1888 he was selected as the miners' candidate for a by-election in Mid-Lanark but was forced to stand as an independent since he had been rejected by the local Liberals. He was defeated, polling a mere 617 votes, but his action paved the way for the formation of the Scottish Labour Party (originally named the Scottish Parliamentary Labour Party) in August 1888. This occurred more or less at the moment that Champion seceded from the LEA in order to use its Metropolitan Section as the basis for a 'National Labour Party'. The Scottish Labour Party was still not socialist but the Scottish Land and Labour League dissolved itself and joined it, espousing an overt commitment to socialist policies.

The SLP, which became the Scottish ILP in 1895, was, however, never a very strong political organisation largely due to the fact that it never had a powerful trade union movement behind it. The exception was the Glasgow area where about two-thirds of Scotland's 147,000 trade unionists were to be found in the early 1890s.[8] Even in Glasgow, the success of the Scottish ILP was precarious for although it helped to return two Labour MPs in 1906 it was barely represented on the Glasgow City Council. It did, however, strengthen its position after 1906 and had fourteen councillors by 1914.[9]

It was in the late 1880s that the British trade union movement began to expand into what has been referred to as its 'new unionist' phase. The fact is that after a number of years of low membership, due to the economic depression, trade union membership expanded as established unions extended their membership and new ones, such as the Gasworkers' and General Labourers, were formed. The result was that many new organisations, with socialist activists, began to increase their representation on the TUC and challenged the position of Broadhurst, who was eventually replaced as secretary of the Parliamentary Committee of the TUC. Prominent 'new' trade unionists such as Tom Mann began to demand the formation of 'One Big Union' with which to challenge capitalism.

However, there were setbacks. The growth of trade union membership was checked from about 1893 onwards, although the older established unions continued to expand their membership gradually while the new 'general' unions began to contract.[10] Champion's *Labour Elector* also collapsed in 1890, whereupon Champion went to Australia, where he remained until 1891.

At this juncture the socialist movement began to move away from London and out towards the provinces and the North.[11] Many small socialist groups had already established themselves in these regions. A small group of secularists and hosiery trade unionists had formed a small branch of the Socialist League at Leicester in the 1880s, providing a platform for a later ILP branch.[12] Edward Carpenter, an anarchist, had set up a socialist society in Sheffield in 1886 and SDF and Socialist League branches had been formed in Bradford and Leeds in 1885 and 1886. Focus was given to these developments by Joseph Burgess who edited the *Yorkshire Factory Times* from 1889 as a paper for the textile workers, although it also encouraged the development of socialism as well as trade unionism.

Yet socialist activities, though important, were not enough. What stimulated the growth of an independent Labour movement in Yorkshire, and the North, was the increasing association of the socialists with the trade union movement and industrial action. Most obviously, as E.P. Thompson and others have suggested, there was the important Manningham Mills strike which took place in Bradford between 17 December 1890 and 27 April 1891.[13] This was one of the most divisive issues in the history of Bradford and the West Riding of Yorkshire. E.P. Thompson has revealed how important the defeat of the strikers was for the political ambitions of the working classes. Contemporaries were also aware of the political importance of the event. In October 1892, Fred Jowett, the first Labour MP for Bradford in 1906, contested the Manningham Ward at the municipal elections and stated that 'In the Lister strike, the people of Bradford saw plainly, as they have never seen before, that whether their rulers are Liberal or Tory they are capitalists first and politicians afterwards.'[14] The point is that the dispute saw the middle classes and employers of Bradford unite behind the Manningham management to force wage reductions of up to 25 per cent on the workforce at the same time as the trade union movement throughout Yorkshire, and the North, united behind the Manningham operatives. The dispute also involved a free speech issue as the Liberals on the Bradford Watch Committee attempted to prevent the strikers holding public meetings near the centre of town, with the events climaxing in disturbances, the deployment of troops and police, and the reading of the Riot Act on Monday 13 April 1891. The annoyance and frustrations which arose over the Manningham dispute are best expressed in the words of Charlie Glyde who, when speaking to the strikers in April 1891, stated that 'We have had two parties in the past, the can'ts and the won'ts, and it's time that we had a party that will.'[15]

The 'party that will' was formed one month later at a meeting at the Firth's Temperance Hotel, formerly Laycock's Temperance Hotel, in East Parade, Bradford. Charlie Glyde, George Minty, James Bartley and W.H. Drew, the strike leader, formulated possible methods of making the working men an effective political entity.[16] Shortly afterwards other Labour unions came into existence, including the Colne Valley Labour Union on 21 July 1891, the Salford Labour Union in August 1891 and the Huddersfield Labour Union on 14 September 1891. Others emerged at Manchester and Salford on 14 May 1892, at Halifax in July 1892 and at Keighley in October 1892. The Scottish United Trades Council Labour Party was formed between August 1891 and April 1892. Joseph Burgess attempted to form a London ILP in the summer of 1892, although with limited success.[17] The Leeds ILP was formed in November 1892 and the Batley and Dewsbury ILP organisations in 1893.[18] Many other labour unions and socialist societies began to emerge.

In October and November 1891 the Bradford Labour Union fought two seats, unsuccessfully, on the Bradford Council and then decided to put forward Ben Tillett to fight the parliamentary seat in West Bradford at the 1892 general election. At this stage, in December 1891, Robert Blatchford, who declined to contest the Bradford East seat for the Bradford Labour Union, began to produce the *Clarion*. Through this medium a cultural aspect of the Labour movement was cultivated with an emphasis upon fellowship and brotherhood, and with an array of organisational activities including the Clarion vocal unions, glee clubs, cycling clubs, scouts and other similar organisations.

The development of the Labour unions certainly encouraged the conversion of the Bradford, Huddersfield, Morley and Keighley trades councils to a socialist perspective between 1889 and 1892, and it was socialists who were instrumental in setting up the Dewsbury and Batley Trades Council, and the Brighouse, Wakefield, Spen Valley and Todmorden trades councils in 1891 and 1892. They converted the Leeds Trades Council to their cause in the late 1890s.[19] Elsewhere, there were similar developments, most notably in Leicester and Manchester, where, respectively, the ILP and the trades councils were allied by 1894 and 1895.[20]

The momentum of independent Labour politics was gathering from the spring of 1891 and its parliamentary breakthrough occurred in the 1892 general election when Keir Hardie won West Ham South and John Burns, now more Liberal than Labour, won Battersea in a straight fight with the Tory candidate. West Ham South was a working-class seat which Hardie won in 1892 against a local Conservative employer largely because of the split within Liberal radicalism. (The seat was lost in 1895.) Ben Tillett also gained 2,749 votes, about 800 more than the number who had indicated in a petition that they would vote for him, in the Bradford West contest.[21] This was only about 600 votes less than Alfred Illingworth, the incumbent and the dominant figure in Bradford Liberalism. In fact, Tillett had chosen to confront Old Liberalism in a direct manner rather than to stand for the Bradford East seat which was where Bradford's trade union strength was to be found and where the Liberals were hinting that they would not put a candidate in his way.

At this juncture several advocates of independent labour, meeting at the 1892 TUC, decided to call a conference for their supporters and Joseph Burgess campaigned to make this a success through the support of his newspaper the *Workmen's Times*. The conference was to be held at Bradford on 13 and 14 January 1893. It drew together many Labour Unions, ILP, Fabian and socialist societies, although the SDF, which claimed 2,000 members in Lancashire alone, adopted a position of 'benevolent neutrality'. In total there were about 120 delegates, who came mainly from the industrial North of England and Scotland and there were no delegates from Ireland, Wales, and from the southern part of England except for London, Chatham and Plymouth.[22] The proceedings began with W.H. Drew, the Manningham strike leader, as conference chairman but his place was quickly taken by James Keir Hardie who, with Ben Tillett, was one of only two Labour leaders of national importance to attend the conference.[23]

It is clear that the new organisation would be socialist, although that word that was kept out of its title, and it adopted a clause committing it to the collective ownership of the means of production, eight hours legislation, free education from elementary school to university, the end of indirect taxation and the extinction of unearned income. Yet it was also a party that was prepared to compromise and obtain the best arrangement for its members, as evidenced by the rejection of the Manchester Fourth Clause which advocated that all members of the party would have to abstain from voting at all elections in which no socialist candidate was standing. Robert Blatchford advocated this but it was a Bradford amendment, committing members to voting in accordance with the decision of their local branch, that carried the day.

The ILP emerged rapidly during the early 1890s. The Bradford organisation had about 2,000 members between 1893 and 1895 associated with 29 ILP clubs or groups in the town. There were between 300 and 400 members of the Colne Valley Labour Union connected with eight local clubs and between 500 and 600 members of the Halifax ILP connected with eight clubs in the 1890s. The seven ILP clubs in Huddersfield had between 780 and 880 members in 1893, although four of the clubs became defunct before 1899 and the other three had only 170 members by 1899. There were about 300 ILP members in Leeds, about 120 in Keighley by 1899 and many others in small clubs and groups throughout the rest of the West Riding of Yorkshire.[24] Elsewhere, the Leicester branch had 120 members in 1897, making it the thirteenth largest branch in the country at that time, and the Manchester and Salford ILP had a listed membership of 693 in 1897, 268 in 1898 and 401 in December 1900.[25] The Scottish Labour Party was soon assimilated into the 'National' ILP.[26] There was a tremendous growth of ILP membership in the early 1890s and the 200 or so clubs and branches of 1893 had risen to over 400 by 1894. Estimates of the ILP membership vary from 35,000 to 50,000 in 1895 but the disastrous 1895 general election reduced these figures to about 20,000 in 1896. From about 1898 onwards determined efforts were being made to organise socialists into the ILP, if not into a 'Socialist Unity' party, and the ILP's fee-paying membership hovered between 11,000 and 13,000.[27]

The ILP was a cultural as well as political movement and operated alongside other cultural movements. The importance of club life can never be overestimated for it 'awakened and developed the self-governing powers of the members'.[28] Club activities were regarded as 'a way of life'. Many clubs ran Sunday lectures and classes in singing, dancing, elocution and political economy. The Bradford North Ward Club entertained its members with the Garrick Orchestral Band on a number of occasions throughout 1895.[29] In 1896 the members of this club arranged an outing to 'Grassington and Kilnsey Craggs, to which they rode from Skipton railway station in wagonnettes'.[30] The Eccleshill Labour Club held regular Labour Church services on Sunday evenings throughout 1895, and attracted speakers such as W. Obank, who gave a lecture on 'The Religion of Socialism'.[31]

The Labour Church movement, organised by John Trevor and Edwin Halford, overlapped with the club life of many ILP supporters. About eighty Labour churches emerged although most of them were small and short-lived. The largest ones were to be found at Bradford and Manchester, both of which had in excess of 300 members each.[32] They focused their activities upon bringing in some national speaker who might give one or two public lectures on the Sunday. Otherwise the movement was immensely varied and ranged from the religious to the secular but most would have echoed the Bradford Labour Church's aim of bringing about 'The Realisation of Heaven in this Life by the establishment of a state of society founded upon Justice and Love to thy Neighbour.'[33] Their efforts were supported by the socialist Sunday schools that emerged. In Yorkshire, and many other areas, these were seen as training schools for the future generation of socialists and they developed the 'Socialist Ten Commandments' which focused upon respect for all and the fourth commandment: 'Honour good men, be courteous to all men, bow down to none.' In Lancashire, Robert Blatchford's alternative socialist Sunday schools emphasised the need for rational debate rather than the inculcation of socialist values. Underpinning the ILP clubs, the Labour churches and the socialist Sunday schools was the Clarion movement which spawned fellowship groups, the Clarion cyclists, vocal unions, glee clubs and a variety of associations with local religious groups.[34]

The extent to which this cultural aspect of socialism was pervasive and lasting has been questioned by historians. Some, such as James Hinton, have regarded it as an irrelevance. Others, like Stephen Yeo, have suggested that it was vitally important until the mid-1890s when the need to win political successes at the local and parliamentary level made cultural activities rather less important.[35] Yet neither explanation would appear to be totally satisfactory for most socialist Sunday schools were not formed until after 1900. Club life did not begin to develop in the important socialist centre of Colne Valley until after 1900 and the Clarion movement was at its peak in the Edwardian years.[36] Indeed, there were many socialists, like E.R. Hartley, who combined political activity with a zeal for the cultural life of the socialist movement. In Hartley's case, he was not only a member of the Bradford ILP and a councillor but also a member of the SDF/BSP and stood for them in the famous Leicester by-election of 1913.[37]

One might also reflect that there were new emerging political figures such as Keir Hardie who were not terribly enamoured of clubs and social organisations which appeared to spend little time on political activities. He was particularly concerned that the social might undermine the political interests of the movement. In Stockport there was evidence that many members were missing the business meetings of the clubs 'while regularly frequenting the Club for purposes of amusement'.[38] Hardie, speaking to the new Labour Club in Leicester, 'warned them against turning the club into a lounge for loafers' as was likely to be the case 'when liquor was sold'.[39] J.B. Glasier was critical of the Darwen Club and suggested that 'some of the men obviously are members merely for the "booze", and have a bad reputation as fathers and husbands'.[40] The sale of drink in clubs was soundly frowned upon in many areas, such as Bradford, but was present in clubs in many other areas such as Bolton. Indeed, Glasier ascribed the ILP's weakness in Bolton to the practice of selling alcoholic drinks in clubs.[41]

Yet there is no doubting that the Clarion movement added to the general mood of debate about socialism in the 1890s. Robert Blatchford's paper, which first appeared in 1891, was selling about 80,000 copies per issue by the end of the 1890s and Blatchford articles to John Smith were collected together as *Merrie England*, sold under the pseudonym 'Nunquam', and had sales of about 750,000 copies in 1894. It, and the *Clarion*, took forward William Morris's message of fellowship, brotherhood and the 'religion of socialism'. It spawned a Clarion Van movement, to travel around Britain and spread socialist literature, which was run by E.R. Hartley and, when he was in New Zealand in 1912 and early 1913, by Gertrude, his daughter.

The work of women was also clearly important to the activities of the ILP. Apart from Gertrude Hartley, mentioned above, there were prominent female propagandists in the ILP such as Isabella Ford, Katherine St John Conway, Caroline Martyn, Enid Stacy and Isabella Bream Pearce. They spoke at Labour Church meetings, helped to organise campaigns, stood for boards of guardians (as did Mrs Hector Munro in Bradford in the early twentieth century) after the 1894 Act removed the property qualification, and campaigned to improve the trade union organisation of women. Enid Stacy (1868–1903) became a member of the Bristol Socialist Society before joining the ILP and risked her livelihood as a high school teacher in order to assist women workers on strike in Bristol. Isabella Ford (1855–1924), the daughter of a wealthy Leeds Quaker, organised the tailoresses in Leeds in the late 1880s and joined the ILP in 1893. She wrote for the *Leeds Forward*, the local Leeds ILP paper, and discussed the role of women in revolutionary movements abroad.[42] This type of activity led Joseph Clayton, secretary of the Leeds ILP in the 1890s, to note that 'in the early ILP women were a great deal more than mere helpers to men, they were quite literally the co-leaders.'[43] It is even suggested that this meant that the ILP was more inclined to support the women's suffrage issue and the 'women's question'. However, June Hannam throws doubt upon some of these suggestions for while the ILP did become deeply involved in the women's suffrage debate the ILP seems to have been far from advanced on matters such as marriage, the family, sexuality, 'free unions' and the legal and economic subordination of women. In other words, the equal rights issue for women was something which feminist socialists favoured though not perhaps the whole of the ILP.[44]

Nevertheless, the ILP was one of the most obvious sources of support for women. Women were allowed to be full members of ILP branches, which was not the case in the Tory and Liberal party branches at that time. It was women in the ILP, and the emergent Labour Party, who went on to form the Women's Labour League in 1906 and separate women's political organisations. Margaret MacDonald, the wife of the Labour leader, was in fact one of the main forces behind it.[45] Women ILPers, such as Sarah Reddish, of Bolton, and Margaret McMillan, of Bradford and London, were to the forefront of the women's question.[46] Indeed, McMillan was returned as an ILP member of the Bradford School Board in 1894 and, in later years, Mrs Hector Munro was returned as an ILP representative on the Bradford Board of Guardians.[47]

Various cultural, social, economic and gender factors helped to shape the rapid development of the ILP. Yet, as already suggested, the 1895 general election was truly a setback for the ILP as it was for the whole socialist movement. The twenty-eight ILP candidates were all defeated, and Hardie lost his parliamentary seat of West Ham South. In addition, the SDF was defeated in four contests. The ILP gained only about 40,000 votes and the SDF less than 4,000. In such a climate the ILP began to consider a number of alternatives. It could move itself back into the Liberal Party, help to form a party of Socialist unity or seek greater support and closer attachments with the trade unions. Too much had gone on for the first to occur while the second alternative was ruled out by the clash between Hyndman and Hardie and the contrasting strategies and policies of the ILP and the SDF. In the end, the ILP, encouraged by its 400 or more local representatives on councils, school boards and other local public bodies, moved towards the creation of a Labour alliance with the trade unions.

What then was the position of the ILP and its associated movements in the 1890s? It is clear that the ILP was the most important socialist party in Britain, having grown to that position by its deep antagonism towards the intransigent attitudes of the 'Old Liberal' party bosses who ran the local and regional organisations of the Liberal Party and who were reluctant to support the selection of working men and trade unionists for local or parliamentary honours.[48] Attracting the support of trade unions it combined this with a commitment to socialism and the development of an alternative way of life, something akin to Morris's 'making of socialists'. What made the ILP distinctive is that it combined the demand for the support of trade unions with a desire to be both a cultural and a political movement.

The ILP was far more important in the growth of socialism in Britain, and in the emergence of the Labour Party, than has often been supposed. Whereas thirty years ago the ILP was considered to be a tributary of the Labour Party, recent research suggests that the impression is simply wrong. Much investigation has been conducted since E.P. Thompson's pioneering work in 'Homage to Tom Maguire' and there have been many local studies on areas of ILP strengths and weaknesses. These have suggested that there were many areas, such as Bradford, Halifax, Huddersfield, Manchester and Leicester, where the trade union movement underpinned significant ILP growth.[49] At the same time, there have been areas such as Keighley and the Colne Valley that depended much more on club life and the cultural activities of the ILP.[50]

There was, indeed, always a split within the ILP between the collectivist and statist approach emphasised by trade unionists and the individualistic approach which saw socialism releasing people to enjoy a wholesome cultural and social life. Philip Snowden was one of the finest exponents of the individualistic approach. He shared with William Morris the view that socialism would allow individual development. This contention appeared in his lecture and pamphlet *The Individual under Socialism* (1905). In this he argued against the view that socialism would sacrifice individual liberty and maintained that by releasing the individual from capitalist exploitation 'Socialism will establish the moral conditions which are necessary for the development of a true individuality, and the exercise of true liberty.'[51] This view was elaborated further in his article 'The Two Salvations' in which he argued that there were two salvations, an individual one and a social one. The Christian religions emphasised the first but it was socialism alone that could deal with the social problems which imposed limitations upon the ability of individuals to develop. Socialism would guarantee individual freedom and not, as some critics argued, threaten it with state bureaucracy.[52]

Yet how much influence did the ILP have and how widespread was its support? There have been two major surveys of the extent of the ILP and Labour influence. David Howell's book, *British Workers and the Independent Labour Party 1888–1906*, contains a section on political spaces which suggests the immense regional and local variations in the ILP experience. He argues that the ILP was a small, but influential, part in the creation of the LRC and the Labour Party. Duncan Tanner's book, *Political Change and the Labour Party*, examines the wider framework and suggests that the ILP and Labour 'had not created a solid "class" vote, based upon cultural unities which were common to working-class voters in all areas. It had not even the uniform support of the trade unionists.'[53] Yet one must remember that few historians who see the growth of class politics favouring the growth of Labour would argue a homogeneity about the response of the working class. Also Tanner's assessment and presentation of local evidence, particularly for Yorkshire, is simply wrong.[54]

Despite Tanner's claims to the contrary, the fact is that the thrust of his work is parliamentary in nature. The success of Labour at the local level, the most immediate source of power, in municipal, board of guardians, county council, urban district council and other local elections is not examined. Between 1906 and 1914 the number of such representatives in the textile district of Yorkshire rose from at least 88 to at least 202, with a surge of success after 1909.[55] Evidence of such growth was widespread throughout England and Wales as a whole.[56] In Scotland, there was a surge of municipal success in the Glasgow area and Smyth concludes that 'It was not the war itself which created the Glasgow labour movement but the contradictions within liberalism prior to the war, demonstrated during the 1908 unemployment agitation (when Liberal support for the 18,000 unemployed Glaswegians was absent).'[57] Tanner has indicated the need to examine municipal results more closely but does not do this in his book.[58] Had he done so, he would be aware that his suggestion that Labour made more progress in Bradford and Leeds before 1906 rather than after is incorrect. In municipal, as well as parliamentary, terms, the opposite is true.[59]

Secondly, it is obvious, as will be suggested later, that the ILP played a vital role in the early development of the Labour Party even though its importance diminished rapidly after 1914. Thirdly, it appears that the ILP attracted significant support from the middle classes. Indeed, there was much encouragement from the business community, the most obvious example of this being the fact that Arthur Priestman, who ran a large textile business in Bradford, led the ILP in Bradford in 1906 at a time when his brother and business partner, H.B. Priestman, ran the Bradford Liberal Party. William Leach, the one-time employer of Fred Jowett in Bradford, was an active member of the ILP and a textile businessman. France Littlewood, the millowner, and T.D. Benson, the estate agent, became the second and third treasurers of the ILP, following in the footsteps of John Lister, the landowner.

The ILP and the cultural attachments that supported it ensured that there was a core of socialist opinion that survived until the end of the 1890s. At this stage, the decision was made that the ILP would create a Labour alliance with the trade unions. The outcome was the Labour Representation Committee, which subsequently became the Labour Party.

THE LABOUR REPRESENTATION COMMITTEE AND THE LABOUR PARTY

The 1890s saw the trade union movement come increasingly under pressure from employers who began to tighten up on work practices as the rising level of foreign competition threatened their economic performance. Court cases, especially the *Lyons* v. *Wilkins* case (1896–9) in which Lyons, a leather-goods manufacturer, took action against Wilkins, the secretary of the Amalgamated Trade Society of Fancy Leather Workers, over a strike and picketing against his premises, effectively made picketing, which became legal in the 1870s, illegal once again. Indeed, Mr Justice Byrne argued that picketing was only legal if confined to communicating information. Picketing to encourage strike action was illegal, a view upheld by the High Court in 1899. Lock-outs, including the famous engineering lock-out in 1897–8, defeated the Amalgamated Society of Engineers, one of the strongest of all skilled unions. In such an atmosphere of oppression from employers trade unions gradually gravitated towards the socialists, and particularly those who both favoured trade unionism and advocated parliamentary politics.

The mining unions were already moving in this direction and the TUC also began to consider the need to promote the parliamentary representation of working men in the late 1890s. The TUC passed a resolution in 1898 calling for the working classes to support socialist parties. At the same time the ILP approached the TUC and the Scottish TUC to take 'united political action'. Eventually in 1899 the executive of the Amalgamated Society of Railway Servants (ASRS) urged that the Parliamentary Committee of the TUC should examine ways in which it could increase the number of Labour MPs in the next parliament. The 1899 TUC accepted the idea by a narrow majority and a voluntary meeting was arranged between the delegates of 570,000 trade unionists (less than half the membership of the TUC) and the representatives of the ILP, the SDF and the Fabians. They met in the Memorial Hall, Farringdon Street, London on 27 February 1900 and formed the Labour Representation Committee. Keir Hardie carried most weight in this meeting which suggested that a distinctive Labour group should be formed in parliament and that the LRC should not base its approach upon the class war. Given that many trade unionists were still Liberal, or Liberal-Labour, in political association this was, perhaps, as much as could be expected at the time.

At first the omens did not look good for the LRC. Its initial home was the back room of Ramsay MacDonald's London flat, and it spent only £33 in supporting fifteen candidates at the 1900 general election, of whom only Hardie was returned for Merthyr and Richard Bell for Derby. What helped to change its fortunes was the decision of the House of Lords, in July 1901, to uphold the claim made by the Taff Vale Railway Company against the ASRS for financial damages incurred by its members during a strike. The decision exposed all unions' funds to similar claims. In this, and other similar cases, the House of Lords had stripped away the financial impunity of the trade unions. With one fell swoop, the Lords had given added impetus to the demand for independent parliamentary representation for the working classes and strengthened the case of the LRC. As L.T. Hobhouse stated, 'that which no Socialist writer or platform orator could achieve was effected by the judges'.[60] The LRC promised to work with the TUC to reverse the judgment and, as many historians have noted, the embryonic Labour Party was rewarded with a substantial increase in membership, from more than 350,000 affiliated members in early 1901 to 861,000 in 1903.

Despite this support, the LRC's impact was limited. It had only five MPs in 1905 and one of these, Richard Bell, changed his sympathies to the Liberal Party. What projected it forward was the secret pact between Herbert Gladstone and Ramsay MacDonald, in 1903, which secured for Labour, as it did for the Liberals, a straight run against the Conservatives in about thirty constituencies. As a result, although some of the Labour candidates were faced with Liberal opponents, the LRC/Labour Party returned twenty-nine, soon to be thirty, MPs in the elections of December 1905 and January 1906. The Liberal Party was no longer the party of the Left, even though the Labour Party was barely any more advanced.

The Labour Party, and its constituent members, was essentially a reformist organisation dedicated to winning the support of the trade unions and temperamentally allied to the Liberal government. The ILP and the Labour Party were evolutionary socialists and reformists at heart. Although the Labour Party was influenced by the Fabians, who became reconciled to operating more closely with it by 1914, it was the ILP's ethical brand of socialism that influenced its thinking and that of its supportive trade unions.

The cultural and ethical approach of the ILP has already been outlined. It was a gut reaction to injustice and simply demanded reform. There was, indeed, in this appeal to the heart and the changing of minds, shades of William Morris's appeal to 'make socialists', even if his objections to parliamentary politics were ignored. There was even a concern that capitalism bred imperialism and would generate war. J. Bruce Glasier, Philip Snowden, Keir Hardie and Ramsay MacDonald, the 'big four' of the ILP, also held such a moralistic approach to socialism. They all revealed their Nonconformist and radical background and, with the exception of Snowden, their grounding in the Scottish land reform movement. With all four it was the Liberal Radicalism of the past, and their desire for more democratic forms, that influenced their thinking. Clearly, the ILP was shorn of any crude Marxist economic determinism. Yet to present the ILP, and its influence upon the Labour Party, in simply a moralistic framework is to ignore what both the ILP and the Labour Party were about.

In one respect they were concerned with the reorganisation of society within an evolving community rather than one that was the product of class conflict. Ramsay MacDonald, a leading figure in both the ILP and the LRC/Labour Party before 1914, attempted to define his socialism in thirteen books written between 1905 and 1921, normally produced by the National Labour Press, the ILP and the Socialist Library rather than commercial publishers.[61] Among them were *Socialism and Society* (1905), *Labour and Empire* (1906), *Socialism* (1907), *Socialism and Government* (2 vols, 1909), *Syndicalism* (1912), *Socialism after the War* (1917) and *Socialism: Critical and Constructive* (1921). These books offered no clear body of integrated thought although they provided some clues to the policies of a future Labour government. For instance, *Labour and Empire* suggested that socialists would run the colonies indirectly, indicating MacDonald's Fabian upbringing in the suggestion of a superior and impartial force operating for the good of the colonies. But the dominant theme of these books was a form of social Darwinism. In the patchwork of ideas that appeared as *Socialism and Society* and *Socialism*, MacDonald rejected the competitive struggle for existence as the chief characteristic of social evolution in favour of the increasing tendency towards cooperation. MacDonald emphasised that economic development was the mainspring of change but that man's reason gave shape and direction to the demands for change. Yet there could be no appeal to narrow class interests for society had to be run for the good of the community as a whole. This was an eclectic set of ideas which drew from Marxist economic determinism and the moral ideals of the ethical socialists but above all reaffirmed the Fabian belief that the central socialist goal of public ownership could be achieved through the gradual modification of existing institutions. The impartial rule of the state arose from the fact that, to MacDonald, 'Socialism is no class movement. Socialism is a movement of opinion, not an organisation of status. It is not the rule of the working class; it is the organisation of the community.'[62] In other words socialism would develop as society emerged and became more enlightened, and not as a result of the development of class conflict and the rise of the working class.

At the same time as MacDonald was giving the impression that the ILP aimed for a society of all the classes, not simply of the working class, there is the undeniable point that Keir Hardie, the only one of the Labour and ILP 'big four' who had trade union credentials, was moving the ILP and the Labour Party towards strengthening the links with trade unionism. Evidently, the Labour Party was becoming the party of class just as its main leaders were claiming to represent the interests of all classes.

This situation had been encouraged by the *Taff Vale* case but was given more substance as it became clear that the Liberal Party was reluctant to become involved in protecting the interests of trade unions. It is true that the Liberal Government's Trades Dispute Act of 1906 nullified the *Taff Vale* judgment but it came too late to staunch the flow of trade union support from the Liberal Party to the Labour Party. The outburst of industrial conflict between 1910 and 1914, which produced national transport and mining strikes, strengthened and speeded up the process of rising trade union support for the Labour Party despite the counter-claims of support made by a small group of syndicalists led by Tom Mann.

In an article on 'Labour and the Trade Unions', Chris Wrigley has also assembled convincing evidence that the Liberal Party could not cope with the demands of trade unions.[63] He acknowledged that the Labour Party was not the only mouthpiece of the TUC in 1906, for the TUC also supported the trade union mining MPs who were Liberal at that time, but argues that it rapidly became so. Many trade unionists were still suspicious of socialists and both the Liberal and Conservative parties vied for their support despite the fact that many trade unions paid political funds to Labour; but the *Osborne* judgment put the matter beyond doubt.

Walter Osborne was determinedly opposed to the Labour Party and extolled the virtues of trade unionism coming to an accommodation with capital, in order to achieve industrial harmony, increased output and improved wages. What he objected to was the socialist type of trade unionism which had emerged to advocate state intervention and the eight-hour day. On an individual basis he campaigned against individual members of trade unions being asked to contribute to the political funds of the Labour Party and used the law to uphold his objection in 1908 and 1909. He took legal action to prevent the ASRS from levying funds for the Labour Party and was supported by the House of Lords. This decision, according to Wrigley, created problems for both the Liberal and Unionist parties. The trade unionists wished for a reversal of the judgment and the Liberals, in particular, were torn between resisting an action which could lead to the strengthening of ties between the trade unions and the Labour Party and presenting too hostile a reaction that would alienate trade unionists.

Both Unionists and Liberals were in a quandary and this is reflected by the split within the Liberal Party. On the one hand, Herbert Samuel detected that if the *Osborne* judgment was not reversed then the result would be 'to increase the separation between labour and Liberalism' while Sir William Robson, a Liberal Attorney General, felt that the conflict between the Liberals and socialists was inevitable: 'Nothing can avoid this conflict. It is also unfortunately too clear that the Socialists are in effective command of the Trade Union organisation, and if they are at liberty to draw on that organisation for funds they may do so up to £80,000 or £100,000 per annum. . . .'[64] To Robson, there was still a majority of trade unionists who objected to the political fund, although this was due to their 'inert assent'.

Lloyd George entered into secret negotiations with the Unionists to block a reversal of the *Osborne* judgment and the 1913 Trade Union Act did not reverse the judgment but, rather, permitted unions to hold a secret ballot on the issue. The fact is that neither the Liberal nor the Unionist party felt much compunction to change the *Osborne* judgment. In the end it rebounded upon them as union after union, holding secret ballots under the Trade Union Act 1913, voted in favour of Labour representation. By the beginning of 1914 about 420,000 trade unionists, from unions with a membership of 1,208,841, had voted on the necessity of establishing political funds for the Labour Party. Of these, 298,702 voted in favour and 125,310 against.[65] The organised trade union movement and its active rank and file were overwhelmingly committed to the Labour Party before the onset of war. As Wrigley suggests: 'These votes ensured Labour's post-First World War electoral finances, and in themselves reflect an element of the explanation for the rise of the Labour party and the decline of the Liberal party in the early twentieth century.'[66]

The Labour Party's political strength was increased after 1906 by the affiliation of more trade unions, and particularly the Miners' Federation of Great Britain in January 1909, and the switch of allegiance of their MPs from the Liberal Party to the Labour Party. After two general elections in 1910 the Labour Party had 42 MPs, although it lost six in by-elections between 1911 and 1914, in many cases with an increased vote. Labour's parliamentary achievements were remarkably good given that six million men and many more millions of women, a substantial proportion of whom would have voted Labour, did not have the vote. Indeed, the increasing political power of the Labour Party and the ILP can be seen in the fact that the tremendous surge in municipal success from 1909 onwards and the vast increase in other local successes, in boards of guardians, urban district councils, rural district councils, parish councils, and other local public bodies, has gone largely unrecorded except for one detailed study of the textile district of the West Riding of Yorkshire.[67]

Although the LRC was quite clearly shaped by the male-dominated trade unions, women did play a part in labour's political growth. Recent work has suggested that many working-class women were drawn into both the activities of the Labour Party and the women's suffrage campaign and that there was something of a fluid, and sometimes conflicting, relationship between the various women's and labour/socialist organisations.[68] C. Collette has also illuminated the history of the Women's Labour League, the only autonomous group of women that has ever existed within the Labour Party. Its history has been obscured, largely because of the male-dominated nature of the political movement and because it was strongly middle class, but it was a body that sought to be a sister organisation to the LRC set up 'by women for women'. At its first conference, in 1906, an amendment of Isabella Ford's was accepted stating that one of the organisation's aims was to 'obtain direct representation in Parliament and on local bodies'. Thus from the very beginning the League was committed to the idea of women's suffrage despite the Labour Party's ambivalence to this issue at the time, and was therefore a credible organisation in the eyes of the contemporary women's movement.[69] It was not, however, a totally independent body for it sought affiliation to the Labour Party from its inception and gained it during the First World War.[70] Its initial intention was also to establish the importance of an agenda of political issues that affected the lives of women. At its annual conference of 1913, the view was expressed that 'We may say that much of the attention given in late years to condition of children is our work. We have . . . directed attention to the need of feeding in the schools . . . we have spoken and agitated about the medical needs of children.'[71] Evidently, its aim was to give 'a channel for the special knowledge and experiences of women of the party'.[72]

Although the Labour Party's political fortunes were attacked, by socialists who were to form the British Socialist Party, it is clear that it did achieve major political success. From July 1907 and through to 1908 it introduced the Unemployed Workmen's Bill and campaigned for the right to work and that local authorities should provide work or adequate maintenance. It had also forced the Liberal government to pass the Trade Union Act of 1913. There is no doubt that it could have done more but the very fact that the Labour Party and the ILP had secured most of the trade union support by 1914, and were achieving significant local and parliamentary political victories, are achievements that should not be slighted given the prevailing political climate of the Edwardian years where Labour was competing with a reforming Liberal administration. It would have been easy for the Labour Party to have become subsumed within progressivism, and authors such as P.F. Clarke and Duncan Tanner have tried to do that, but in effect its connections with the trade unions cut across the harmonious aspirations of the New Liberalism and obviously conflicted with the Old Liberalism. Yet the Labour Party had only loose socialist connections and it is clear that other socialist organisations were also making political advances.

THE SDF, FABIANS, AND OTHER SOCIALIST GROUPS, c. 1890–1914

The ILP was the dominant socialist organisation in Britain at this time and experienced significant growth between 1890 and 1914, having a paying membership of well over 20,000 in 1906 and of 30,000 in 1912, when it also had 1,070 local government representatives. The ILP easily exceeded the total paying membership of all other socialist groups in Britain.[73] Yet it was not the only socialist party to experience significant success. The SDF, despite some fluctuations, made steady progress, particularly between 1906 and 1908, and the Fabians also expanded their influence into the provinces.

The national membership of the SDF had fallen to 453 in 1890, organised in 34 branches, with 368 of these being members of 25 branches in London and 50 in 4 branches in Lancashire. It grew steadily thereafter, reaching 3,259 members in 1897. By that time it was clear that the SDF was strong in two main areas, London and Lancashire. Indeed, Lancashire, with 1,021 members in 19 branches in 1894, had more members than London at the same time although the London membership was normally the larger. SDF membership fell away fairly significantly at the end of the century and dipped further in 1902 and 1903 when the SLP and the SPGB split away;[74] the SDF lost eighty members to the SLP and eighty-eight to the SPGB.[75]

There were numerous issues, apart from the major one of Socialist Unity, that were to dominate the SDF's activities between 1890 and 1914. First, it was involved in the formation of the LRC in 1900, but was annoyed at the way in which the ILP helped to ensure that James Ramsay MacDonald became its secretary and at the SDF Annual Conference of August 1901 it voted 54 to 14 in favour of secession from the LRC. Although the general argument was that within the LRC they were supporting a man and ideas they did not support, most historians agree with the later view of H.W. Lee 'that the decision was a sad mistake' and that

All the propaganda that we did afterwards, all the influence we were able to bring to bear in a Socialist direction, would have been much greater indeed had we carried it on and exercised it as an integral part of the LRC, and not as an outside body at which many supporters of Independent Labour Representation looked a trifle askance because of our withdrawal from the LRC.[76]

The second major feature of this period was the fact that the SDF did gain some political success outside London, most particularly in Lancashire. Martin Crick's main argument is that the SDF did well where it put its resources. The organisational work of J.J. Terrett, Tom Mann, Dan Irving and Herbert Burrows ensured that many of Lancashire's industrial towns, most particularly Blackburn, Burnley, Nelson and Rochdale, had well-developed SDF organisations. Terrett was in fact a paid organiser of the Federation in 1893 and delivered 363 lectures and established 24 new branches in the North in that year. Dan Irving, a Bristol man who had lost a leg in an accident on the Midland Railway, was a member of the Starnthwaite Labour Colony, a farming commune set up by the Revd H. Mills, who was a Fabian. Irving campaigned regularly in Burnley and Nelson and, in the course of 1893, accepted an invitation from the Burnley SDF to become its full-time secretary.

All this organisational work resulted in the formation of the Lancashire District Council of the SDF, which comprised 21 branches in August 1893. In the same month the Federation held its annual conference in Burnley, where the local branch claimed a membership of 600 which rose to 1,000 by the end of the year. The branch appointed a committee of 36 members who invited Hyndman to stand as its prospective parliamentary candidate.[77]

A small number of SDF town councillors were returned in Blackburn, which had four in 1905, Salford South was contested in the 1892 and 1895 general elections; Hyndman contested Burnley in 1895, 1906 and December 1910; and Dan Irving contested Accrington in 1906, Manchester North West in 1908, and Rochdale in 1900, 1908 and December 1910. He later contested Burnley in the 1922 and 1923 general elections. Despite the fact that all these parliamentary contestants were defeated some, such as Hyndman and Irving, polled remarkably well. As Hill and Crick have suggested, their success was based partly upon the close working between the trade unions, the ILP and the SDF and the decision of many Lancashire SDF branches not to leave the LRC at the end of 1901, although this may have contributed to a lack of distinctiveness in the local policy of the SDF. Alan Kidd makes much the same point, stressing that the SDF was not dogmatic and inflexible and noting that in Manchester there was a 'diversity of political philosophy and practice' that sustains this view.[78]

Hill and Crick, quite rightly, suggest that there was a close relationship between the ILP, the SDF and the trades councils in some areas of Lancashire but one cannot ignore the fact that there were also serious tensions, as in Rochdale where in July 1901 the ILP feared that the SDF would 'steal a march' in the selection of a joint Socialist candidate.[79] Such sentiments were not unusual among ILP branches in Lancashire.

Outside Lancashire and London the major area for SDF success was Northampton, where a variety of SDF candidates contested parliamentary seats in 1895, twice in 1906 and twice in 1908.[80] Areas like Leicester saw an SDF/BSP challenge in the parliamentary by-election of 1913 but it was never an established stronghold of SDF influence. Also despite Harry Quelch's contest in the Dewsbury parliamentary by-election in 1902 there is little evidence that the SDF had much lasting influence there or in the rest of Yorkshire.

The third major development is that the SDF continued to shed members as a result of the Boer War and the dominating policies of Hyndman. The SDF's policy towards foreign nations and colonialism was intensely nationalistic and any criticism it had of the famous Jameson raid of 1895–6 was tempered by its anti-Semitic and anti-German references. On the outbreak of the Boer War in 1899 the SDF became instinctively critical and aware of the class implications of the conflict. At first the SDF held anti-war demonstrations. Yet Hyndman began to see the war as a product of the efforts of a few, mainly Jewish, capitalists. The longer it went on the greater was his inclination to praise the British troops and the less equivocal the SDF became in its hostility to the war. The problem was that the SDF was clearly divided between those who were advocating a more international approach to imperialism and the Boer War and those, like Hyndman, who were instinctively nationalistic. This conflict, and the increasing feeling that the movement was 'dictated by the old man [Hyndman] which varied with his moods', led some minority groups to leave the SDF.[81]

Indeed, the Scottish District Council of the SDF was fiercely opposed to the Boer War and also opposed to the SDF's membership of the LRC. When the SDF left the LRC at the end of 1901, it was only partly appeased and immediately found itself opposed to those, such as many rank-and-file members in Lancashire as well as some national leaders, who felt that departure from the LRC was unwise. The SDF began to divide between those who wanted the SDF to be a pure revolutionary support with revolutionary trade union connections, those who wished to remain a vanguard party working within the existing trade unions and those who wished to rejoin the LRC.

Theodore Rothstein opened up this debate after the 1901 Conference, proposing a synthesis between political and economic action, and attacked the Scottish views which favoured industrial action. He regarded these 'impossibilists' as political 'virgins who, for the sake of their immaculate chastity, are ever ready to immolate themselves on the altar of sterility'.[82] He advocated the capturing of trade union support though not the return to the LRC. Others offered a variety of shades of opinion all of which were anathema to the Scottish impossibilists. From then onwards, matters moved apace.

The Scottish SDF began to go its own way and the Scottish District Council produced its own paper, *The Socialist*. Three impossibilists got on to the SDF Executive at the end of 1902 and close links were set up between the Scottish SDF and some sections of the London SDF branches. In open conflict with the national organisation, two groups seceded from the SDF. In May 1903 *The Socialist* announced the formation of the Socialist Labour Party and set up four branches in Edinburgh, Falkirk, Glasgow and Leith, with others forming elsewhere later. This organisation became committed to industrial unionism and became important in Clydeside during the First World War. The London rebels remained within the SDF until they decided to leave and form the Socialist Party of Great Britain on 12 June 1904. It refused to offer palliatives and seems to have adopted the idea that it should act as a publishing company spreading the gospel of socialism and contest parliamentary elections, turning over the entire political and social system once it had a majority in parliament. It survives today, and produces its *Socialist Standard* but, as yet, has not won a single parliamentary seat.

The SDF faced constant argument and division. The Fabians were less divided by political and economic wranglings but equally found their political influence waxing and waning. In the early 1890s the Fabian Society began to expand its influence beyond London and into the provinces. There were a dozen provincial societies in 1890, 42 in 1892 and 72 in 1893. Many of these merged into the ILP and there were only 18 such societies by 1896 and 4 by 1900, excluding 4 university societies with 185 members. In effect there were between 100 and 150 provincial Fabians in 1900 plus about 600 or so London Fabians. It was not until 1906 and 1907 that the position of the Fabians began to revive in the provinces when 39 provincial societies were formed alongside 11 university societies. Permanence was not a feature of the provincial Fabian societies for only the Liverpool Fabian Society could claim a continuous existence between 1890 and 1918. Many societies, such as those in Bradford, Halifax, Sheffield and the Yorkshire Federation of Fabians, had merged into the ILP during the mid-1890s.

The big question is how influential were the Fabians between 1890 and 1914? The impression given by the Webbs, the Coles and other Fabians is that they were immensely important in this period.[83] This is not a view supported by many more recent writers, most particularly Alan McBriar.[84] While admitting that the Fabians sold hundreds of thousands of their Fabian Tracts and Fabian Leaflets, apart from 46,000 copies of *Fabian Essays in Socialism* before 1914, McBriar suggests that their political influence was very limited before 1914. The Fabians carried little influence within the ILP, although they provided some blueprints for the municipal policies they advocated, and they carried even less weight within the LRC/Labour Party to whom their attitude was one of 'benevolent passivity'. Part of the problem was that Fabians were uncertain about which political party would best bring about the change in the social structure that they envisaged and thus they focused increasingly upon a policy of 'permeation' in connection with the Liberal Party and London Liberals on the London County Council and the London School Board. It was here where they seemed to exercise most influence, returning three members to the London School Board in 1888 and one in 1891. To the London County Council they returned six Fabians in 1892, three in 1895, six in 1898 and still had five representatives in 1913.

The performance of socialist societies, other than the ILP, was not terribly impressive in the years 1890 to 1914. An average of about 9,000 SDF members 1,100 or 1,200 Fabians, and 150 to 200 members for both the SLP and the SPGB was poor testimony to socialism in a period when the ILP and the Labour Party were bringing about significant political change. It is hardly surprising then that the issue of Socialist Unity should emerge with regularity from the SDF from the early 1890s until the First World War.

SOCIALIST UNITY, c. 1893–1914

Socialist Unity became an issue for the British left within a year of the formation of the SDF due to the secession of William Morris and the formation of the Socialist League. The formation of other socialist parties, such as the ILP, led to further disunity within the British socialist movement. Nevertheless, notwithstanding the proliferation of British socialist societies with their distinctive credentials, there were several attempts to form a united socialist party in Britain between 1893 and 1914. They were normally encouraged, on the one hand, by the advocates of the 'religion of socialism' such as Morris, Blatchford and Victor Grayson, and, on the other hand, by Hyndman and the SDF. The aim of these efforts was to strengthen socialist organisations, whether in periods of success or failure, but in every instance they failed due to the intractable problem of bringing together socialists of distinctively different persuasions under the umbrella of one party. These failures have led recent historians to debate two major questions. First, they have asked at what point Socialist Unity ceased to be a viable alternative to the Labour Alliance between the ILP and the trade unions. Stephen Yeo feels that Socialist Unity became impossible after the mid-1890s; David Howell suggests that this 'suppressed alternative' became unlikely about five to ten years later, as the leaders of the ILP opted for the trade union rather than socialist alliance; while Martin Crick feels that Socialist Unity was still a viable alternative until at least 1911, if not 1914, when a determined effort was made to form the BSP, the one socialist party and the forerunner of the Communist Party of Great Britain.[85] Thus 1895, 1900 to 1906 and 1911 to 1914 are offered as alternative years when the prospects of Socialist Unity in Britain reached a watershed. Historians have been equally divided on the second, and related, question of why Socialist Unity was not achieved. In particular, they have focused upon two subsidiary questions. First, why did the Independent Labour Party choose the alliance with trade unions and the parliamentary route to power rather than Socialist Unity? Secondly, how important was the intransigence and narrowness of the SDF in thwarting moves towards Socialist Unity? Some writers have noted the steadfast opposition of the ILP leadership as the main problem while others have focused upon the inflexible and domineering nature of Hyndman and the SDF, offering the 'image of the Social Democratic Federation as a narrow and dogmatic sect unsuited to the rigours of British politics'.[86]

The argument presented here is that there was little real prospect of Socialist Unity being achieved in Britain after the mid-1890s and that the reason for the failure of Socialist Unity is to be found in the diverse and compromising nature of the ILP and the continued intransigence of the SDF. Even if the domineering influence of Hyndman has been blown up out of all proportion into a marvellous myth, it is clear that even in 1912 his antipathy towards industrial action was a block to Socialist Unity, as was his attitude towards defence and foreign policy.

As Yeo suggests, by the mid-1890s, with the political failure of the ILP in the general election of 1895 which Beatrice Webb dubbed 'the most expensive funeral since Napoleon',[87] Keir Hardie and the other ILP leaders were forced to choose between the business of 'making socialists' and the need to make a political party. Up to the 1890s socialism was in the business of 'making socialists' and it did not matter to which socialist organisation an individual belonged. Yeo argues that after the 1895 general election and the death of Morris in 1896, the ILP and other socialist groups chose to become entrenched in an alliance with trade unions that focused upon parliamentary and local political organisation. The need to win elections, and electioneering, replaced the ethical aspects of socialism which had focused upon leading the ethical life of a socialist. The general drift of Yeo's argument seems fair, even if the fine detail has proved contentious. Indeed, Yeo has argued that party connections became much more important to socialists towards the end of the 1890s. Howell accepts much of this and feels that the alliance with trade unions meant that Socialist Unity became a less likely option.[88] This view seems plausible but what is difficult to accept is the argument put forward by Martin Crick who seeks to extend the Socialist Unity debate to at least 1911 and possibly 1914. His argument is that many socialists were unattached, that the ILP and the SDF worked closely together in Lancashire, and that the socialist revival of the 1904 to 1909 period ensured that there was an alternative to the alliance with trade unions on the eve of the First World War and that the SDF was far more flexible and less sectarian than is often supposed. Nevertheless, his argument and supporting evidence could be interpreted in another way. As Jeff Hill has noted, the SDF in Lancashire appeared to be detached from the policies of its parent organisation and it success may have been despite the actions of its national body.[89] It was also possible that the vibrancy of socialism was just as likely to produce sectarian rigidity as it was to engender a desire for Socialist Unity, as each organisation viewed its own individual successes as confirmation of the correctness of its policies. In the final analysis, the intransigence of both the ILP and the SDF, and the success of the ILP and trade union alliance in 1906, made Socialist Unity a highly unlikely proposition and confirmed the experience of the previous twenty years that socialism in Britain was to be characterised more by schism than by unity. Indeed, there was little prospect of Socialist Unity being achieved in the 1890s and none after 1906, once the LRC/Labour Party had established its trade union credentials and parliamentary achievements.

In August 1911, Victor Grayson wrote that 'The time for the formation of the BRITISH SOCIALIST PARTY has definitely come.'[90] He then called for others to follow his example and to withdraw from the ILP, vowing never to join another socialist organisation until the BSP, the 'one socialist party', had been formed. Grayson's appeal worked briefly. There was a period of ecstatic enthusiasm leading to the Socialist Unity conference in Manchester in September 1911, when a clamour of support emerged. Within a week of his appeal Grayson was writing that 'The British Socialist Party is practically an accomplished fact . . . the response has been extraordinary.'[91] After the Unity Conference, Grayson wrote that it 'was the most harmonious and unanimous Conference of the kind that has ever been held'.[92] It seemed that the dream of uniting socialists of all persuasions under the umbrella of one organisation was going to become reality. The attempt had been made several times previously but this moment seemed propitious, for Britain was experiencing a period of serious industrial unrest and both the ILP and the Labour Party were under attack because of their failure to lead in the fight for socialism. Yet support for the BSP seemed to evaporate almost as quickly as it appeared. The vast majority of ILP members were not attracted to it and the BSP was soon little more than the old SDF/SDP. Yet for a brief moment, carried forward by the impetus of Grayson's enthusiasm, the BSP promised to be something more. The BSP was eventually undermined and destroyed by the bitter disagreements that had blighted earlier moves towards Socialist Unity.

The idea of forming a united socialist party was, clearly, not new in 1911 and, indeed, it was fitting that Grayson should begin his campaign in the *Clarion* for it was Robert Blatchford, its editor, who had set the precedent by his staunch advocacy of the ideal during the 1890s. In 1894, Blatchford had called for the formation of 'One Socialist Party'. He desired that the ILP, SDF and the Clarion Scouts should submerge their differences and unite all genuine socialists into one party. It was an extension to the provinces of ideas that had already occurred in London in 1892 and 1893 when Morris and the Hammersmith Socialist Society promoted the idea of a union between themselves and the SDF and Fabians. The result of the Morris initiative had been the rather vague and imprecise *Manifesto of English Socialists* issued on May Day 1893. The main weakness of the document is that it excluded the national ILP. Blatchford's appeal was an attempt to rectify this omission. Nevertheless, the campaign proved to be mistimed and misplaced, and Blatchford's faith was unfounded. The idea of creating some type of mass party concerned more with fellowship than political organisation simply did not appeal to Hyndman or Hardie.

Nevertheless, socialist defeats in the 1895 general election revived the prospects of Socialist Unity. Keir Hardie was rather reluctant to push the ILP in this direction, preferring to work for an alliance with the trade unions, but agreed to support the idea of an 'Informal Conference' with other Socialist organisations on 29 July 1897. At first, the SDF was reluctant to respond to these overtures but financial difficulties forced its leaders to think anew. As a result it decided to send five delegates to the 'Informal Conference' where it was agreed that a joint committee would be set up until decisions were made about the nature and name of the new arrangement. An additional committee was formed to deal with arbitration in election disputes. Subsequently, H.W. Lee, secretary of the SDF, gave his support to attempts to create real unity between socialists.[93] There was then a referendum of the joint membership of the ILP and the SDF which voted 5,158 to 886 in favour of fusion. Yet the decision was never implemented.

Hardie intervened to inform the ILP that less than a third of its paying membership had voted and a decision on the ballot was delayed until the next annual conference. In the meantime he campaigned strongly against fusion and suggested that the methods of propaganda of the SDF and its stagnant membership would 'check rather than help forward our movement'.[94] This was a view supported by J. Bruce Glasier, whose paper to the ILP Conference in Birmingham, of April 1898, maintained that federation and continued separate existence would be advantageous to the ILP for 'the ways of the SDF are not our ways. If I may say so, the ways of the SDF are more doctrinaire, more Calvinistic, more aggressively sectarian than the ILP.'[95]

The National Administrative Council of the ILP (NAC) supported Hardie's demand for federation rather than fusion. It called for a vote of ILP members in July 1898, which resulted in 2,397 voting for federation and 1,695 for fusion. The ILP leadership had thus blocked the prospect of creating a united socialist party and the issue expired when Lee stressed that the SDF was 'in favour of fusion'.[96] The belated efforts of Blatchford to revive negotiations failed, even though a poll of the *Clarion* readers produced a vote of 4,429 for fusion and 3,994 for federation.[97]

The ILP leadership had thwarted the attempt to form a united socialist party but there is much evidence to suggest that the rank and file of the ILP were very mixed in their attitude towards Socialist Unity. There appears to have been support for the Socialist Unity idea in many parts of Lancashire. Littleborough ILP called for 'one militant socialist party' while the branches of Droylsden and Preston refused to enter the ILP's second ballot because they had already voted decisively for fusion. Bolton West, Everton and Blackburn opposed the NAC and Stockport announced its intention 'to withdraw from the party' as a result of the 'undemocratic action of the NAC'.[98]

At the other extreme there was far less support for Socialist Unity in the textile regions of the West Riding of Yorkshire. In 1898 and 1899 there were about 11,000 to 12,000 members of the ILP who paid fees on a regular basis and about 2,700 to 3,000 of these came from the West Riding.[99] The National ILP was strongly influenced by the ILP branches in the West Riding, and in particular by the powerful branches in Bradford and Halifax. In Bradford the ILP's rejection of Socialist Unity was based upon the fact that, even in decline, it had about 1,000 members, while the SDF was almost powerless, having started in Bradford in August 1895 with six members, averaging fifteen members, and expiring in 1897. The ILP had nothing to join. Not surprisingly, in 1896, the local Labour paper argued, with some justification, that 'The time has not come for the thorough fusion of forces which the creation of such a party would demand. . . . The formation of such a party before the time was ripe would bring nothing but mischief.'[100]

There was little support for the idea of fusion within the Bradford ILP and equally little support for the idea in Halifax. The July 1898 issue of the *Record*, the organ of the Halifax ILP, did refer to the 'One Socialist Party' campaign going on in Bradford but played down its importance, doubting its 'practical superiority' to the existing situation. The report suggested that the term fusion indicated a hardening of social policies which did not fit the more general approach favoured by the members of the Halifax ILP. Also most ILP members spent a working week protected by trade union surveillance, and weekends attending Labour Church activities, glee club meetings and rambles. Satisfied with their achievements they were not inclined to join forces with a society which had little presence in Halifax and which appeared to play down the importance of trade unionism. On the whole one is left with the impression that Socialist Unity barely merited serious consideration in the ILP strongholds of Bradford and Halifax. Also, the Yorkshire Divisional Council of the ILP had rejected the idea, by 32 votes to 16, as early as October 1894. In Bradford, Halifax and more generally throughout the West Riding of Yorkshire, there was little or no inclination to join with an organisation that carried almost no political support. Martin Crick has suggested that the movement for Socialist Unity was probably a movement from the bottom up, but even this is partial and barely evident in some areas, most notably in the West Riding of Yorkshire.

It would appear that there was little prospect that Socialist Unity would be achieved in the late 1890s. There were four main reasons for this. In the first place, the ILP leaders and many of their supporters had attached their flags to the trade union mast which the SDF had ignored. Secondly, there were intense rivalries within the broader socialist movement between Hardie and Blatchford on the one hand and between Hardie and Hyndman on the other. Thirdly, if the ILP was driven by political expediency so was the SDF, whose leadership showed no inclination towards Socialist Unity until it began to lose members in the late 1890s and once it was faced with financial embarrassment. Fourthly, while just under half the rank-and-file members of the ILP favoured fusion, the other half, possibly the majority, favoured federation and it was the second body, firmly based in Yorkshire, which carried most political clout with the ILP leaders. Given these facts it is not surprising that the attempts at Socialist Unity in the 1890s ended in failure, and that future efforts would be blighted.

It is true, as Martin Crick suggests, that there was nothing unusual in socialists having dual membership of the ILP and SDF. Quite clearly it didn't matter to many socialists which organisation they joined, for to them a socialist Britain was imminent. But after the 1895 general election defeats it was more difficult to sustain hope for the immediate success of socialism and electioneering and leadership considerations got in the way of sustaining any hopes of socialist success. Indeed, the experience of Lancashire should not be emphasised too much for, as Jeff Hill suggested, there were two factors that needed to be taken into consideration. One is that the Lancashire SDF branches acted more flexibly than the parent organisation, and some branches still continued to remain in the LRC. Secondly, they paid a price for their flexibility for, as Hill suggests, 'Though on the one hand local autonomy was a source of strength in that it allowed social-democrats to adapt to their immediate environment, on the other hand, it produced a movement notoriously prone to internal divisions over strategy and one which ultimately was unable to preserve its identity as a united socialist force.'[101]

Even if Socialist Unity had been achieved it seems unlikely that it would have survived. Most probably the ILP would have split, with Hardie leading his West Riding of Yorkshire contingent and other supporters into an alternative organisation. In effect the SDF would probably have been left with its own supporters and a few other socialists, much as occurred when the BSP was formed in 1911.

There was a second phase in the development of Socialist Unity at the beginning of the twentieth century. The LRC was formed as a result of a conference held in February 1900 and, at first sight, it appeared to have met the needs of both alternative strategies for the progress of the Labour movement. On the one hand, it was an alliance between the trade unions and the socialist parties, and, on the other, it brought the socialist parties, including the SDF and the ILP, within one organisation. Although the LRC was not a socialist organisation at this time, five of the twelve members of the Executive Committee were socialists and there was a prospect that this alliance could be the basis of closer cooperation between the SDF and the ILP. Yet within eighteen months of the founding conference the SDF voted to secede. This decision was taken because 'We were being committed to the support of men and measures with which we do not agree.'[102] Indeed, the ILP and the SDF clashed from the outset when the ILP failed to support the SDF resolution committing the LRC to socialist objectives.

The SDF's secession from the LRC was a mistake for it now cut itself off from the most influential independent political organisation of the working classes, although its action is explicable in terms of the internal difficulties within the Party which led to the secession of two groups who formed the SPGB and the SLP organisations, usually dubbed the 'Impossibilists'.

At this point the SDF seemed to have revived an interest in Socialist Unity but, according to David Howell, such a prospect had effectively been ruled out by the formation of the LRC: 'The logic of national events . . . combined with local developments . . . to erode the United Socialist alternatives, even in an environment where it had developed a significant presence.'[103]

Only Martin Crick seems to doubt this judgement, basing his assessment upon the situation that existed in Lancashire, which has already been referred to, and upon the Dewsbury parliamentary by-election of 1902 where Harry Quelch obtained 1,597 votes as the SDF candidate, 517 votes more than Hartley had secured in the 1895 general election despite the hostility of the ILP. Referring to the Dewsbury contest, A.M. Thompson, of the *Clarion*, wrote that it was

> a crushing blow to the conflicting 'Leaders' and a triumphant vindication of Socialist Unity. . . . The rank and file of Dewsbury have shown the way. Socialists of all denominations have shut their eyes to the scowlings and nudgings of rival party officials and stood shoulder to shoulder for Socialism.[104]

The problem with Crick's approach is that the Lancashire SDF began to decline after the departure of the national SDF from the LRC and the Quelch affair produced a damaging conflict between the SDF and the ILP rather than the climate that would have produced Socialist Unity. In any case, this second phase of Socialist Unity, if it can be regarded as such, did not get very far.

Crick is quite correct to suggest that there were strong moves towards its further advocacy between 1904 and 1911, although this is not to suggest that it was a viable proposition. The SDF certainly changed its attitude towards Socialist Unity and fully embraced the Amsterdam

Conference resolution in 1904, which instructed socialist parties in all countries to amalgamate. It made approaches to renew negotiations with the ILP in 1907, 1909 and 1910 but the ILP laid down the precondition that the SDF should re-affiliate with the LRC. It would also appear that the SDF became internally divided over the issues of industrial conflict and international relations as new figures in the party, such as Zelda Kahan, began to challenge Hyndman, Quelch and the old established leaders of the SDF/SDP. Undoubtedly, the rising emphasis which the SDF placed upon Socialist Unity was a distraction from these internal conflicts but it was hardly going to offer a solution to the conflicts of the SDF/SDP nor to the problem of policy as it emerged in the BSP. The SDF/SDP may have become less narrowly economically deterministic in its attitudes but the dominating influence of Hyndman's view was still present in the vital years when the BSP was being formed.

There were quite clearly other factors which encouraged the idea of reviving Socialist Unity apart from the convenience it offered to the SDF/SDP. The membership of all socialist organisations rose between 1906 and 1909 and the return of twenty-nine LRC MPs to parliament brought an optimism about social change that was not going to be realised, even by a Labour Party working upon a reforming Liberal government. The contrast between Labour Party inaction and rising socialist ambitions certainly increased tensions between some members of the ILP and the Labour Party.

Victor Grayson echoed this disillusionment with parliament following his success in the Colne Valley parliamentary by-election in 1907. His views were outlined in a book entitled *The Problem of Parliament – a Criticism and a Remedy*, published in 1909 and dedicated to 'H. M. Hyndman, Robert Blatchford and J. Keir Hardie, who can give this country a Socialist party tomorrow if they care to lead the way'. At much the same time, E.R. Hartley was arguing in a debate at Manchester that the ILP was 'swamped' within the Labour Party.[105] Indeed, between 1909 and 1911, forty-six branches of the ILP collapsed. The moment seemed propitious for a renewal of the Socialist Unity debate.

Indeed, the criticism of the ILP intensified. Towards the end of 1910 four of the fourteen members of the NAC of the ILP signed the pamphlet *Let Us Reform the Labour Party*, better known as the 'Green Manifesto'. Written by J. McLachlan, a Manchester councillor, introduced by Leonard Hall, and contributed to by C.T. Douthwaite and the Revd J.H. Belcher, it attacked the ILP and the Labour Party for sacrificing socialist principles in order not to embarrass the Liberal government.

Subsequently, Fred Jowett criticised these men for their lack of loyalty and all lost their seats on the NAC at the ILP annual conference in 1911.

Also, social representation committees were emerging in towns such as Birmingham and Manchester to unite socialists of all persuasions, including many who were not attached to any particular organisation. The United Socialist Propaganda League was formed to combine them together and to spread the message to the rural areas.[106] Indeed, there was sufficient evidence to encourage Grayson, now free of parliamentary duties and the political editor of the *Clarion*, to think that a call for Socialist Unity would be well received. Within three months he was claiming that about 30 per cent of the ILP members had joined the BSP.[107] This seems excessive and percentages of 20 per cent for Yorkshire and about 25 per cent for Lancashire seem more accurate.[108] Within a couple of years these levels were to diminish significantly as individuals and branches drifted out of the BSP. Ultimately, the BSP was to become the SDF/SDP under a new name.

In the meantime the Socialist Unity Conference was held at Manchester on the weekend of 30 September to 1 October 1911 at which delegates claimed to represent 35,000 members coming from 41 ILP branches, 32 Clarion clubs and fellowships, 85 SDF/SDP branches, 50 local socialist societies and 12 branches of the new BSP plus other organisations. It was later to claim 40,000 members and 370 branches, although its total dues of £650 based upon 1s (5p) membership subscription suggests that there were only 13,000 paying members.[109] Matters went well but the Provisional Committee that was set up soon had trouble when Grayson realised that the SDF/SDP was not going to cease to exist immediately. Grayson left the BSP and many of his supporters did the same.

Other problems were added when Hyndman addressed the first annual conference of the BSP in April 1912. While noting the success of the new body he admitted that there had been problems and he attacked the syndicalist ideas, on the need for industrial unionism, and noted that 'of the futility of resuscitated syndicalism it is needless to speak. There is nothing real and nothing ideal in the floundering and hysterical propaganda of segregated grab.'[110]

Such a statement from the chair made the 'old guard' position clear. They would concede that 'The political and industrial organisations of the working class must be complementary to each other', but their view that the main function of the BSP was 'the organisation of an independent political party of the working class' remained unchanged. Leonard Hall, a syndicalist, moved an amendment at the first annual conference to gain equal recognition for industrial as well as political action but it was defeated by 100 votes to 46. The syndicalist debate continued for several months but they broke from the BSP in October 1912 when the BSP *Manifesto* was issued, emphasising the primacy of political over industrial action.

Many BSP branches were divided on the issue. The Huddersfield BSP, led by Arthur Gardiner, was a strong advocate of industrial action, partly owing to the pioneer propaganda work of syndicalist E.J.B. Allen, who lived locally. It passed a resolution committing itself to socialist representation and 'to assist in the building up of a powerful union movement'.[111] In other areas there was serious division within the local BSP branch. This was most evident in the case of Birmingham where H.B. Williams, secretary to the local branch, found himself in conflict with Leonard Hall, Thomas R. Wintringham and others over industrial unionism and the 'Graysonian clot' on the party.[112]

This split was just one of several tensions that divided the BSP, the other major one being the conflict over increased government naval expenditure between Hyndman and Zelda Kahan.[113] The end product was that the BSP declined. It faced financial problems with Twentieth Century Press, which produced *Justice*, and the 'enrol a Million Socialists' campaign, begun in April 1912, failed to get anywhere near the 100,000 members it wished to win in less than a year, never mind the one million it hoped for in five, and in fact its total membership fell from a claimed 40,000 in 1912 to a mere 15,313 by 1913.[114] In 1914, the BSP was forced to change tack and it began to woo the Labour Party and the ILP, and worked to form the United Socialist Council, organised joint socialist demonstrations with the ILP and the Fabians, and voted by 3,263 to 2,410 in favour of affiliating to the Labour Party.[115] As a result the BSP applied to join the Labour Party on 23 June 1914 and affiliated in 1916. In October 1916 a not very effective United Socialist Council was also formed.

Stephen Yeo has written that the formative socialist period of the 1880s and '90s was 'too exciting to last' and added that 'Socialism in that period had not yet become the prisoner of a particular elaborate machine – a machine which would come to associate its own well-being with the prospects of Socialism.'[116] He was right, for by the mid and late 1890s party electioneering was rapidly taking the place of the task of 'making socialists'. By that time, also, the ILP and the SDF had become almost sectarian in their approach, which meant that there was little prospect of obtaining Socialist Unity. If it was the ILP leaders who were intransigent opponents of Socialist Unity in the 1890s, as they sought the support of trade unions, it was equally the case that the

SDF/SDP leaders in the 1911 and 1914 period were also intransigent for there was little evidence that Hyndman was going to change his mind on the issue of industrial action and defence. Hyndman's control of the SDF/SDP might not be total but it was still sufficient to thwart attempts to unite and keep socialists in one mass party.

In the final analysis, Socialist Unity was a non-starter after the formation of the LRC in 1900, if not before, and was killed by the rigidity of both ILP and SDF leaders. The fact that there were close relations between the ILP and SDF branches, and dual membership, in some areas like Lancashire is of little significance because, as Hill noted, the sheer flexibility of the Lancashire SDF branches made them prone to internal strife and compromise. Areas like the West Riding of Yorkshire, dominated by the powerful Bradford and Halifax ILP organisations, would have no truck with Socialist Unity and were soon operating a trade union alliance. As the CPGB was to find, mass party socialism within a united socialist party in Britain has proved to be an appealing illusion. Syndicalism, which emerged most forcefully on the eve of the First World War, was no more successful in paving the way for a socialist Britain.

SYNDICALISM AND GUILD SOCIALISM

Industrial conflict began to increase dramatically immediately prior to the First World War and continued apace throughout the wartime years. To many contemporaries, the rise in strike activity that occurred at this time was associated with the rise of syndicalism, but the balance of recent opinion has played down these events. Instead, recent research suggests that syndicalism was a minor and incidental occurrence.

Until the 1970s the traditional view about British syndicalism was that it was a rather limited movement which had a fitful impact upon British society between 1910 and the summer of 1912.[117] Such attempts to minimise the syndicalism were then challenged by Bob Holton.[118] He maintained that its influence extended between 1910 and 1914, noting that many workers acted in a proto-syndicalist manner and stressing that many workers began to feel that they could change society through industrial rather than political action. To Holton, British syndicalism was just as alive and vital as that on the Continent and in the United States. More recently, however, Professor Clegg has noted that, apart from the Cambrian mining dispute in 1910–11 and the dockers and seamen's strike in Liverpool in the summer of 1911, there is little to suggest that syndicalism held much sway in the fourteen major industrial disputes that occurred between 1910 and 1914. Although it was coal mining that provided fruitful ground for syndicalism there was practically no support for it at all in areas such as south and west Yorkshire, and even in South Wales, which produced the main British syndicalist document *The Miners' Next Step* advocating the organisation of industrial unionism and the general strike, the support seems to have been limited after the spring of 1912. The protracted Cambrian dispute and the conflicts at Tonypandy might be the stuff of British syndicalism but the fact is that when faced with a ballot on a national strike in 1912 the South Wales miners voted, by two to one, in favour of accepting the government's Minimum Wages Act, while all other coalfields voted to reject the government's bill and, thus, were in favour of strike action. Even Holton has to admit that 'this undoubtedly represented a setback to the syndicalists of the Unofficial Reform Committee. . . .'[119] One must also reflect that the *Syndicalist Railwaymen* may have appeared in 1911 and claimed to have converted the ASRS to workers control in 1912 but the suggestion that it forced the amalgamation of four railway unions into a pro-syndicalist National Union of Railwaymen (NUR) is simply not supported by the evidence. The amalgamation movement was emerging well before the development of British syndicalism and was separate from it.

Notwithstanding this failure, it is clear that syndicalism was part of the debate going on within socialist ranks. After 1903 the industrial unionism it advocated, and the general strike it anticipated, was being pressed forward by the Socialist Labour Party. It established the British Advocates of Industrial Unionism (BAIU) in February 1906 in order to set up the British equivalent of the American Industrial Workers of the World. There were other strands of influence as well. Socialists in the United States had moved to form the Industrial Workers of the World in 1905 and through their main leader, Daniel De Leon, had come to the conclusion that craft trade unions in the United States did not represent the interests of all the working class and that revolutionary industrial unions, outside the existing craft unions, had to be formed. This was not entirely appropriate in the British situation, where trade unionism was stronger than in the USA, but it meant that groups of miners in South Wales set up their Unofficial Reform committees within the existing trade unions. They were influenced further in the direction of 'boring from within' trade unions, rather than developing De Leon's dual unionism, by the formation of Tom Mann's Industrial Syndicalist Education League in Manchester in September 1910. This was influenced more by French revolutionary trade unionism than it was by its American socialist counterpart.

Industrial unionism or syndicalism was simply one attack upon the dominant statist conception of socialism in Britain and, as already indicated, emerged to blight the efforts of the BSP to gain a meaningful party of Socialist Unity. Yet it was not the only one, for the rather less important guild socialism also emerged at this time. In 1912 A.R. Orage's journal *The New Age* published some articles by S.G. Hobson which expounded the idea that future society should be shared by consumers, who would be represented by the state, and producers organised into industrial unions, who would be responsible for production. The state would set the production targets and the workers, in industrial unions, would determine how that production was to be achieved. There would be no conflict of interest in the sense that every person would exert influence as a consumer and a producer. There would be no general strike because unions would simply extend their power and undermine managerial rights. The ideas, which were later developed by other middle-class intellectuals like G.D.H. Cole, were partly influenced by William Morris and Ruskin but above all by A.J. Penty's *Restoration of the Guild System*, produced in 1906.

Penty was an architect who, despite being a Fabian until 1902, was greatly influenced by William Morris's *News from Nowhere*, and presented a vision of a small-scale agricultural economy of the Middle Ages dependent on hand production and skill rather than machine production. His ideas lacked a sense of reality and the guild socialist movement they spawned was sifted out as irrelevant to the future of socialism in Britain during the First World War. What it represented, however, was part of the growing concern that syndicalism had about the imposition of state power which, if it was not checked, could substitute state power for capitalism and bring about little in the way of democratic rights for the workers.

They reflected the concern of Hilaire Belloc who was worried about the possible creation of a 'servile state' which would emerge as employers were forced to attend to the welfare of their workers, a situation which could easily make workers simply well-fed employees who exercised no real power or influence. Guild socialism was to be a means by which real democratic rights were established and whereby the sectionalism implied by syndicalism's tendency to proliferate numerous industrial unions operating numerous workers' control schemes would be avoided. In the end, like syndicalism it carried little force within British Socialism as collectivism began to overwhelm the more individualistic approach to socialism.

SOCIALISM ON THE EVE OF WAR

In the decade before the First World War it became obvious that the Labour Party, and the ILP to a lesser extent, carried the real hope of achieving socialism in Britain. The SDF/BSP and other socialist parties and alternatives were of very limited influence. For this reason, Lenin intervened in 1908 to ensure that the Labour Party remained a member of the International Socialist Bureau. Like other more overtly socialist organisations, the Labour Party had accepted an internationalist view whereby upon the outbreak of a European or world war it would coordinate working-class action to overthrow capitalism and end the conflict. There was, of course, no unanimity of support for such a position within British socialism. While MacDonald and the Labour Party played lip-service to the notion it is quite clear that both Blatchford and Hyndman were intensely nationalistic and anti-German and would not support such a position.

The outbreak of war in 1914 came with startling suddenness. As late as 1 August 1914 Continental socialist leaders were still not convinced that it was even a likely possibility. As Haupt suggests, they were captives of their own myths about their ability to prevent war and unaware of the depths of national chauvinism.[120] They were caught short by events, pushed on to the defensive and literally became disorientated spectators, waiting to be submerged by the gathering wave of nationalism.

Arthur Henderson spoke against the war the weekend before it started but within a week had declared that all must support the war of national defence. The Labour Party moved from opposing the war to supporting the war effort within days and Ramsay MacDonald, having wanted Britain to remain neutral on 3 August, resigned as chairman of the Labour Party on 5 August 1914 because his party had supported war credits. In other words, the Labour Party was divided on the war issue as was the ILP and the BSP.[121]

CONCLUSION

Socialism in Britain made great strides forward between 1890 and 1914 in terms of supporters, policies and political effectiveness. The 2,000 active socialists of 1890 had risen to 50,000 or more by 1914, although many of them carried wider influence within the broader political organisation of the Labour Party. Most of the socialist parties were statist organisations which believed in political rather than industrial action but new democratic and individualistic forms of industrial socialism were beginning to emerge by the Edwardian years, albeit on a small scale and without much impact. The most significant developments were in terms of political alliances. The ILP, by far the largest socialist organisation in Britain, had identified its political future in an alliance with the trade unions which spawned the LRC/Labour Party. It was this parliamentary route, based upon the political support of the trade union movement and with the prospect of some form of state control, that was to reap reward. The Labour Party and the ILP may have been subject to strong criticism between 1910 and 1914, particularly about their lack of political independence from the Liberals, but that usually came from organisations that carried remarkably little political or industrial clout and whose prospects of bringing about a socialist Britain were remote. To some socialists the Labour Party was not the ideal vehicle for bringing about a socialist Britain, because it appeared to threaten individual and democratic rights with the statist views it adopted, but the fact is that it made enormous political strides between 1900 and 1914. Ostensibly, it was not a socialist party, although it had a socialist core. This was to change with the challenge of the First World War. However, it should be noted that the political Labour movement, and the Labour Party in particular, had firmly established itself before the First World War and was seriously challenging the Liberal Party as the progressive party of British politics.

SOCIALISM AND THE CHALLENGE OF WAR, 1914–18

The First World War exerted a major impact upon socialism in Britain; it contributed to the growth of state intervention, divided the Liberals, directed the progressive vote to Labour, galvanised the link between the Labour Party and British trade unionism, and provided the climate from which the Communist Party of Great Britain was to emerge. It may have even weakened and fragmented socialism in Britain. In a specifically socialist context the war saw four major developments. First, it reduced the influence of the ILP over the Labour Party, despite the fact that the ILP was not the pacifist and unpatriotic organisation it was often made out to be and even allowing for the growth of the ILP in Scotland. Secondly, it helped to reshape the Marxist organisations in Britain in the wake of the Bolshevik Revolution. Thirdly, and more important, it saw the Labour Party produce a new constitution, in 1918, which committed it to the public ownership of the means of production. The importance of this particular event has divided historians between those who feel that this was a conscious decision, arrived at after the sifting of socialist alternatives, and those who feel that it was an afterthought which carried little significance. In other words, was there dichotomy or continuity in Labour and socialist politics? The answer is by no means clear although the impact of Clause Four at the time was less than is often supposed. Fourthly, it is possible that the war paved the way for Labour's growth by either galvanising the class politics it had already established or by dividing the Liberal Party and creating a hiatus in progressive politics into which the Labour Party could slip. Potentially, the most important of these four developments was the acceptance of socialism by the Labour Party, although it was not certain that this was meant to be more than a rallying cry for those who were committed to establishing greater equality in society.

THE LABOUR PARTY AND CLAUSE FOUR

The origins and importance of Clause Four have been debated in the works of Arthur Marwick, Philip Abrams, Ralph Miliband and many others. It was put into sharp focus in 1974 with the publication of J.M. Winter, *Socialism and the Challenge of War: Ideas and Politics in Britain, 1912–18* and R. McKibbin, *The Evolution of the Labour Party 1910–1924*, who disagreed over whether or not Clause Four should be taken seriously as a statement of Labour's socialism.[1]

It was Winter who developed the orthodox view that the First World War brought about significant changes in British society. Building upon Marwick's study of the volcanic impact of the First World War upon British values, organisations and ideas, Winter argued that the improved incomes and employment prospects of all workers resulted in the blurring of distinctions within the working class and between classes. He argued that the deep involvement of all sections of society in the war effort led to a decline in the deferential attitudes of the working class and the rising prospect of political and social change. In this environment, Labour leaders were forced to conclude that the restructuring of the Labour Party was essential and they were forced to sift through a variety of socialist policies in order to select those which would be most apposite to its post-war growth. In the final analysis, the wartime conditions favoured the collectivist policies of the Webbs and paved the way for the 1918 Labour Constitution and Clause Four, its clear commitment to a future socialist state. The more democratic guild socialist policies of G.D.H. Cole and the long-term educational approach of R.H. Tawney did not offer the clarity, immediacy or wartime context that seemed essential to the Labour leaders. The Marxist alternative was never considered.

Such an interpretation is entirely alien to Ross McKibbin who rejects the view that the wartime economy made much difference to the potential of Labour politics, and cannot believe that the men who drew up the new Labour Constitution, most of whom were in their fifties and sixties, were capable of dramatic conversion or that Clause Four was anything other than an 'uncharacteristic adornment' of the new constitution. To him, the trends in British Labour development were evident before the war and Clause Four was simply a response to the wider electorate which was to be created by the Representation of the People Act of 1918. He believes that it is inconceivable that it could have been otherwise given that the Labour Party was moving to the right not the left, during the war, a fact evidenced by the increased trade union control of the National Executive Committee of the Labour Party under the 1918 Labour Constitution.[2] Thus

> in Britain alone the left wing of the working-class movement did not emerge from the war in some way stronger than it entered it. It is true, certainly, that the unions disliked socialists more than they disliked socialism and it is true also that dislike of socialists was generated by a highly developed class-consciousness. Were socialists suspect because they were socialists or because they were supposedly not working-class? – it is often hard to tell. But in a way the result was the same, and if the war did not necessarily mean the defeat of socialism in Britain, it did mean the defeat of socialists.[3]

His views are not unlike those expressed by Ralph Miliband, who referred to Clause Four as a form of labourism rather than socialism and that *Labour and the New Social Order*, the Labour Party's statement of policy, was a Fabian blueprint for piecemeal collectivism.

Although both Winter and McKibbin differ in many respects there are only three vital points of divergence. The first is the extent to which the trends evident in the Labour Party were apparent before the First World War. The second is whether or not the wartime economy led to the creation of a homogeneous working class. The third is the degree to which the Labour Party seriously discussed the socialist alternatives; put more bluntly, was the Labour Party conscious of the need for a distinguishing ideology, concerned with offering a genuine socialist ideology, or simply responding to the political exigencies of the time?

The first sub-debate stems from the emphasis which McKibbin placed upon the growth of the Labour Party before the First World War. McKibbin sees that Labour was growing before 1914 with the support of the working class while Winter sees the pre-war Labour Party as being a 'rudderless' organisation. The second debate is concerned more with the way in which the wartime conditions narrowed the pay differentials and the social divides. However, it is the third sub-debate which is vital to the present discussion.

According to Winter, the lack of direction from the Labour Party on many issues forced socialists 'to work out anew political ideas which they hoped would give form and purpose to the growing protests of the labouring population'.[4] This led to a debate about the socialist direction of the pre-war Labour Party, having been clarified by the war which helped to sift the socialist alternatives. Through the agency of the War Emergency: Workers' National Committee, the gradualist and statist policies of the Webbs were to become dominant in the discussion of the 1918 Constitution of the Labour Party and in *Labour and the New Social Order*, Labour's reconstruction programme which was written by Sidney Webb and published in 1918. This interpretation contrasts sharply with McKibbin's view that Clause Four has hogged the limelight of debate to the detriment of the corpus of the 1918 Constitution which 'embodied not an ideology but a system by which power in the Labour Party was distributed'.[5] To McKibbin, it is the practical considerations of the time, with Labour in the wartime coalition governments, events in Russia and the 1918 Representation of the People Act, that dominated Labour's approach to the 1918 Constitution. The demands of trade unions were to the fore in the formulation of the new constitution and socialism was very much an afterthought.

In contrast, part of the sense of greater working-class unity and possible improvements in living standards, which Winter refers to, may have come from the activities of the War Emergency: Workers' National Committee. Winter feels that this body did much to promote the state socialist ideas of the Webbs within the Labour Party. His views are not shared by McKibbin, who simply ignores them, nor by Ralph Miliband, S.H. Beer, or Royden Harrison, who see the structure of power within the Labour Party to be more important than the proclamation of socialist intent in Clause Four.[6]

The War Emergency Committee (WEC) was drawn together on 5 August 1914 after Arthur Henderson, Secretary of the Labour Party, had called a special meeting 'to consider what action should be taken in the very serious crisis in Europe and any other business that may arise'.[7] It was formed in the context of a Labour Party committed to peace but within a day it was being called to act for a movement which was committed to the war effort. Its prime function became the defence of the rights and interests of the working class from unreasonable encroachment. It quickly evolved to include not only the Labour Party but the Co-operative Union and the Co-operative Wholesale Society. Its policy of co-option led to invitations to Ramsay MacDonald, and several hundred individuals, to join it, and the absorption of the representatives of many trade unions, the ILP, BSP, the National Socialist Party, the Fabian Society and many other organisations. In short, it soon became the most representative body in the British Labour movement incorporating both pro-war and anti-war organisations, although its 'heterogeneous membership ought not to obscure the fact that it was an extension of the Labour Party's national office'.[8] Its membership included Sidney Webb, H.M. Hyndman, Ramsay MacDonald, Arthur Henderson, J.S. Middleton, as well as other leading Labour figures.

The primary objective of the WEC was to keep the Labour movement from disintegrating under the impact of war. To achieve this end, the WEC concentrated its efforts on assuming a leading role in defending the living standard of the population. It protested at the 70 per cent inflation that occurred between 1914 and 1916, participated in the campaign to raise old age pensions from 5s to 7s 6d (25 to 37½ pence), worked for rent restriction in 1915 and to ensure that there was an adequate distribution of food supplies. One of its number, R. Smillie the miners' leader, was offered the position of Food Controller in the Lloyd George wartime administration. He refused, pointing out that he would have soon had to resign, for he would have demanded 'plenary powers to deal in my own way with the food profiteers. Some I would be content to send to prison, others I should feel obliged to hang.'[9]

Towards the end of the war, however, the WEC became far more positive in its policies and more aggressive in its approach. The introduction of compulsory military service in 1916 brought about a fundamental change in its strategy. It protested against the Military Service Act in 1916 and developed a campaign for the Conscription of Riches as a *quid pro quo* for labour's contribution to providing manpower for the trenches. Evolving from a resolution put forward by Hyndman, which was considerably modified by Sidney Webb, the WEC's policy was essentially one for the 'Conscription of Wealth', through income tax, supertax, capital tax and sequestration of all unearned income, and the nationalisation of all industries then under government control for the duration of the war.[10]

Up to this point there is little disagreement between the various interpretations of the value and the work of the WEC, if one discounts McKibbin's total disregard of its role. Both Winter and Harrison agree that the work of the WEC was important. For Winter it meant that the Webbian thought was projected forward, for in the wake of the proposal being formed it was accepted by the Labour Party Executive and various other Labour organisations: 'we may see a complete acceptance of

Webbian thought on this measure – the first independent Labour programme during the First World War.'[11] It followed that, with Webb's deep involvement in formulating the new Labour Party Constitution, the WEC programme had a direct bearing upon the formulation of Clause Four. Harrison agrees that Webb was the dominant spirit behind the new policy and that 'In short, the Conscription of Riches demand led on to clause 4.'[12] But from that point onwards there is disagreement. While Winter sees the growing influence of Webbian socialism as the basis of the new constitution of the Labour Party, Harrison accepts the view of Miliband, and anticipated the approach of McKibbin, in suggesting that Clause Four has to be seen within the context of the political pressures being placed on the Labour Party at this time.

Why did the Labour Party commit itself to the socialist goal? Was it because of the growth of Webbian socialism, thrust forward by war, or was it simply a product of political expediency?

There is no doubting that the socialist ideas of the Webbs were attractive to some sections of the Labour movement. The ILP and the Fabians had already declared their commitment to both vague and broad resolutions connected with the common ownership of the means of production. It is also possible, as Winter suggests, that the Russian revolutions of 1917, and particularly the Bolshevik Revolution which occurred soon after Arthur Henderson's ill-fated trip to Russia, forced Labour leaders to adopt a resolution that would offer a less violent and a more democratic way to socialism. There is also the suggestion that the professional middle classes were being drawn to such a policy in the wake of the government collectivisation policy. In addition, the Lloyd George coalition government set up a Ministry of Reconstruction to prepare policies for the post-war years. Of the nine members of the central Advisory Council attached to the Ministry two, Ernest Bevin and J.H. Thomas, were trade unionists and active members of the Labour Party. Apart from being in the coalition, Labour was being drawn into efforts to prepare schemes for housing, health and social welfare policies on a broader front in the post-war years. It must have appeared that old *laissez-faire* capitalism was dead and that socialist policies, particularly those of the Webbs, were now more appropriate than ever. To many Labour activists, it must have seemed that the wartime collectivism would not be dismantled, especially after the formation of the Ministry of Reconstruction. Clause Four (or Party Object 'd') ran as follows:

To secure for the producer by hand or by brain the full fruits of their industry by the Common Ownership of the Means of

Production and the best obtainable system of popular administration and control of each industry and service.

It was a very imprecise statement of socialist intent, though it was the Labour Party's first official commitment to socialism. McKibbin suggests that it was untypical of the new Constitution of the Labour Party and was not meant to be taken seriously. That may be so, but presumably it meant something to someone. If it is assumed that it was useful in order to distinguish the Labour Party from the Liberal Party, to indicate Labour's political independence, then it is fair to assume that this socialist ideology was important to some sections of the Labour Party and its supporters. If not, why should it be included at all?

Winter has established a clear link between the WEC, the Webbs and Clause Four. What he has failed to do is explain how this related to the ideology of the new class consciousness of the working class. Indeed, there is still little published which examines the evolution of class consciousness in the First World War and explains why it was possible to offer Clause Four in 1918 and not in 1913. McKibbin's suggestion that it was there as a sop to the professional middle class, who had found socialism through the wartime experience, seems unconvincing.[13] One might note that Bernard Barker's attempt to explain why some prominent Liberal MPs, 'the 1918 Liberals', moved over to the Labour Party, suggested that they had many motives.[14] Some, like C.P. Trevelyan, were apparently won over to socialism. Others, like Cecil Wilson, hoped to do some good for the party they had joined. All seem to have concluded that the Liberal Party was a spent force. Such evidence hardly suggests the attractions of socialism were irresistible but that the new ex-Liberal members were primarily concerned to join a growing party. This might also be the motivation behind the rising level of support for Labour emerging from the middle classes.

If Winter's explanation is still wanting then why did Clause Four find its way into Labour's Constitution? It has been suggested that it served a useful purpose in sharpening the divide between the Labour and Liberal parties. McKibbin offers a variety of reasons: the professional middle class were evidently enamoured of socialism, it was of secondary importance to the issue of who controlled the Labour Party and the trade unions were not much interested in it, and its vagueness and lack of rigour permitted it to unite a party where there was otherwise 'little doctrinal agreement'.[15] The first of these suggestions has already been dismissed. The second seems plausible, given that the trade union movement, with its block vote, was the dominant force in the Labour Party and enhanced its control of the NEC under the 1918 Constitution. Yet it is the third, barely examined by McKibbin, which appears to offer the best answer.

It was the vagueness of Clause Four which permitted it to act as a unifying force within the Labour Party. The various Labour and Socialist organisations which accreted to the Labour Party exhibited widely different views about socialism and war. Some favoured a type of workers' control while others wished for an extensive programme of nationalisation. Many were pro-war but some, like the ILP and the BSP, after 1916, associated with the Peace Campaign of 1917 and were represented at the Workers' and Soldiers' Conference at Leeds. The WEC managed to unite these interests through the defence of living standards and via its 'Conscription of Riches' campaign. Clause Four could be seen as an extension of this approach. As Harrison suggests,

> It is better regarded as a rallying point around which the adherents of different ideologies and representatives of different interests assembled. . . . The adoption of Clause Four did not imply that the whole membership came to have a common objective, but rather that an objective had been proclaimed which both accommodated and concealed a large diversity of particular concerns.[16]

It was detailed enough to distinguish Labour men from the Liberal Party but sufficiently vague to avoid serious conflict over the variety of socialist programmes on offer.

Indeed, there is little evidence that Clause Four excited much interest at either the national or local level, beyond the recognition of the fact that, by accepting it, the Labour Party had formally declared its commitment to socialism. In the West Riding of Yorkshire it was other issues, such as war and the protection of the standards of living of the working classes, that attracted most concern.[17] In the end, Clause Four proved a useful point of common agreement between socialists of all shades of opinion but it should not be seen as more than an acceptable flag of convenience which helped to detach the Labour Party from the progressive end of the Liberal Party. The emergence of class politics and the war itself might also have had a more direct impact.

CLASS POLITICS V. IMPACT OF WAR

Whether or not the First World War paved the way for the Labour Party to replace the Liberal Party as the progressive party in British politics is another debate entirely. It poses the conflict between those historians who point to the tremendous growth of Labour before 1914, noting the rising connection between the trade unions and the Labour Party, and those who argue that it was the split between David Lloyd George and H.H. Asquith in 1916, which saw Lloyd George become Prime Minister, that divided Liberalism and opened the way for the Labour Party. It is more relevant to the issue about the rise of the Labour Party and thus has subsidiary value in the discussion about the rise of socialism in Britain.

The evidence presented in Chapter 2 suggests the rapid and dramatic rise of the Labour Party in the decade before the First World War due to the growth of working-class support for it through the medium of trade unionism. The fact that many working men did not have the parliamentary franchise might also have affected the potential parliamentary performance of the Labour Party, a view accepted by D. Powell and R. McKibbin, if not by Duncan Tanner and P.F. Clarke.[18] Four million, or more, working men were denied the vote as compared to about 350,000 single men of the middle classes who lived at home with their parents, and it is undoubtedly the case that many of them would have voted Labour as they began to do in the immediate post-war years. There have been many regional studies that have indicated the rapid local growth of the Labour Party and that New Liberalism, with its emphasis upon social reform, seems to have carried little weight outside Lancashire and Westminster.[19] In other words there was significant Labour growth in many areas and little evidence that New Liberalism, with its emphasis upon social harmony, was checking Labour's growth.

Indeed, as already indicated, Labour's parliamentary growth was quite substantial and from 1909 onwards the Labour Party and the ILP were making significant local political gains. Indeed, Labour seems to have made an increasing number of local political gains from 1909 onwards.[20]

There is strong evidence to suggest that Labour was developing before 1914 as a result of its rising working-class support and that it was not just the First World War that projected it forward by causing the split within Liberal ranks. None the less, the idea that the Labour Party arose as a result of the accident of war is a view held by a number of historians, including P.F. Clarke, Trevor Wilson, Roy Douglas, and others.[21] They explain the demise of the Liberal Party in terms of the cultural and social changes brought about by the First World War and the internal conflict within the party resulting from the replacement of H.H. Asquith as Prime Minister by David Lloyd George in 1916. The 'rampant omnibus of war', not class politics, is thus propounded as the explanation for the interwar decline of Liberalism, for the war initiated a process of disintegration in the Liberal Party which began in 1916 and was complete by the 1930s.[22] The point was stressed more recently by Michael Bentley when he wrote that 'the First World War not only buried the Liberal future but rendered hopeless the past by which Liberals had charted the course which took them there.'[23] This has led these historians to suggest that the Liberal Party was performing well in 1914 and that the Labour Party was doing badly. This desire has led Clarke to suggest that New Liberalism was the key to the Liberal revival between 1906 and 1914.[24] Others have suggested that Old Liberalism was still doing well before 1914 or note that Labour's parliamentary by-election results were poor between 1910 and 1914.[25]

Nevertheless, the fact is that Labour was doing well before 1914, its by-election results were not bad, and the Liberals split as a result of war. Given Labour's pre-war growth all one can conclude is that the Liberal split speeded up the process of Labour growth and Liberal decline. This was not immediately evident in the 1918 general election, called under peculiar circumstances in the immediate wake of the armistice. Yet a new Labour Party, committed to some vague socialist objectives, did emerge in 1918, based upon its working-class support in the years before 1914 and galvanised by the experience of war. Other socialist groups had not done so well even with the increased interest in Marxism stimulated by the Bolshevik Revolution.

THE ILP, THE PEACE MOVEMENT AND THE WAR

Contrary to the general impression given by the Tory and Liberal press, there were few members of the ILP who adopted an outright pacifist stance. At the national level the main advocates of pacifism were Bruce Glasier, Clifford Allen, Arthur Salter and Fenner Brockway, with Philip Snowden on the edge of the group although he was never a fully committed pacifist.[26] This group was composed largely of writers, journalists, academics and doctors, in other words the professional middle class. They took the pure pacifist line that all war was wrong, and some of them supplemented their hostility to war by forming the No-Conscription Fellowship and working with the Union of Democratic Control.[27] Despite its limited support, this group managed to gain some measure of control at the ILP national conference in 1917.

While there tended to be few pacifists in any particular region or district, those there were often held prominent positions within local ILP branches. Arthur Priestman, a Bradford Quaker, businessman and one of the leading figures in the Bradford ILP, carried pacifist sentiments into the Bradford ILP.

William Leach, an employer who joined the Bradford ILP in the mid-1890s and became a councillor, was similarly important and acted as editor of the *Bradford Pioneer*, taking over from the increasingly pro-war Joseph Burgess in June 1915. In October 1915, Leach articulated the paper's policy:

We hate all war, especially the present one. This is a pacifist or peace journal conducted among other purposes, with the object of stating as well as we can, the ILP position on the hideous tragedy now being enacted in Europe. . . . Human life is the most sacred thing we know, and its preservation, its development, its best welfare, must therefore be our religion on this earth.[28]

The pacifist section of the ILP was always a small minority and the dominant strand within even the anti-war section of the Bradford ILP was not pacifism. The majority seem to have followed the example set by Fred Jowett, the leading ILP figure in Bradford, and Keir Hardie in that they accepted the need for National Defence but opposed the secret treaties that led to war. Jowett argued, in his chairman's speech to the 1915 ILP Conference at Norwich, that 'Now is the time to speak and ensure that never again shall the witches' cauldron of secret diplomacy brew the war broth of Hell for mankind.'[29] In an important article in the *Bradford Pioneer* he explained that

I believe that the war would never had arisen if the government had carried out an open and honest foreign policy and disclosed to the people who had most to lose the relations between themselves and foreign governments with whom they were acting in collusion.[30]

His constant theme was that the war had been caused by the secret treaties which had been arranged, though frequently denied, by the British government. 'His fad', as the *Standard* said of Jowett, 'is the democratic control of foreign affairs.'[31] In this connection Jowett also demanded that the government should specify its war aims and be forced to the negotiations table.

To Jowett, the First World War was caused by the secret treaties arranged by the British government and should be settled as quickly as possible. But on numerous occasions he declared that he was in favour of a British victory over 'Prussianism' and that he could not agree to the settlement of the war without 'the restoration of Belgium to complete sovereignty'.[32] He maintained that a nation had the right to defend itself and frequently paid homage to those who had given their lives in the war.[33] In many respects, Jowett's policy resembled the views expressed by Keir Hardie in his famous article 'We must see the War through, but denounce Secret Diplomacy'.[34] Although Jowett's position on the war, as with the stance adopted by Hardie, often appeared ambiguous and at odds with the ILP's declared opposition, he was categorical in his wish to see the First World War concluded speedily and successfully by the Allies. On his attitude towards the anti-war resolution passed by the 1916 ILP Conference, of which he was chairman, he reminded one critic:

> The ILP resolution to which you refer only expressed the view that Socialist Parties as organised bodies should support no war. It did not attempt to lay down such a policy for individuals. If it did I should be opposed to it in principle.[35]

Such a distinction between the actions of individuals within the party and the policy of the party was confusing to many critics of the ILP and permitted Jowett to both support and oppose the war in different guises. Here was a classic case of having one's cake and eating it. But in many respects, Jowett's position was clearly understood by many members of the Bradford ILP and offered some common ground between the warring factions within the local party.

The fact is that many members of the ILP were committed to the war effort, either on the negative grounds of the need for national defence or on the more positive grounds that Prussianism needed to be destroyed. Indeed, in Bradford a number of the ILP members who were trade unionists seemed to have supported the war for both reasons. J.H. Palin was one of the most obvious examples. Chairman of the Amalgamated Society of Railway Servants at the time of *Taff Vale*, and later an MP for Newcastle, he opposed the resolution, presented to the 1916 ILP Conference, which advocated that all socialist parties of all nations should refuse to support every war ever entered into by any government. Palin cut across the comparative equanimity of the meeting and stated bluntly that

> We do not want the Germans here. Assume that the workers of this country had carried out this resolution at the beginning of the war, and the Socialists of other countries had not, and had rallied or been forced to join the army, where at the moment would Great Britain have been? At any rate, it seems to me that more time is required to get considered opinion to start afresh after the war.[36]

Palin later went to France to help in war transportation.

The fact is that Palin seems to have stood for the views of a very large proportion of the membership of the ILP. This is indicated by the situation in Bradford, recognised as one of the centres of the ILP Peace Campaign. When the *Bradford Daily Telegraph* attacked the ILP's resistance to the war effort and their inability to 'raise a finger to help the country to prosecute the war successfully', Jowett replied that 'In proportion to its membership the ILP has more adherents serving in the army and navy by far than either of the two other political parties.'[37] Censuses of the Bradford ILP membership confirm this impression. One census in February 1916 indicated that of the 461 young men in the local party membership of 1,473, 113 were in the trenches, 4 had been killed, 1 was missing, 9 had been wounded, 3 were prisoners of war, 118 were in training in England, 6 were in the Navy and 207 were attested under the Derby Scheme as necessary home workers.[38] A similar survey conducted in 1918 found that of 492 members liable for service, 351 were serving in the forces while 48 were conscientious objectors or were on national work.[39]

The false impression that the majority of the ILP membership supported the 'Peace Campaign' and were pacifists certainly encouraged many trade unionists to move their allegiance to the Labour Party rather than the ILP by 1918. With the development of rising working-class loyalty it was the Labour Party, not the ILP, that was to be seen as the liberating force for the working class in future and the ILP was left to dwell upon the role of socialists inside, and outside, the Labour Party.

There was, of course, the exception of Clydeside, where the ILP became the dominating force in Labour politics, a fact which enabled it to exert some impact upon Labour Party politics in the early 1920s. Joseph Melling, in a perceptive and critical article, has highlighted the vital, but often ignored, role of the ILP in the Clydeside area. Noting that the ILP was involved in the industrial conflicts on the Clyde during the war, and had strong links with officials in the engineering unions, he stressed that the ILP transformed the Liberal stronghold of Glasgow into an ILP and Labour stronghold by its involvement in, and organisation of, the rent strike in Glasgow and the campaigns against rising prices. Indeed, 'Here the ILP made its greatest contribution to the wartime unrest by organising the rent strikers in local groups, under the umbrella of a general committee but encouraging autonomy in each district.'[40] The activism of the ILP in the workplace permitted it to make the connection with the householders on Clydeside and helped in the post-war success of the ILP. However, Melling feels that the switch from Liberalism to the ILP in Glasgow was more than a transition from traditional Liberalism to constitutional Labourism, in which the rent strike gave Labour a 'strong constituency of support for housing reform'.[41] Rather, the traditional landmarks of Liberalism had been destroyed by the war, there was political flux and socialist ideas were being debated intensely between 1917 and 1920. Protest against the repressive wartime actions of the state was not simply the 'residue of Liberalism but an authentic theme in socialist discourse'.[42] Indeed,

The ILP captured the leadership of different campaigns because it practised a form of dual politics, simultaneously rooted in everyday life and conventional political arenas, which ignored party boundaries and was based only on the discipline of the specific project, not the party card. This meant that a broad coalition of social groups could be assembled in support of various speakers on Glasgow Green. The emphasis upon 'making socialists' allowed the ILP to avoid some of the more bitter sectarian squabbles over political doctrine during the war and appeal for a more moral stand on the war. Even more important was the ILP's firm grasp of organisation strategy and the presence of high-calibre activists like Harry Hopkins and Andrew McBride. By their leadership of popular struggles in the war these people associated the ILP with a clear alternative to the Liberals who dominated pre-war Glasgow politics.[43]

The fact is that the ILP on Clydeside appears to have realised that in order to build up its power base it needed to go beyond the Shop Stewards' movement and to develop its connections with the unions, the housing movement and the Labour Party. The sabotage of production would not deliver political power. This is something which the Shop Stewards' movement did not comprehend.

THE SHOP STEWARDS' MOVEMENT AND GUILD SOCIALISM

Arthur Balfour, the British Foreign Secretary during the war, wrote two papers on the themes of 'Democracy and International Relations', in April 1918, in which he admitted that trade unions and the Labour Party were important developments in the wartime situation and that 'It would probably be impossible . . . for our Government to make a peace greatly different from the declared war aims of the Labour Party.'[44] The claim may have been exaggerated but it did reflect the enhanced position of Labour and the trade unions within the government. Arthur Henderson was given a seat in the wartime cabinet, and both John Hodges (Steel Smelters' Association) and George Barnes (Amalgamated Society of Engineers) were given ministerial office in Lloyd George's wartime cabinet. The Asquith wartime government concluded a voluntary agreement with the trade unions to suspend trade union rights until the end of the war, which the government transformed into a statutory measure with the passing of the Munitions of War Act in June 1915. This action by the government led some unions to refuse to comply. The miners' leaders refused to work with the Act and within two weeks of the passing of the Munitions of War Act the South Wales miners were on strike. Other unions followed suit.

Nevertheless, the engineering unions operated closely with the government's war effort. Their union officials worked with the new legislation. Yet, despite the obvious commitment of most trade unionists to the war effort, from which they benefited financially, there has been significant controversy about the importance of the dissident Shop Stewards' movement for both the trade union movement and for the evolution of socialism. During the First World War the radical and militant action which it took on 'Red Clydeside' was celebrated, with somewhat exaggerated importance, by Willie Gallacher in his book *Revolt on the Clyde* (1936). James Hinton has examined the events on Clydeside, in Sheffield and other engineering centres, and fitted them most firmly into the response of engineering craftsmen to the threat of the new technologies.[45] Apparently, faced with such a threat, and led by an able group of shop stewards, the rank and file ignored their moderate leaders and adopted other strategies, including opposition to dilution and the demand for workers' control, in a desire to protect their craft privileges, although this gradually developed into a conflict between capitalism and organised workers in which the skilled engineers moved from narrow sectionalism to class leadership as a result of their shopfloor conflict in the munitions workshops. Imposed upon these events were subsidiary issues, such as hostility to conscription and anti-war sentiments. In addition, some of the leading shop stewards increasingly associated themselves with the movement which eventually became the CPGB.

This view of 'Red Clydeside' has, however, been challenged by Iain McLean whose book, *Legend of Red Clydeside* (1983), suggests that our understanding of Scottish society has been distorted by the myth that there was a class struggle on the Clyde. He suggests that the Clyde Workers' Committee was isolated and confused and represented the conservative and defensive strand of trade unionism. He argues that Marxist shop stewards were of marginal influence on Clydeside and that socialism emerged from other factors in Clydeside, such as the rent strike.

Since McLean's book appeared, there have been several contributions to the debate about 'Red Clyde'. Alistair Reid has argued that Hinton has exaggerated the importance of the dilution campaign and suggests that dilution, by the introduction of female labour, did not damage the control of the craft workers in the engineering trades.[46] Gerry Rubin's work on the Glasgow Munitions Tribunal, in *War, Law and Labour* (1987), also suggests that moderate and state-inclined policies emerged from the tribunals as trade union officials were converted by their experience of legal regulation under the munitions Act to the need for state regulation. In the end it appears that trade union leaders were converted to moderate state reconstruction which encouraged the evolution of the politics of the Labour Party.

These revisionist views have been questioned by Joseph Melling and John Foster.[47] While accepting some of the views of the revisionists, they argue that the struggle of the skilled workers contributed to the growth of Labour politics on Clydeside. As already indicated, Melling argues that the various industrial struggles certainly influenced the ILP, which, through the rent strike and related campaigns, came to dominate Clydeside after the First World War.

Most certainly the Treasury Agreement and the Munitions of War Act of 1915, the 'Shells and Fuses' agreement, which produced a situation whereby unions agreed to suspend free collective bargaining and to introduce compulsory arbitration, created a situation which was ripe for local rank-and-file conflict with employers since national union officials were now irrelevant for the duration. Vigilant shop stewards on the Clyde in 1915 and 1916, in Sheffield in 1916, Barrow in May 1917, and in the great engineering strike in May 1917, took over control of the rank-and-file concerns. The history of these events, the way in which the government defeated the Clyde workers with the use of 'leaving certificates', arrest and dilution is well documented.[48] The important point to stress, however, is the link the Shop Stewards' movement developed with socialism and how it fitted in to the socialist developments that were occurring during the war.

The Shop Stewards' movement represented an alternative trend to that being developed by the Labour Party. It had arisen out of the breakdown between the national union leaders and some skilled engineers in a few of the engineering centres of Britain and, by and large, was defused and isolated by the government. It was, thus, very much a minority activity against the trend of normal wartime trade union activity. Its socialist credentials were equally limited.

On the Clyde the ILP, which was the dominant local political force, only had David Kirkwood and John Muir on the Clyde Workers' Committee. The BSP was represented by William Gallacher. Most of the rest of the leading figures were members of the SLP which was still a relatively small party committed to industrial unionism and industrial democracy.

The English equivalent of the SLP was the Amalgamation Committee Movement, which waged its campaign through its journal *Solidarity*. Its leading exponent was J.T. Murphy, secretary of the Sheffield committee, who publicised his views through the journal and outlined them in detail through *The Workers' Committee* (1917), which sold about 150,000 copies. This pamphlet advocated that all workers should be balloted on important decisions, which should not be left to the officials of the union. His participatory democracy scheme was to be based upon the workshop committee and build up to working through a national structure of elected committees. Yet such a policy proved almost impossible to implement. A National Shop Stewards' and Workers' Committee Movement (NSSWCM) was set up in August 1917 when a National Administrative Council was formed. Yet it never got much support beyond engineering and it faded into insignificance during the early 1920s. In any case, the October 1917 Revolution in Russia led to the development of the idea of state control coming before workers' control and the acceptance by the Shop Stewards' movement of the Soviets as a model for workers' self-government in 1920. The creation of the CPGB and the economic situation soon undermined the influence of the Shop Stewards' movement.

Guild socialism fared no better. A National Guilds' League was formed in 1915 by 500 members who had seceded from the Fabian Society. Its only significant success occurred in 1920 when the National Building Guild was formed, although it wound up in 1923. During these years it was greatly influenced by G.D.H. Cole and Harold Laski, both of whom believed that the state was the political machinery of the community and had to be made the representative of the people, and that this depended upon the elimination of capitalism. The way in which this would be accomplished was set out in the Storrington Document of 1915 which envisaged the disappearance of capitalism as industrial unions pursued workers' control and as socialists won a parliamentary majority and nationalised the key industries. In effect it would be a federation of trade unions that would represent the producers who would share power with a pyramid of consumers' organisations represented by parliament. This system assumed a well-informed citizenry and that there would not be conflict between the consumer and some of the producers over output levels.

Yet this participatory democratic system never caught on. There were far more attractive alternatives, such as the party building of the Marxist Leninists. In addition, it is clear that guild socialism was edged too much with assumptions about the goodness and reasonableness of human nature that were unrealistic. The BSP was to develop a much more party-state approach as the First World

War wore on and as the Bolshevik Revolution occurred. Its approach proved much more popular although even it faced major difficulties in the war years.

THE BRITISH SOCIALIST PARTY

The First World War brought to book the policies that had dominated the Second International ever since it was founded in Paris in 1889. The International condemned, in a consistent manner, the use of standing armies and favoured the creation of citizen armies, on the assumption that the members of these armies would prevent the occurrence of war. The reality is that up to the First World War there was no socialist government to implement such policies, that the International was divided between socialists of the right, left and centre and that socialist leaders were naïve about the opportunities a war would offer.

The outbreak of war on 4 August 1914 brought the anti-war unity among British Socialists to a halt. The Labour Party, as already indicated, supported the war effort while the ILP leadership, if not the majority of the rank and file, felt their way to a peace campaign. Hyndman, firmly to the right of the socialist spectrum on the question of war and intensely nationalistic, led the 'old guard' of the SDF/BSP towards a pro-war position. This provoked fragmentation and conflict within the BSP between Hyndman and the internationalist section led by Zelda Kahan. There were five regional conferences in February 1915 instead of the national gathering, and all had to consider the pro-war outpourings of Hyndman.

The two groups within the BSP were finely balanced. In Glasgow and London the opponents of war held the upper hand but it was those in favour of the war who dominated the Leeds conference. The internationalists won a majority of 5 to 4 on the Executive but the Hyndmanites ran *Justice* and remained in control of the Central Branch of the BSP.[49]

The situation worsened when, following a Conference of the Allied Socialists, held in London, the Allied internationalists met at Zimmerwald in September 1915 to reconstruct the Second International. They produced the Zimmerwald Manifesto which blamed war on imperialism and capitalist greed and suggested that socialists of all nations should fight for peace.[50] Hyndman rejected the Manifesto but other sections of the BSP were supportive, although Zelda Kahan considered the proposals to be impracticable since they did not consider how to stop wars under capitalist conditions.

Those sections of the BSP who supported the First World War began to form into new organisations, most particularly into the Socialist National Defence Committee which became the British Workers' League en route to becoming the National Democratic Party. This organisation attracted many national socialists including A.M. Thompson and Robert Blatchford, from the *Clarion*, and E.R. Hartley, Dan Irving, Bert Killip, Ben Tillett, J.J. Terrett and Will Thorne of the BSP. Some members of the Labour Party also joined. Hyndman gave his support, if not his membership but he, like many of the BSP figures, soon dissociated themselves from this organisation.

There were many other incidents and points of conflict between Hyndman and his international socialist opponents, many of whom had themselves not made an unequivocal stand against war. They culminated in the BSP Conference at Salford on 23 and 24 April 1916, attended by 106 delegates representing 91 branches. The Executive of the BSP, no longer dominated by Hyndman, asked for a vote to hold the meeting in secret because of fear of arrest under the Defence of the Realm Act and, though opposed by Hyndman who was by now considered to be almost a spy of the state, this was supported by a vote of 76 to 28. As a result, and following a pre-arranged plan, 22 pro-war delegates from 18 branches walked out of the conference. Hyndman led them to the Deansgate Hotel, Manchester, where he announced the formation of the National Socialist Advisory Committee which was soon to become the National Socialist Party. By that time its national organiser was Joseph Burgess, ex-President of the Bradford ILP, and it claimed 43 branches. It was supported by a mixture of nationalist members of the ILP and the SDF, including Bert Killip and E.R. Hartley, although Hartley later joined Victor Fisher's ultra-patriotic British Workers' League. It is ironic that the remaining internationalist section of the BSP became affiliated to the Labour Party in 1916.

By 1917 the BSP was down to 6,435 paying members and the NSP was never able to command 2,000 members.[51] The SDF/BSP brand of socialism, like that of the ILP, was weakened by war. Yet the First World War was the catalyst for issues that had divided the movement since its development in the 1880s, although it gave the BSP hope for the future with the occurrence of the Bolshevik Revolution of 1917.

THE BOLSHEVIK REVOLUTION AND THE WORKERS' AND SOLDIERS' COUNCILS

The downfall of the Tsar in February/March 1917 and the creation of a Provisional Government in Petrograd, offering the prospect of a democratic government in Russia, attracted the support of just about every shade of political opinion in Britain. The Conservatives and Liberals lined up with Labour in support of the change and even the anti-war socialists hoped that this Russian Revolution would prepare the path for peace. Arthur Henderson visited Russia in May 1917 on behalf of the British government, was attacked by the Bolsheviks and came back convinced that the Russians would only stay in the war if a conference of all socialists was held at Stockholm. He also became convinced that the Labour Party had to find a peaceful way to socialism. Having exceeded his brief, the war cabinet forced him to resign and replaced him with G.N. Barnes, another prominent Labour figure.

In this atmosphere of euphoric support for the Russian (Menshevik) Revolution, the ILP and the BSP, through their United Socialist Council, organised the Leeds Convention in June 1917 to celebrate the March Revolution. It was a vast meeting of about 1,150 delegates who brought together all the sections of the Labour movement. It passed four resolutions: hailing the Russian Revolution, advocating moves towards establishing a general peace based upon the rights of nations to decide their own affairs, demanding the creation of a charter of liberties by the British government, and advocating the formation of a Council of Workers' and Soldiers' delegates in every town, urban and rural district. Philip Snowden was responsible for putting forward the second resolution and for drafting the resolution which was sent to the Petrograd Soviet, informing it of the conference and its support for the Russian Revolution, endorsing Russia's foreign policy and pledging efforts to obtain a democratic peace.[52] Snowden talked of painting Britain red, W.C. Anderson urged the formation of 'Councils of Workmen and Soldiers' Delegates' and Robert Williams favoured 'the dictatorship of the proletariat'. However, what they anticipated was rather less revolutionary than the Russian Soviets. Indeed, Stephen White suggests that the Workers' and Soldiers' Council movement was designed to press for a negotiated settlement to the war rather than to bring about revolutionary change.[53]

Despite the support which the Leeds Conference elicited, it was generally distanced from organised labour and never captured the public imagination. By July 1917 the Labour Party had declared that none of its branches should have anything to do with the Workers' and Soldiers' councils. But even before this occurred, doubts had been expressed about the efficacy of the putative organisation. Many of the delegates who attended as trade union and trades council representatives were immediately doubtful of the value of the conference. Even before the conference was held, the Leeds Labour Party had expressed its support for the first three resolutions but had refused support for the fourth. These embryonic soviets were rejected by the Labour Party organisation before the conference and by trade unionists afterwards.

The main concern of trade unionists appears to have been that the Workers' and Soldiers' Council might challenge their hegemony in organising workers. Returning from the Leeds Conference, the President of the Halifax Trades Council, G. Kaye, reported his disquiet:

> He was not at all satisfied with the Conference. . . . personally, he did not support the resolution of a Workmen's and Soldiers' Council, taking the view that the place for these people was in the Labour and Socialist movement and that if multiple organisations were formed there was a great risk of wasting energy on side issues. The conference ought to be followed up by something on the lines of drastic and revolutionary action. His faith lay in the organised industrial workers backed up by political action if they liked.[54]

When an attempt was made to set up a District Organisation of the Workers' and Soldiers' Council in the West Riding of Yorkshire in the autumn of 1917, the Leeds Trades Council rejected the move for similar reasons to those referred to by Kaye. It was unanimously resolved that the propaganda work of the Soldiers' Council 'can and will be done by the existing Labour organisations'.[55] This was an attitude which was prevalent throughout the nation's trade unions and Labour organisations.

This situation did not change dramatically when the Bolshevik Revolution occurred in October 1917. This *coup d'état* made the Bolsheviks the single most important section of the international socialist movement and attracted widespread support from all sections of the British labour and socialist movement: there was a spontaneous singing of the 'Red Flag' at the Labour Party Conference in January 1918 and cheers at the mention of the names of Leon Trotsky and Maxim Litvinov. There was similar support among members of the ILP, although the general feeling was that Bolshevik Russia should be supported but that conditions were different in Britain. At the more extreme level the BSP gave its full-hearted support to the Bolshevik Revolution and the Socialist Labour Party claimed to be the 'British Bolsheviks'.

BSP links with Russia were strengthened when Chicherin and Peter Petroff were deported in January 1918, only to assume prominent roles in the Revolutionary Government in Russia. Joe Fineberg also returned to Russia and prepared the way for the arrival of Bolshevik propaganda in Britain. Theodore Rothstein, who had spent many years in Britain, became the chief Bolshevik agent in Britain and directed the Russian funds to British revolutionary movements. The BSP, above all, became far more involved in agitation on both the industrial and political fronts, paving the way for its later involvement in the formation of the CPGB.

The position of Russia became of increasing importance to the Allies with the fear that she would withdraw from the First World War and assume the 'revolutionary defencism' policy of Lenin, which meant that she would not fight as long as her borders were not threatened. The Treaty of Brest-Litovsk, which the Bolsheviks were forced to conclude with the Germans in March 1918, saved the Soviets and ended Russia's participation in the war. It reflected the weak situation of Bolshevik Russia at this time and it provoked a significant attack upon Russia by the Prime Minister, David Lloyd George, who was seeking the rapid defeat of Germany. At that time there was much confusion in the ranks of the Labour Party about what the Bolshevik Revolution meant and the attitude they should develop towards Russia. Yet following the Armistice in November 1918, and the general election a month or so later, it was clear that despite the Labour Party's political hostility to the type of regime created in Russia, Ramsay MacDonald, Philip Snowden and many Labour Party members were urging the recognition of Soviet Russia and anticipated the subsequent 'Hands of Russia' campaign to stop the intervention of the Allies in Russian affairs.

CONCLUSION

The First World War brought about significant changes in the position of socialism in Britain. Above all, it forced the Labour Party to declare itself to be openly socialist, even if its commitment amounted to relatively little. At the same time, it weakened both the ILP and the BSP, the two leading socialist organisations in Britain who were divided on the issue of war, although it strengthened the ILP's position in Scotland. It was only after the two Russian Revolutions of 1917 that Marxist and more extreme socialist parties in Britain began to recover to any degree. Although the ILP, the BSP and the SLP might have been able to muster about 35,000 supporters in 1918, somewhat down on 1914, it is significant that while they all offered some support for Lenin's views, little of it flowed into the CPGB which had only 3,000 to 4,000 members when it was formed in 1920. The Shop Stewards' movement had relatively loose ties with socialism, and guild socialism was practically stillborn. Perhaps McKibbin is right to suggest that socialism was weaker and more fragmented in Britain in 1918 than it was in 1914, despite the fact that the Labour Party was now adorned with Clause Four. Indeed, the interwar years do not seem to have provided British socialism with much more to hope for, despite the formation of the CPGB, the creation of two minority Labour governments and the late flowering of socialism as a result of the reaction against fascism in Europe and Spain in the mid- and late 1930s.

CHAPTER

4

THE INTERWAR YEARS: LABOURISM AND SOCIALISM, 1918–39

During the interwar years British socialism was faced with many opportunities to expand its influence, particularly as a result of the creation of the Communist Party of Great Britain, the formation of two Labour governments and the challenge posed by European fascism. None the less, the Labour Party, the mass agency of socialism in Britain, was little more advanced in 1939 than it had been in 1918 and the CPGB was still a relatively isolated body even though it may have exerted more influence upon trade unionism than has hitherto been supposed.[1] Given the major national and international forces at play, the influence of the Soviet Union and the United and Popular fronts against fascism, the major question is: why did socialism in Britain remain so static during the 1920s and '30s? The answer may have something to do with the conservative nature of the British trade union movement, which greatly influenced the Labour Party, committed itself to public ownership and was partly nurtured by Ernest Bevin, who was decidedly hostile to the CPGB. This was not necessarily a situation of trade union domination of the Labour Party, although there was an element of this present, but one of conservative trade unionists working together with moderate socialist politicians to isolate the political impact of the Communists and Labour's left wing. As Lewis Minkin has noted, the Labour Party and the trade unions often operated in separate spheres but were interconnected by a set of evolving rules which saw the Labour Party support the trade unions' right to collective bargaining, and the trade unions recognised that the Labour Party and Labour governments needed to maintain a degree of independence.[2] These forces of the trade unions and the Labour Party, nevertheless, seem also to have united at the national level to minimise the impact of the Communist Party in a society which, in any case, inhibited its development and restricted its significant influence to a few areas where a peculiar mixture of circumstances and leadership allowed it some local success.[3]

THE LABOUR PARTY, THE TRADE UNION MOVEMENT AND THE WOMEN'S VOTE

By 1918, if not before, the Labour Party was shaped, even if it was not totally dominated, by the trade unions. In 1900 the LRC Executive included seven trade unionists and five socialists. In 1902 it had nine trade unionists, one representative of the trades councils and three socialists (two ILP and one Fabian).[4] The Labour Party Constitution of 1918 had allowed it to elect thirteen of the twenty-three members of the new National Executive Committee and to have a say in the election of the rest. Throughout the 1920s, and particularly after 1926, the Joint Council of Labour, which brought together the Parliamentary Labour Party (PLP), the TUC and the Labour Party, became increasingly important in making the decisions for the 'constitutional' Labour movement. In 1934 it became the National Council of Labour and the TUC was the most important force on this body, in the shape of Ernest Bevin (from 1932) and Walter Citrine. Both Bevin and Citrine were opposed to the Communists, before, during and after the General Strike of 1926, and shaped Labour's policy of non-cooperation with Marxist forces in the 1930s when the threat of European fascism loomed large. By that time, the TUC was on good terms with the National Government and it was Bevin's commitment to defend the working class of Britain against fascism that led the TUC and the Labour Party to give some support to the National Government's rearmament programme in the mid and late 1930s and to endorse the campaign to construct air-raid shelters. If the Labour Party had become the party of the working class, regardless of Ramsay MacDonald's protestations that it was a party of all the classes, it had become so through the agency of the trade union movement and the price it had to pay was the restriction of its policies to a pale version of Clause Four introduced gradually and selectively over a lengthy time span. Using the large block vote of the Transport and General Workers' Union (TGWU) and other unions, Bevin was able to dominate the Labour Party conferences throughout the 1930s on issues such as the threat of fascism. Indeed, Bevin remarked that the Labour Party 'grew out of the bowels of the TUC'.[5] This is not to say that the Labour Party did not have its opportunities to extend its socialist planning, for this often operated in a different sphere from trade unionism, although Bevin and the TUC Economic Planning Committee (1932) were part of the process.[6]

The relationship between the Labour Party and the trade unions was complex and not without major difficulties. Lewis Minkin, in a monumental work, has suggested that while the Labour Party and the trade unions are often seen as working closely together they often developed different policies and strategies, and operated in different spheres, which sometimes developed into a contentious relationship. He argues that the metaphor that the Labour Party was the 'offspring of the TUC' is misleading because there has often been a disparity in the policies adopted by both organisations.[7] Nevertheless, he maintains that the two bodies built up a common set of attitudes and rules between 1900 and 1948 – based upon loyalty and anti-communism – and that these operated effectively in some type of 'golden age' between 1948 and 1959 before becoming subject to the increased strains and changes of recent times. For the interwar years, then, there were difficulties as the ground rules were being built up and it is not surprising that there should have been some sharp disagreements in their relationships. The Labour Party's 1918 Constitution provided the potential for conflict between the broad socialist goals and the narrower base of trade union objectives. The use of the Emergency Powers Act by the 1924 Labour Government to deal with industrial disputes created tensions with the trade unions. The reluctance of the Labour Government of 1929–31 to abolish the Trades Dispute and Trade Union Act of 1927, which made sympathetic strike action illegal and restricted the flow of trade union funds to the Labour Party, provided another source of conflict. The fact is that the Labour government was dependent upon Liberal Party support to continue in office and the Liberals were opposed to the withdrawal of the 1927 Act. The deflationary policies of the Labour governments of 1924 and 1929–31, their failure to tackle the issue of unemployment and their willingness to reduce unemployment benefits in 1931 also added to the strains of this contentious relationship.

The different spheres of influence and responsibilities between the Labour Party and the trade unions have been recognised by many contemporaries and was well put by W.J. Brown, of the Civil Service Clerical Association. Reflecting upon the 1924 Labour Government, he expressed the view that there was a general assumption that the Labour cabinet would apply the policy of the TUC in industrial matters but that the reality was that

. . . there would be a permanent difference in point of view between Government on the one hand and the Trade Unions on the other: and that difference in point of view did not arise from any wickedness on the part of the political side, or on the part of the industrial side, but arose from the fact that the Trade Unions had different functions to follow than the functions of Government.[8]

Smethurst, the Secretary of the Amalgamated Engineering Unions, reflecting upon the end of the first Labour government stated that 'they had their little fads and feelings', that 'the members of the Labour Government individually and collectively gave excellent service' and that 'when Labour representatives again take up the reins of Government – as they most assuredly will – the experience gained in 1924 will not be lost sight of.'[9]

Other trade union leaders made much the same point. Walter Citrine, General Secretary of the TUC, wrote that the trade unions did not dominate the Labour Party and suggested that the Labour Party and the trade unions 'work together and consult from time to time when any matter of policy is in question'.[10] Trade union leaders did not seem to expect too much of the Labour Party in government and in June 1931 the TGWU admitted that 'the results of the work of Government can rarely be seen in its own lifetime'.[11]

The development of these different spheres of influence was also a product of the fact that trade union leaders were not inclined to combine the office of MP with the leadership of a trade union. Before 1914 many trade union leaders such as Ben Pickard and Mabon, leaders of the miners, acted as MPs. After 1918 this was a rare occurrence. Ernest Bevin ran the TGWU throughout the interwar years without parliamentary duties, although they were thrust upon him in the wartime conditions of 1940. Jimmy Thomas, of the NUR, became the political secretary of his union when he went into parliament, with C.T.T. Cramp acting as industrial secretary between 1920 and 1931 before acting as secretary from 1931 to 1933, owing to the political defection of Thomas to the National Government. Indeed, only the General Union and the Workers' Union were led by parliamentarians.[12] This was a situation which permitted the political and industrial sections of the Labour movement to act in different spheres despite the dominant financial and voting link which the trade unions held.

Nevertheless, from 1918 until the early 1930s, whether because of the problems of the trade union alliance, or owing to the cautious nature of Labour's socialism, there was little evidence of any advance in the socialism offered by the Labour Party. There were political and industrial successes for the

Labour movement and the Labour Party, but most of these were exaggerated and more than tinged with a failure to enhance its socialist objectives.

Some success could be gleaned from the 'Hands off Russia' campaign. Yet one must remember that the PLP had resisted many rank-and-file requests that it should proclaim support for Soviet Russia although it considered taking action when, in the spring of 1920, the Poles invaded Russia and took Kiev. However, it was at this moment that the London dockers refused to load the *Jolly George*, a ship that it was believed was laden with a cargo of weapons for Poland. By August it appeared that Britain might declare war on Soviet Russia and on 9 August the TUC warned that 'the whole industrial power of the organised workers will be used to defeat this war'.[13] On 13 August a Council of Action was formed and empowered to call a general strike in the event of Britain declaring war on Soviet Russia although two days later the Red Army's march was stopped outside Warsaw and the crisis was over. It was the trade union movement, rather than the Labour Party, that had taken action and it is not at all clear that how far their actions carried weight in shaping events.

As already suggested, it was the two Labour governments of 1924 and 1929 to 1931 that created most tensions within the Labour Party. The first of these, formed after Stanley Baldwin's defeat on the issue of protectionism, lasted about ten months in 1924 before being ousted in the furore over the Campbell case, when J.R. Campbell, assistant editor of the *Workers' Weekly*, was arrested and charged with incitement to mutiny by the Attorney General and then released because he was only sub-editor of the paper. The resulting debate and vote of no confidence in the House of Commons led to MacDonald's resignation and an election which saw the publication of the infamous and potentially damaging Zinoviev Letter, which suggested that the Communist Party was using the Labour Party to achieve its objectives. The first Labour administration achieved very little, other than the introduction of John Wheatley's Housing Act which encouraged local authorities to build houses for rent to the working classes. Indeed, it alienated both trade unionists, over the use of the Emergency Powers Act against strikes, and advanced socialists with regard to the rest of its policies. Its attempt to reveal itself as a responsible government, its dependence upon Liberals, and its gradual and parliamentary approach meant that it was almost unable to further socialism in or outside Britain. MacDonald's administration had nine members who were or had been associated with the Union of Democratic Control (UDC) but it did nothing to change the Treaty of Versailles, which the UDC saw as the cause of political instability in Europe, and it supported the Dawes Plan, an

American scheme for helping the Germans to pay their reparations. Its only significant international achievements were that it established diplomatic relations with Soviet Russia and offered the prospect of trade with Russia as a partial solution to unemployment in Britain. Not surprisingly, given its limited achievements, R. Palme Dutt, a leading member of the CPGB, referred to MacDonaldism as 'the greatest enemy of the working class at the present stage'.[14]

The second Labour government also offered little to the furtherance of British socialism. It came into power in May 1929 at a time when the economy was improving and unemployment falling but was set back by the Wall Street Crash of November 1929 and its disastrous economic impact upon world trade. Faced with rising unemployment, increasing expenditure and financial imbalances, MacDonald's government was forced to accept the May Committee examination of the national finances in 1931 and the need to introduce massive public expenditure cuts. It was its attempt to balance the budget that raised the prospect of the 10 (initially 20) per cent cut in unemployment benefits, which divided the Labour cabinet on 23 and 24 August 1931, and paved the way for the formation of MacDonald's National Government. The very fact that the Labour cabinet discussed a cut in unemployment benefit demonstrated that its commitment to a decent standard of living for those who could not be guaranteed work, something the Labour Party had stressed since the 'Right to Work' campaign of 1908, was meaningless. It also demonstrated that the second Labour government and Philip Snowden, its Chancellor of the Exchequer, were slaves to the Treasury dogma of balancing the budget.

Yet even before the economic crisis there had been strong indications that the Labour government was not going to further British socialism. The fact that there was no Labour majority in parliament was interpreted by Labour leaders as evidence of the fact that they had no mandate to introduce socialist measures. The second Labour government's reluctance to act was evident in respect of the expansionary economic measures and political devices that Oswald Mosley outlined in his Memorandum to Government Departments, which appeared in the press as the Mosley Manifesto in December 1930.[15] His suggestion that the cabinet should be reduced to five and that there should be a system of cabinet committees to deal with the economic crisis went against the prevailing acceptance of the old machinery of parliament and government.

When the financial crisis did occur the issue was not the future of socialism but the issue of a conflict between the second Labour government, committed to operating the gold standard and free trade and thus faced with reducing government expenditure and unemployment benefits, and a TUC which felt that any such action would be a betrayal of the interests of the working classes. Indeed, on 20 August 1931 a deputation from the General Council of the TUC, along with a deputation from the Labour Party Executive, met with members of the Labour cabinet, including Snowden and MacDonald. There was certainly no meeting of minds between MacDonald and Snowden, on the one hand, and E. Bevin, W. Citrine, A. Hayday and A. Pugh, on the other. Citrine denied that the economic situation was desperate for 'There are enormous resources in this country.'[16] It was clear that neither the Labour cabinet nor the TUC were going to come to an accommodation and the Labour cabinet split soon afterwards and paved the way for the formation of a National Government.

Until 1931 it seemed that the state was to be the Labour Party's vehicle for achieving British socialism and the Webbs embroidered this with the idea of a 'Social Parliament' which would administer the major industries and services through many tiers of committees. Those who challenged this commitment to statist socialism were ignored. R.H. Tawney, whose more educational and democratic ideas cut across the statist ideas of the Webbs, carried little influence. Yet even that statist approach to socialism had taken time to develop.

At the 1920 Labour Party Conference resolutions were carried, demanding the more effective publicising of the Labour Party's plans for the nationalisation of land, gas, water, electricity and banking and for the creation of workers' committees, district councils and national boards to this effect.[17] In 1922 the party conference established this by a commitment to the nationalisation of land, mines and 'other essential public services' in the party's election programme.[18] The ILP attempted to drive the Labour Party into committing itself to more radical proposals in its 'Socialism in Our Time' campaign of 1926 and 1927 but the Labour Party would not be pushed. Instead it responded with its own programme *Labour and the Nation* (1928) which accepted some of the demands of 'Socialism in Our Time', including public ownership, though not of the Bank of England and the joint stock banks. It adopted a 'step by step' approach and stated that the Labour Party would 'without haste, but without rest, with careful preparation, with the use of the best technical knowledge and managerial skills, and with due compensation to the persons affected' socialise the basic industries. Of the ideology of the party it spoke of 'tentative doctrineless socialism' brought about 'by experimental methods, without violence or disturbances'.[19] Despite some criticism from ILP members, *Labour and the Nation* was accepted by the party conference in 1928.[20]

By 1931, the Labour Party had built upon its general commitment to public ownership by identifying a number of industries it wished to nationalise, with due compensation, in the fullness of time and after some trial and error. The progress to socialism was going to be determined but slow and plodding. Yet the collapse of the second Labour government, the departure of MacDonald, Snowden and Thomas, and the dramatic collapse of Labour's parliamentary representation with the general election of October 1931, led to the questioning of the 'inevitability of gradualness' and to the recognition that Labour lacked a policy on many of the important domestic issues.

At that juncture it appeared that there had to be a more detailed commitment to public ownership and that some alternative socialist strategy had to be developed in place of the discredited policies of Labour's old leaders. Indeed, Labour's 1931 general election manifesto, *Labour's Call to Action: The Nation's Opportunity*, revealed a modest leftward drift, blamed the crisis on capitalist breakdown and advocated public ownership and planning as the solution to Britain's economic problems.

The ILP had already begun to develop a more revolutionary approach to socialism. Its 'Socialism in Our Time' programme of 1926 resulted in *The Living Wage* pamphlet which suggested that Britain was suffering from underconsumption and that this could only be cured by a programme of family allowances, statutory wage minimums, public ownership and the printing of money in the attempt to redistribute wealth. By the 1930s its policies were becoming even more revolutionary but at this stage its leaders forced it to secede from the Labour Party in 1932 and it made no contribution to the new debate on socialist policy.

Labour Party intellectuals and theorists also began to develop alternative socialist strategies. Harold Laski was concerned that state power threatened democracy but hoped that the development of voluntary associations would help to maintain both political and industrial democracy.[21] Yet he asserted that there was a decline in democratic trends within trade unionism and that there remained the corrupting influence of big property owners to contend with. After Hitler's rise to power in Germany in January 1933, he began to move towards Leninist ideas, maintaining that parliamentary democracy had arisen when capitalism was competitive but that the emergence of monopoly capitalism had accentuated the economic crisis and class conflict. He argued that class antagonism could only be settled by class conflict and that fascism was a demonstration of the necessity of this because it revealed that capitalists would rather extinguish democracy than see it turned against their interests. To Laski, then, the conflict was between socialism and fascism, in which conflict socialists should use constitutional methods until fascism made that avenue impossible.[22]

It was Laski's fear of fascism that drove him to support the Unity Manifesto of the CPGB, the ILP and the Socialist League in 1937. The objective of this campaign was 'unity of all sections of the working-class movement within the framework of the Labour Party and the Trade Unions in common struggle against fascism, Reaction and War, and for the immediate demands of the worker, in order to develop the strength and unity of the working-class for the defeat of the National Government'. This was to be 'built upon the basis of day-to-day struggle for immediate limited objectives by mass action, industrial and political, and through the democratisation of the Labour Party and the Trade Union Movement'.[23] Laski signed the Unity Manifesto along with Aneurin Bevan, Harry Pollitt, John Strachey, Palme Dutt and Sir Stafford Cripps and was hopeful that a meaningful alliance against fascism would be organised, although his hopes were soon to be dashed by the disbanding of the Socialist League, the conflict between the CPGB and the ILP over Spain, and the effective collapse of the Unity Campaign.

Like Laski, G.D.H. Cole failed to see the point of nationalising industries, especially if they were in poor economic health, and believed that there was a need to restore capitalist viability through a National Investment Board, which would help existing firms and form new ones, to ensure that socialism could be built upon the foundations of successful capitalism. If necessary, these could develop into nationalised industries, although he was generally opposed to state controls at this point. In other words, the expert, the entrepreneur and the professional would assume a bigger role whereas under public ownership it was the impartial administrator who was more important.[24] Cole was obviously advocating a form of monopoly capitalism.

R.H. Tawney and Stafford Cripps also began to consider the need for a more speedy transition to socialism on the grounds that slow change was unlikely to undermine the capitalist base from which it would emerge.[25] Yet the problem all these intellectuals faced was that of reconciling their schemes with the demands of a far more cautious trade union movement dominated by Bevin, who, in particular, wanted a programme of practical policies which could easily be applied to reduce the high level of unemployment. Indeed, Bevin had produced his *My Plan for 2,000,000 Workless* in 1932 which advocated a variety of schemes including lowering of the retirement age, the raising of the school leaving age and the creation of work by starting major building schemes. His focus was extremely narrow and social rather than socialist and one is reminded of Minkin's suggestion that there were, in the 1920s, some obvious disagreements between the trade union leaders and the Labour Party, but often with no obvious victor. The one stressed the democratic right to decide about wages and conditions of employment while the other claimed and operated a system of parliamentary privilege.[26]

This may explain why the trade union domination of the Labour Party in the 1930s did not inhibit the social planning that was evident within the intellectual socialist groups. In the end the moderate and right-wing socialists in the Labour Party prevailed and developed their policies under the guise of planning, the need for which had been discussed by Oswald Mosley at the ILP summer schools in the mid-1920s and had been outlined in his book *Revolution by Reason* (1925).

Evan Durbin,[27] Hugh Gaitskell, Douglas Jay and Hugh Dalton were particularly important in shaping the Labour Party's new strategy, which was one largely based upon reducing internal conflict and of offering a limited programme of public ownership designed to raise living standards and to reduce unemployment. This strategy, and their influence, emerged from the planning exercises of the Labour Party.

Labour's social planning was conducted mainly by the New Fabian Research Bureau (1931), the TUC Economic Committee (1932) and a new policy committee of NEC, with four sub-committees, created for the purpose in 1931. The most important of these NEC sub-committees was that for Finance and Trade chaired by Hugh Dalton, who virtually wrote Labour's economic and financial policy in the 1930s. None the less, few of these policies would have had influence without the support of the National Council of Labour (the old National Joint Council) and therefore the support of Ernest Bevin and Walter Citrine, who dominated this body, was vital. Thus there was never likely to be a commitment to full-scale reorganisation since that would require a complete change in the relations between the state and the economy which Bevin was not prepared to contemplate in the short term.

The Labour Left always wanted rather more direct state intervention than the Labour Right was willing to accept.[28] As early as 1932, E.F. Wise, chairman of the newly-formed Socialist League, essentially a group of ex-ILPers, asked the Labour Party Conference for the nationalisation of joint-stock banks, a policy which Cole's New Fabian Research Bureau (NFRB) also felt was necessary if planning was to work. Conference approved the Wise amendment by 2,241,000 votes to 984,000. Yet such radicalism was not to last as, over the next few years, Labour restricted itself to a policy of nationalising the Bank of England and became increasingly attracted to the policies of J.M. Keynes, who suggested that economic policies could achieve full employment through indirect controls.

Hugh Dalton was the powerhouse behind Labour's new moderate, but planned, socialist policies. Essentially Fabian in outlook, he dismissed the various alternatives put forward by Laski, Cripps and Cole and argued that 'Labour needed better policies and better people'.[29] At first, he joined the NFRB as a member of its directing body but he disliked Cole's disdain for politicians and objected to some of the NFRB publications, most notably a paper called 'A Labour Programme for Action' in which Harold Laski and William Mellor argued that socialists should arm themselves against the possibility that capitalist parties would prevent a victorious Labour Party taking office. The document had suggested the need to nationalise joint-stock banks and went well beyond what Dalton and many of the leading Labour figures were advocating, even though it was accepted at the 1932 party conference.

While briefly associated with the NFRB, Dalton visited the Soviet Union with a group of New Fabians in the summer of 1932. He returned convinced that the First and Second Five Year Plans of the Soviet Union indicated that planning could work and that Britain required something similar, though not under a communist regime. From then onwards, planning socialism in Britain became Dalton's central aim. He wanted to redistribute the resources of Britain in order to tackle the horrendous problem of unemployment. He took this commitment into the NEC's eight-man Policy Committee where he emerged as chairman of the Finance and Trade Sub-Committee. Only Herbert Morrison, who chaired the Local Government and Social Services Committee, rivalled him in importance. Dalton developed the idea that planning was to be free from market pressures and had to have the ability to overcome official resistance, should call upon experts and, according to his Labour Party document *Socialism and the Condition of the People* (1933), should be a well-planned rush.[30] This document, debated at the conference that year, accepted the need to nationalise joint-stock banks, the steel industry and other vital industries. Nevertheless, there was a mixed economy element in it for Dalton was partly influenced by Barbara Wootton's book, *Plan or No Plan*, which suggested that there was room for both socialist planning and Keynesian expansionism.

Dalton's influence was further evident in Labour's new policy document *For Socialism and Peace*, accepted by the party conference in

1934, which made specific commitments to planning and nationalisation while not specifying which industries would be subject to public ownership. This was a very contentious document which was criticised for being rather vague and general, but it had gained widespread support at the 1934 conference for it was 'based on a concordat between political moderates and their trade union counterparts'.[31]

The policies outlined in *For Socialism and Peace* were more closely examined by Dalton in his *Practical Socialism for Britain* (1935). This emphasised that planning under capitalism was possible and maintained that it could speed up the transition to socialism. It played down the importance of Keynesian expansionism but acknowledged the importance of a National Investment Board to control the direction and level of long-term investment. The emphasis was, however, to be placed upon the nationalisation of basic industries.[32]

These schemes were played down during the 1935 general election but shortly afterwards the TUC presented specific plans for the socialisation of the cotton industry to the 1935 Labour Party Conference. A plan for the socialisation of the coal mining industry, *Coal: The Labour Plan*, was accepted at the 1936 conference.[33]

The ideas that emerged were finally put into shape, under Dalton's direction and strongly influenced by Evan Durbin and Hugh Gaitskell, in a short manifesto called *Labour's Immediate Programme* which was adopted at the party conference in 1937. It removed the Labour Party commitment to nationalise joint-stock banks, which had been made by the party conference in 1932, and was altogether less radical in tone. Indeed, the CPGB felt that Labour's new programme would simply strengthen capitalism. Yet *Labour's Immediate Programme* committed Labour to a programme of nationalisation, narrow and limited as it was, in a more specific manner than had ever occurred before. It also committed it to direct intervention stating that 'The State must accept responsibility for the location of industry' and that 'Labour will bring new industries into these areas, . . . develop local resources and improve communications, assist Local Authorities and relieve the crushing burden of local rates.'[34]

Labour's socialist programme was thus laid down for the next eight years since *Labour's Immediate Programme* provided a blueprint for the post-war Attlee governments. In almost twenty years the Labour Party had moved only from an unspecified commitment to public ownership to offering a modest programme of nationalisation and state intervention. It lacked the radicalism that some socialists had hoped for and there were no new radical ideas, but five years of policy discussions had at least committed Labour to a specific, if restricted, set of proposals for public ownership. The unity between the Labour Party and the trade unions, despite the tendency to operate in different spheres, prevented the intrusion of more radical socialist proposals. In particular, it kept at bay some of the alternative revolutionary ideas of the CPGB.

From its formation in 1920 and until 1928, the CPGB attempted to affiliate with the Labour Party. This caused much consternation within the Labour Party which, while rejecting the CPGB's application at its annual conferences, found it impossible to exclude individual communists from its proceedings. The problem is that the Labour Party was dominated by the trade unions which could, and did, send a small number of Communist delegates to the Labour Party conferences and, indeed, to local Labour Party constituency meetings much against the wishes of their national trade union leaders. Faced with its own version of 'the enemy within', the Labour Party sought to remove the offending delegates and began a long process of finding the right formulation of resolutions which would exclude Communists without offending some rank-and-file trade unionists.

Labour's first main attack upon Communist infiltration began at the Labour Party's Edinburgh conference of 1922 when it was agreed that every person nominated to serve as a delegate 'shall individually accept the constitution and principles of the Labour Party'.[35] This decision was supported by a resolution that delegates could not be associated with any party wishing to return MPs who were not approved by the Labour Party.

The Edinburgh amendments directly challenged the right of trade union organisations to determine who would be the representatives at Labour Party conferences and called upon local parties to exclude properly accredited Communist representatives from their ranks. Even though Communists were very thin on the ground, local labour parties began to jib at the prospect of excluding 'tried and trusted' members and delegates from trade union branches, simply because they were members of the CPGB.

Such was the hostility to the Edinburgh amendments that the London conference of the Labour Party, held in the summer of 1923, agreed to drop the second amendment and to rely upon the first, which simply asked that all delegates should individually accept the constitution of the Labour Party. In December 1923 the NEC of the Labour Party decided to form a sub-committee to examine the whole issue. It first reported to the full NEC on 2 September 1924 and later that month endorsed the view that the affiliation of the CPGB had to be refused and that no member of that party could be eligible for endorsement as a Labour candidate for parliament or any public body.[36] The sub-committee emphasised the great variance between the Labour and Communist parties: 'The Labour Party seeks to achieve the Socialist Commonwealth by means of Parliamentary democracy. The Communist Party seeks to achieve the "Dictatorship of the Proletariat" by armed revolution.'[37] It saw no way in which a party which favoured 'tyranny' could be affiliated to the Labour Party. The NEC endorsed this decision in December 1924 and reminded local Labour parties that it would be a breach of the Labour Party constitution for them to ignore the decision to exclude Communists. The debate continued throughout 1925 and 1926 until the party conference of 1926 reiterated the decisions first taken at Edinburgh in 1922.

This policy has remained the basis of the Labour Party's attitude towards the CPGB ever since. Throughout the rest of the interwar years, however, the attitude of the CPGB towards Labour changed on two counts. First, the General Strike of 1926 led to a conflict between the CPGB and the TUC which permitted Bevin, Citrine and other trade union leaders to isolate and reduce Communist support within the trade union movement. Secondly, in 1928 the Comintern, the Third International, decided to withdraw from its 'United Front' policy and attack the Labour Party in its 'Class Against Class' policy, accusing it of being the third capitalist party in Britain.[38] In one fell swoop 'Class Against Class' killed off Communist support within the Labour Party and put Communist candidates against Labour candidates at the 1929 General Election, as the CPGB declared its new revolutionary programme.[39]

The CPGB attempted to revive its links with the Labour Party in the 1930s but with little success, although, as will be suggested later, it gained some modest success in winning trade-union support.[40] In 1933 the threat of European fascism led to the CPGB reinstituting the United Front, in this case against fascism. By 1935 the CPGB was even attempting to operate a Popular Front, willing to work with any anti-fascist party. Once again, the CPGB was attempting to affiliate to the Labour Party but without any success, despite the fact that there were often hundreds of declarations of support for such a policy at the Labour Party conferences.

Hitler's accession to the Chancellorship of Germany in January 1933 and the Spanish Civil War between 1936 and 1939, brought into the open the Labour Party's continued antipathy towards the CPGB. The Labour Left was particularly interested in the Communist-inspired United Front and Popular Front campaigns against fascism; the former hoped for an alliance between socialist and communist groups while the latter (of the late 1930s) was more an ethical alliance of progressive interests against the failures of British foreign policy aimed at an alliance with all anti-fascist organisations.

Recently, however, there has been some questioning of the extent to which the Popular Front owed its origins primarily to the CPGB. It is David Blaazer's contention that the Popular Front emerged in Britain not as a result of the pressure of the CPGB, but as a result of the desire by the Labour Left, Liberals and progressives to strike a temporary alliance on a limited and immediate programme to change British foreign policy from its dilatory approach in dealing with the rising threat of European fascism. This desire, Blaazer argues, dated back to an earlier tradition of alliances between progressive groups which were forged in connection with the Boer War, the First World War and the Treaty of Versailles. In essence, then, Blaazer rejects the 'myth' that the Popular Front was a campaign engineered by the Communists for it had good credentials in earlier crisis movements.[41] Be that as it may, the fact is that the Labour Party saw the United Front and the Popular Front as part of the Communist challenge to its position, and was unwilling to be involved.

This became more obvious in the case of the Spanish Civil War. The United Front and Popular Front evoked little support from the Labour Party leadership and the TUC. Labour leaders participated in the general humanitarian concern for Spain but did not wish to unite with the CPGB in campaigning for a more active involvement in Spanish affairs. Indeed, because of its support of the Popular Front against fascism the Socialist League was forced to disband in 1937.

Yet it is not at all clear that the Labour Party/TUC opposition to the Popular Front in connection with Spain was entirely about hostility to the CPGB. Tom Buchanan has noted that it was also about problems within the trade union movement. Indeed, he makes the point, of the Spanish Civil War, that 'The Labour Party did not see it as the "last Great Cause" but as a problem to be overcome', and that 'the Catholic minority . . . acted as a storm-centre for opposition to the Spanish Republic.'[42] Indeed, he notes that Ernest Bevin's sympathies were with the Republicans but that he refused to be influenced by the emotions generated by Spain because of the problems within his own union, the TGWU. The fact is that the TGWU had a strong core of Catholic supporters among the Liverpool dockers, who were being encouraged by the Catholic priests to criticise Republican actions, including the murder of priests, in Spain. This section objected to the TGWU sending about £10,000 of humanitarian aid to Spain. At the same time, and among many of the so-called rank-and-file Communist members of the TGWU in London there were equally vociferous demands to give more trade-union support for the removal of the National Government's embargo against arms being sent to Spain, which was particularly damaging the position of the legitimate Republican government.[43] Ernest Bevin and his union were thus criticised for both doing too much for the Spanish Republican government and for doing too little.[44] Other trade unions, and the Labour Party, faced similar criticisms.

Thus, it could be argued that the Labour Party was not prepared to put its full weight of support behind the Spanish Republican government. This may have had something to do with the fact that it was a government run by communists but it should be remembered that Spain did pose a problem for both the Labour Party and the trade unions and the support for the Republican side was more muted and circumscribed than it might otherwise have been, even allowing for the symbolic visits to Spain by the Labour leaders such as Clement Attlee. As far as the Labour Party was concerned the presence of what were perceived to be Communist-inspired United and Popular Fronts did not help matters. The Labour Party was not prepared to accept communists at the national level and this was an attitude that they sought to pass on to constituency Labour parties by the late 1930s.[45]

Nevertheless, in the mid and late 1930s communists were present within the local trade union movement and hence the local Labour party constituency organisations. The Socialist League, a body of about 3,000 members, was one organisation which encouraged this development for it associated itself with the Popular Front demands in the 1930s.[46] Indeed, there was significant support for the United Front and the Popular Front from the Labour Left and Kevin Morgan is probably correct in suggesting that 'the dividing line between the Communist Party and the Labour Left was virtually indefinable, not least because an unknown number of communists pursued their Popular Front activities within the Labour Party.'[47] Yet the Labour Party had shut the door on the CPGB and, by the end of the 1930s, had developed a fairly extensive system of proscription, by excluding individuals and organisations who supported the CPGB or its official line. The Socialist League was forced to disband in May 1937 and Cripps, Aneurin Bevan, and those who supported what were referred to as 'Crippisms', were expelled from the Labour Party in a flurry of activity in early 1939.[48]

Local Labour parties began to take action and watched their dissentients more carefully. The Leeds Labour Party, for instance, was particularly concerned about the Leeds branch of the Militant Labour League. Formed about 1938 by Lancelot Lake, the Leeds branch of the League attacked the local Leeds Labour Party, focused upon the need to face up to both fascism and capitalism, campaigned for the setting up of an International Workers' Socialist Republic and called upon 'Socialists not to leave the Labour Party . . . but to join with us in building the Organised Socialist Left Wing'.[49] The Leeds Labour Party kept a file on this branch and had A.L. Williams, secretary of the Leeds Labour Party and editor of its flagship the *Leeds Citizen*, keep a check on this organisation, and other suspected Communists. The relationship between the Labour Left and the Communists was clearly an issue of great importance to the Labour Party and will be examined later in this chapter.

While socialist planning and Communist challenge were the issues that came to dominate the Labour Party it also had to adjust itself to the mass entry of women into politics. Like all the other political parties, Labour had to address the issue of the women's vote once the 1918 Franchise Act had given the vote to all women over the age of 30, and especially when the age limit was reduced to 21 in 1928. It took its first step when the Women's Labour League, formed in 1906, fused with the Labour Party in 1918, to form the basis of the women's section of the Labour Party. By 1922 more than 100,000 women had joined the 650 women's sections of local Labour parties and there were about 35,000 women in the Women's Cooperative Guild which acted with the Labour Party although it was an independent body.[50] These developments raised serious gender issues since the presence of these women's organisations began to challenge the Labour Party's commitment to the 'equality of the sexes', for women now helped to define the political agenda. Marion Phillips, of the Labour League, who became the Chief Women's Officer within the Labour Party, emphasised the need for the women's section to integrate with Labour Party politics whereas Margaret Llewellyn Davies, of the Women's Cooperative Guild, emphasised that the Labour Party was offering women very little. As a consequence the Labour Party was faced with division and debate over the need for specific policies for women in the 1920s, in which Phillips played down the gender issue and in which Davies played it up.

The most obvious points of conflict were to be associated with the female demands for both birth control and family allowances. On the issue of birth control, there were many women within the Labour Party who saw it as the way to release themselves from a cycle of poverty and from constant ill health. The issue emerged strongly in May 1924 when a women's deputation went to John Wheatley, Minister of Health in the first Labour government, asking him to lift the ban that made it illegal for local health authorities to distribute birth control information.[51] Marion Phillips, however, felt that birth control should not become a political issue to divide Labour. There was also the fear that the Catholic members within the Labour Party would be upset by the dissemination of information on birth control.[52] This was a view on which the NEC of the Labour Party agreed and it reported at the Labour Party's Liverpool conference, 1925

> That the subject of birth control is in its nature not one which should be made a political Party issue, but should remain another upon which members of the Party should be free to hold and promote their individual convictions.[53]

Similar divisions developed in connection with the demand for family allowances, which many trade union leaders, such as Ernest Bevin, objected to. Marion Phillips felt that such a provision would 'increase the irresponsibility of fatherhood' in opposition to the fulsome report of the Women's Cooperative Guild.[54]

Throughout the 1920s there was little evidence that the Labour Party had taken women's issues on board in the gradualist socialist programmes it offered. There was even less evidence of such commitments in the 1930s. With the collapse of the second Labour government in August 1931 the main purpose of Labour came to be the maintenance of unity in order to recover political power and gender issues became less important than they had been in the 1920s. In the final analysis the Labour Party found itself incapable of fully integrating gender issues within its social democratic structure as planning, the survival of the party, and the rejection of communism became more important than women's issues.

THE COMMUNIST PARTY OF GREAT BRITAIN

At the end of July 1920 members of the BSP, the SLP, the Workers' Socialist Federation, the Shop Stewards' movement, the Plebs League, and other socialist groups, came together to form the CPGB in London. The CPGB's combined strength was between 2,000 and 3,000 at that time but had fallen to 2,000 when it was relaunched at Leeds in 1921. It is almost axiomatic that it was formed because of Lenin's pressure rather than because of the desire of British Marxists, always notoriously divided, to unite. The intention was to form a mass party and the main question facing historians is: why did the Communist Party fail to become the party of the working classes? Many suggestions have been made, ranging from the poor economic conditions of the interwar years to the suggestion that Marxism was alien to the British social and political system, manipulated as it was by Moscow. There may be some truth in these explanations but of more importance may be the fact that the CPGB was formed too late to exert much influence on the trade union movement and to make good the connection which previous Marxist organisations had often neglected. Without the trade union movement the CPGB was unlikely to win the support of the working classes and it is patently obvious that it gained few members from the working classes when compared with the Labour Party.

Nevertheless, there were some areas of Communist support, the 'Little Moscows' , which Stuart Macintyre suggests may have been the tip of a proletarian culture based upon Marxism.[55] There is no doubt that communist communities, such as Mardy, in South Wales, and Lumphinnans and the Vale of Leven, in Scotland, emerged but why did such areas of support emerge? Such islands of support were untypical of Britain as a whole but may have been rooted in the peculiar problems of the community and the strength of local Communist leadership taking up local issues such as unemployment. Even then one cannot assume a continuity of Communist influence for it had to be fought for against a background of police prosecutions and the expulsion of members from the trade unions and the Labour Party.

Indeed, Macintyre admits that the creation of a strong Marxist area like Mardy was dependent upon a strong sense of community and the nature and strength of the local political leadership which took up the issues vital to the community. However, Communist leaders had to fight for their position and Macintyre rejects the notion of outside commentators who put down the 'extraordinary mentality' of the Mardy inhabitants to the fact that 'they have no experience of any towns except Mardy [and] they are unable to realise the weight of public opinion against Communism in the country generally and they believe that soon other towns will be controlled by Communists.'[56] Indeed, this was far from being the truth for there was little political unity in Mardy and the Communists were in a constant struggle with their opponents.

The CPGB was formed as a result of the creation of the Third International, the Comintern, in Moscow in 1919. Through this organisation, which had emerged despite the resurrection of the Second International, Lenin, Trotsky, Zinoviev, and other leading Bolsheviks, had sought to bring together Marxists of all countries to be inducted into the finer points of Marxism. It was essential, of course, that a communist party should be formed in every country including Britain. As Walter Kendall and Raymond Challinor have stressed, it was Lenin and the Comintern who pressured British Marxists, such as Willie Gallacher, to form the CPGB.[57] In Gallacher's case, he answered yes to Lenin's request that he should persuade his Scottish comrades to join the CPGB, and toned down his opposition towards affiliation with the Labour Party. The Soviet Communist Party directed 'Moscow money' to certain Marxist groups and dictated the policies. This would appear to be the case despite the revisionist ideas of some historians, most obviously Kevin Morgan, who challenges the notion that the CPGB closely followed the Comintern line.[58] It was only those organisations that seemed likely to toe the line that were to be admitted to the Comintern, which laid down twenty-one conditions in its 1920 Congress that were designed to keep communist organisations in and others out. There were always groups within the CPGB who were prepared to criticise the official line, as laid down by the Comintern, who might seem to be ahead of the changes that occurred but once the Comintern changed its line the official line of the CPGB changed quickly to come into line. This was evident in the case of 'Class Against Class' in 1928 and in the case of the change in policy towards fascism brought about by the Soviet–German pact in 1939 – both of which will be discussed later.

From the outset, the Comintern, and its satellite organisations, felt that the great danger was monopoly capitalism which created tensions, wars and instability. It therefore maintained that reformist trade unions and socialists were merely appendages of the bourgeois state inside the workers' movements. It also suggested that the capitalist state, no matter how democratic it was, was merely a reflection of the control and dictatorship of monopoly business and finance. True democracy could only be established in a soviet or council of democracy. Therefore the thing that mattered was the conquest of power by the revolutionary party for this was the measure of progress towards socialism. The gradual extension of state collectivism was considered not to be an effective measure of the move towards socialism.

Leninism was thus to turn British Marxism into a doctrine of action focused upon the construction of a mass CPGB. No longer were British Marxists to await the inevitable economic collapse of capitalism, in the classic style of the SDF, but were now committed to revolutionary action. Rajani Palme Dutt and Harry Pollitt in their famous *Report of Organisation* (sometimes known as the Organisation Committee Report of 1922 but better known as the 'Dutt–Pollitt Report') sought to Bolshevise the CPGB by getting rid of inactive party branches, geared to the almost dormant task of listening to letters on party business, and by creating in their place active groups of members who would be responsible for promoting the campaigns of the CPGB. The slogan of the report was 'down with the old style branch' and the aim was to set up a 'network of influences through the working class and its organisation'. The *Workers' Weekly* appeared in February 1923 to replace the fading

Communist, and quickly increased the circulation from 19,000 to 51,000 in eight weeks.[59] But organisation and propaganda alone would never be sufficient. The problem was how to achieve mass support in Britain, where socialist developments were increasingly dominated and controlled by the trade unions and the Labour Party.

Lenin encouraged the CPGB to apply for affiliation to the Labour Party, partly in order to gain access to the trade unions which were deemed essential to its growth and success. The Labour Party rejected such overtures and the CPGB and the Comintern were forced to attempt other measures. In 1921 the Comintern established the British Bureau of the Red International of Labour Unions (Profintern). Then, in 1923, the CPGB was encouraged to form the National Minority Movement in order to organise trade unions sympathetic to the communist cause. This was formed in January 1924 and declared its aims in August 1924, including:

> a wage increase of £1 a week, with a minimum wage of £4; a 44-hour week, and no overtime. Workshop and Factory Committees with members guaranteed against victimisation; Workers' Control of Industry; a stronger TUC, with control over the Labour Party; industrial unionism; the affiliation of the National Unemployed Workers' Committee Movement and the trades councils to the TUC; . . .[60]

It also committed itself to more revolutionary aims with the following objectives:

> to organise the working classes of Britain for the overthrow of capitalism, the emancipation of the workers from the oppressors and exploiters, and the establishment of a Socialist Commonwealth; to carry on a wide agitation and propaganda for the principles of revolutionary class struggle . . . and against the present tendency towards social peace and class collaboration and the delusion of the peaceful transition from capitalism to socialism; to unite the workers in their everyday struggles against the exploiters; to maintain the closest relations with the R.I.L.U. [Red International of Labour Unions] . . .[61]

In 1925 a National Left Wing Movement was also developed within the Labour Party, the purpose of which was to develop a link between the left wing of the Labour Party and the CPGB. Effectively, the CPGB was attempting to penetrate the mass Labour movement through the trade unions and the constituency Labour parties.

Neither of these movements carried much impetus in the 1920s. Roderick

Martin has demonstrated that the National Minority Movement exerted little influence, despite claiming almost a million trade union supporters in 1926, and it expired in 1933 claiming only a few thousand.[62] Part of its problem was that the General Council recognised that the National Federation of Trades Councils, formed in 1922, had been taken over partly by the Communists and so decided in 1924 that the trades councils should be local agents of Congress. In 1926 the TUC decided that trades councils could not be members of the National Minority Movement. This decision was enforced on the trades councils in 1927 and, in May 1927, the Communist majority was removed from the executive of the London Trades Council. These actions were approved by the TUC, Herbert Smith and many other trades union leaders.[63] The National Left Wing Movement also gathered some support but was killed off by the CPGB itself. This body had developed support in South Wales and London, and shortly after the General Strike of 1926 the Greater London Left-Wing Group formed the National Left Wing Movement which had held its first national conference at Poplar Town Hall, London, in September 1926. By the time of its 1927 conference it was claiming 150,000 members. But it did not develop further, for in February 1928 the Comintern decided to withdraw from its United Front policy and to achieve reformist and socialist parties. Eventually, the CPGB abandoned the National Left Wing Movement by 1929.[64] The NEC of the Labour Party also cut its links with twenty-seven constituency associations connected with the CPGB between 1926 and 1929 and threatened dozens of others with similar terminations.[65]

Nevertheless, John Callaghan suggests that the real problem runs deeper than the failure of communism to develop trade-union and left-wing connections, for there were no bitter and massive splits comparable to those that occurred to Labour movements in Europe during the First World War. British quasi-Marxist organisations were small and had failed to detach the working class from the political system. Lenin's revolutionary approach was thus a non-starter in Britain even though it offered a coherent strategy for change.[66]

As already noted, the Labour Party made a determined effort to thwart the ambitions of the CPGB and was not prepared to be used as part of its power struggle. Equally, the trade union leaders generally operated against communists, although many of their local members might have accepted them from time to time as good trade unionists. Indeed, in the early 1920s there was some support for communists from trade unionists. However, the failure of the General Strike of 1926 undermined any meaningful link between communism and the

British trade union movement and without that link there was very little prospect of creating a mass CPGB.

At the outset of the General Strike the CPGB had, despite its criticism of the failure of the Triple Alliance in 1921, given its support to the General Council of the TUC using the slogan 'All Power to the General Council'. The force of this commitment was undermined by the fact that a dozen of the CPGB's leading figures had been arrested for seditious libel, found guilty and imprisoned some months before the dispute began. Nevertheless, the remnants of the CPGB leadership hoped to get the support of a number of members of the General Council, most notably A.A. Purcell, Alonso Swales, Ben Turner and George Hicks, as well as the more general support of the Labour Left and the ILP Clydesiders. That support held good until the General Council called off the General Strike on 12 May 1926, after only nine days. Immediately, the CPGB attacked this action and its most vitriolic criticism appeared on 13 May 1926:

> The General Council's decision to call off the General Strike is the greatest crime that has ever been permitted, not only against the miners, but against the workers of Great Britain and the whole world. The British workers had aroused the astonishment and admiration of the world by the enthusiasm with which they had entered upon the fight for the miners' standard of living. But instead of responding to this magnificent lead by a call to every section of organised labour to join the fight against the capitalists, the General Council has miserably thrown itself and the miners on the tender mercies of the workers' worst enemies – the Tory Government.[67]

The General Council was being accused of betraying the miners, of not being committed to the struggle and of abandoning a winnable dispute. Soon afterwards, A.J. Cook, the secretary of the Miners' Federation of Great Britain, produced his somewhat constrained but critical account of events in a pamphlet entitled *The Nine Days*. The TUC, on the other hand, attempted to maintain a rule of silence until it rebutted the charges made against it at the Conference of the Trade Union Executives held on 20 and 21 January 1927.[68]

The CPGB attack upon the TUC, and incidentally upon A.J. Cook on another occasion, made it difficult for it to maintain any significant support within the trade union movement. Admittedly, the CPGB membership rose to about 10,000, mainly as a result of recruitment in the mining areas of the South Wales and the north-east coalfields, but those figures soon dwindled away as the TUC attached itself more firmly to the political ambitions of the Labour Party.

Martin Jacques, a Marxist writer, has argued that 1926 proved to be a decisive turning point in the development of the working classes for 'it marked the end of the last great period of working-class militancy and it saw a massive shift in outlook and orientation of the trade-union movement.'[69] He maintains that the trade unions were on the offensive between 1918 and 1926 but that the situation changed dramatically thereafter, for trade unions began to accept that they could do little about unemployment and moved towards improved industrial relations with the employers, through the Mond–Turner talks (1928–30) between the TUC and the representatives of the larger employers, and by working with the government. Other writers, such as Chris Wrigley, would tend to suggest that there was a more continuous history of improving industrial relations which was interrupted, temporarily, by the General Strike.[70] Perhaps the radical and parliamentary potential of the working classes was never really there.

The CPGB had never had much of a parliamentary presence, returning only two MPs, J.T. Walton Newbold (Motherwell) and S. Saklatvala (Battersea) at the 1922 general election. Newbold was a rather unpredictable figure who, having been beaten in the 1923 general election, drifted out of the CPGB, since he was disaffected by its Comintern-inspired move to establish the Communist-led National Minority Movement.[71] His resignation provoked the CPGB leadership to criticise his 'political confusion' and his 'gross political cowardice'.[72] Saklatvala was thus left as the sole Communist MP in Parliament. The CPGB won another parliamentary seat in 1935 when Willie Gallacher was returned for West Fife in 1935.[73]

Lacking a significant parliamentary presence the CPGB had hoped to work through the Labour Party to extend its influence but increasing criticism of this United Front policy from J.T. Murphy and R. Palme Dutt, Reg Groves and others was supported by the action of the Sixth Congress of the Comintern (July to September 1928) which abandoned that policy. From now on the Labour Party was to be regarded as the third capitalist party in Britain according to the 'Class Against Class' pamphlet; it stated that the Labour Party 'lays claim to the title of Socialist Party but has nothing to do with socialism', and put forward a 16-point programme for a Revolutionary Workers' Government which would declare Britain to be a Workers' Socialist Republic, nationalise banks, repudiate the National Debt, establish a seven-hour working day and nationalise all educational institutions.[74]

Although it is clear that 'Class Against Class' did undermine the CPGB influence within the Labour Party and the trade unions it is argued by Nina Fishman that it paved the way for a more determined assault upon the trade unions in the 1930s.[75] There had been some Communist dissatisfaction with the leadership of both the trade unions and the Labour Party in 1926 and this had been taken up by the 'Young Turks', especially Willie Rust and John Mahon, who strongly supported the new Comintern line in 1928. Nevertheless, there were some within the CPGB who felt this policy to be a mistake and saw red revolution as the basis of the declining support for the CPGB. Harry Pollitt, Walter Hannington (leader of the Communist-dominated National Unemployed Workers' Movement) and Arthur Horner began to question the value of the leftward move of the CPGB. Indeed, it was out of their regular meetings that Pollitt and Campbell began to develop the alternative strategy of winning the support of the trade unions by keeping the rank-and-file movements in check. Their cause was strengthened as the CPGB membership declined to 2,555 in 1930. Pollitt and Campbell continued to emphasise the importance of 'daily mass work inside factories and pits' and developed what became known as 'revolutionary pragmatism'.[76] Once the Comintern changed its policy and moved towards both a United Front against fascism in league with other socialist organisations, and a Popular Front, with all anti-Fascist parties, Pollitt and Campbell became more assertive and the 'Young Turks' lost their influence.

The year 1933 was, indeed, a vital transitional moment in the history of the CPGB. During January and February, the party seemed content to carry out the 'Prague resolution' of 1931, whereby the Comintern had instructed all Communist parties to take mass revolutionary activity. Rank-and-filism was to the fore. This was encouraged by the busmen's strike and conflict with the London General Omnibus Company and the creation of the London Busmen's Rank and File Movement in October 1932.[77] The Central Committee of the CPGB was committed to supporting the mass revolutionary trade unionism and to implementing the decision of the 12th Plenum of the Comintern which 'placed before the Parties as a principal task in this period the development of the revolutionary trade union movement into an organisation capable of independently leading the struggle of the workers against capitalism'.[78] At this stage, the 'Class Against Class' policy was still in operation and the rank-and-file movement was being encouraged and developed through the *Busman's Punch* and the *Railway Vigilant*, and other Communist papers, which were critical of the trade union leaders. Factory-based organisations were being encouraged and Walter Hannington was in trouble with the Central Committee and the Political Bureau of the CPGB because of his failure to introduce a form of collective leadership within the National Unemployed Workers' Movement (NUWM)[79]

Yet this mood of aggression was tempered when Hitler came to power in Germany in January 1933. German fascism dealt a death blow to the proletarian movement in Germany and forced the Comintern to produce its manifesto outlining its new policy of a United Front against Fascists. The mood of the CPGB changed as it quickly aligned itself with the new position of the Comintern. There were some critics who felt that the new instruction to work with social democratic parties could be used as a weapon against them and the *Daily Worker* reproduced the statement that 'Should the Social democrats not accept the Communist offer the whole working class, even its most backward strata, will know that it is social democracy which interferes with the rejection of fascism and the defence of the working class.'[80] This was a view which was quickly rejected by Harry Pollitt (speaking under the pseudonym of Comrade Brisker) who emphasised the new positive tone that had been adopted by the United Front Manifesto. In a lengthy speech to the Central Committee of the CPGB he made the new policy clear.

> What is the situation now. The proletariat suffered a terrific defeat as a result of the triumph of Fascism in Germany. If we can't see that we can't see anything. The second most important point is that the CI [Communist International] declares that it is permissible for the Communist Parties to approach central organisations of the reformist Parties. This isn't merely a figure of speech. This is not something to be put in there lightly. It is one of the most important things that is in the Manifesto and there isn't one comrade who read it but didn't immediately understand that this was something big.[81]

He then went on to argue for a concrete programme of action and that there was a need to be positive about the United Front, for any suggestion that it would expose the failures of social democracy would appear in every factory paper and every Communist cell and would be seen by other socialist groups as an attack upon them. Unity, not discord, was what was required. The new policy was something which supported the strategic course he was following in attempting to win support among trade union officials and within the Labour Party. There is no doubt that it did help the CPGB to improve its fortunes.

From 1933 onwards the CPGB began to see its membership increase because of its stand against fascism and because of the Spanish Civil War (1936–9). This revival in fortunes, recent evidence suggests, was partly the result of increasing influence within the trade union movement. Kevin Morgan alerted historians to this possibility in 1989 when he wrote:

> There was more continuity to Communist influence in the trade union movement than is usually recognised, and if there was a decline of influence

between 1928 and 1932, it was probably due to the chronic level of unemployment among Party members as much as it was due to sectarianism.[82]

Since then, two writers, Richard Stevens and Nina Fishman, have sought to examine the rise of Communist influence within the trade unions in the 1930s, although they each tend to adopt slightly different approaches.

Stevens, examining the traditionally moderate area of the East Midlands, suggests that a small number of Communists were to be found in the trades councils at Derby, Nottingham, Leicester and the surrounding areas. They were small rank-and-file groups who appear to have exerted some influence upon their respective trades councils from time to time. It does not appear to have been the case that the Communists could advance only if their membership was kept secret. In fact, their Communist membership was usually well known and the trades councils normally paid lip-service to the 'Black Circular' (there were in fact two, one for the trades council, number 16, and one for the trade unions, number 17) of 1934.[83] In the case of the Nottingham Trades Council there were between six and nine Communist delegates in a body of just over a hundred, with between one and three acting in an official position throughout the period from 1933 to 1938. Their position improved slightly in the early 1940s.[84] The Trades Council chose to ignore 'Black Circular' 16, one of about eighty to do so, when it was circulated by the TUC but were forced to accept it in April 1935, by 29 votes to 8.[85] Despite that decision the Nottingham Trades Council did nothing to force Communist delegates to resign, although Dan Mahoney of the NUR left for other reasons. The pattern of Communist influence varied from trades council to trades council in the East Midlands, although it is clear that the Communists were always a small but active minority. Stevens suggests that these rank-and-file members generally went their own way, were not always responsive to the leadership of the CPGB and survived within trades council activities by virtue of the fact that trades councils were increasingly being urged by the lesser TUC figures, such as Vic Feather, Vincent Tewson, Edgar P. Harris and others, to confine themselves to industrial rather than political activity.[86]

While Stevens is primarily concerned with the rank-and-file developments, and admits to the variable and limited impact of Communists within the trades councils in the East Midlands, Nina Fishman focuses much more upon the attempts by the national leadership, and particularly Harry Pollitt and Johnny Campbell, to improve the relationships between the CPGB and the British trade union movement. Despite some obvious difficulties connected with the CPGB's attempt to curb the activities of some of its rank-

and-file members, it would appear that the new, more positive, approach by the CPGB to trade unionism was perceived as being immensely successful by Fishman, while it seemed rather less so to Stevens.

Fishman's main theme is that 'It is difficult to avoid the conclusion that by 1945 Pollitt and Campbell had achieved their ambition, conceived in 1929–30, to make the Communist Party an important force inside the official trade union movement.'[87] Refining, and confining, the argument further, it is clear that the spadework for this was done in the 1930s, even if the Second World War pushed success along more rapidly. Yet Fishman acknowledges that Harry Pollitt and Johnny Campbell, the main shapers of CPGB policy, were always on the horns of a dilemma between wishing to support rank-and-file movements, in their struggle with unions against employers, and their desire to work with the existing unions in order to extend Communist influence. In the final analysis, however, they 'had no hesitation in placing union loyalty before rank-and-filism'.[88] They often worked to get the rank-and-file movements to discontinue their campaigns. Loyalty to the trade union leadership did not, however, bring a substantial increase in the CPGB's membership at first. Indeed, realising that tens of thousands of militants had not joined the Communist Party, Pollitt announced in his New Year statement of 1937 that he wished these activists 'would only realise that joining the Communist Party does not mean weakening the Labour Party, the trade unions or the co-operative organisation in which they are already working, but will actually strengthen it'.[89] Pollitt felt that this sense of cooperation was important as the Communist Party attempted to build up its alliances and united fronts against both 'the bosses' and against fascism.

Fishman's major argument is elaborated in three subordinate themes. First, she suggests that the pragmatic approach of Pollitt and Campbell worked. They did build up the strength of the Communist activists in the industrial workplace and most trades councils ignored, even if they accepted in principle, the 'Black Circular' of 1934. Secondly, she believes that the industrial pragmatism of the Communist leaders was justified by the ultimate prospect of revolution, even though it was not a popular response with 'rank-and-filism' and 'highly embarrassing and potentially embarrassing for King Street's credibility'.[90] Indeed, this problem was evident in the case of the London busmen's strike and the Aircraft Shop Stewards' National Councils' planned strike, both of which occurred in May 1937. The Harworth colliery strike of May and June 1937, which sought to challenge the Spencer unionism in the Nottingham coalfield, did, however, go some way to redeeming the Communist Party if only through the willingness of Communist activists to risk victimisation and imprisonment. Thirdly, Fishman argues that the Communist activists in the trade unions ignored the stated aim of the King Street headquarters that the Communist Party should be a party of the masses and accepted, instead, that they were the vanguard of change. Indeed, this seems to be a view that most Communist activists had come to accept by the 1920s and the 1930s.

There is no doubt that the CPGB established a more powerful presence within trade unions and trades councils during the 1930s. Nevertheless, the work of both Fishman and Stevens suggests that while the CPGB improved its relations with official trade unionism it was, none the less, limited in its impact. The TUC sought to isolate the Communist influence through its Black Circulars, which did not work effectively, and also by encouraging trades councils to focus upon industrial rather than political activities. In many cases the CPGB found itself in conflict with its rank-and-file activists who, in any case, often saw themselves as part of a vanguard movement and were often not in tune with the views of Pollitt and Campbell. The Comintern and the CPGB found themselves opposed to the Second World War in September 1939, due to the non-aggression pact between Germany and the Soviet Union, which also damaged the Party and saw Pollitt relieved of his role as general secretary of the CPGB. This undoubtedly damaged the CPGB, although the Soviet Union's entry into the war, as we shall see later, led to the 'golden age' of British communism.

The fact remains that, despite all their efforts and their increased influence, the communists remained a small, vanguard group within the trade unions. They, perhaps, carried influence beyond their numbers, but even that influence was extremely limited in relation to the entire British trade union movement. Callaghan is right, the CPGB was unable to capture significant trade union support or to offer a realistic alternative to the moderate socialist policies developed by the Labour Party. Even if they had penetrated trade unionism further they may still have been faced with the problem of breaking down the ties and links which bound the British working classes to the very institutions that communism was attacking.

THE INDEPENDENT LABOUR PARTY

The ILP, the second major socialist party (behind the Labour Party) in British politics for most of the interwar years, also found that its influence was limited. Its problem was that it had lost most of its trade union support to the Labour Party by the end of the First World War and that during the interwar years it became increasingly isolated, being too reformist for the CPGB and too revolutionary for the Labour Party. This situation was reflected accurately in the title of R.E. Dowse's book on the ILP, *Left in the Centre* (1966), a study of the ILP during the interwar years.

At the end of the First World War the ILP was faced with three major problems. First, it had lost much political support as a result of both its official opposition to the war and the fact that the trade unions had now attached themselves more firmly to the Labour Party. Secondly, the Labour Party had introduced Clause Four into the 1918 Labour Party Constitution and there was now serious discussion about its continued existence as a separate organisation. Thirdly, there was the fact that the war had stimulated the formation of a Marxist or Bolshevik section within the ILP. Conflated, these three developments produced several years of instability within the ILP in the immediate post-war years.

Between 1919 and 1922 there was much division within the ILP between those who felt that it should cease to exist and those who wanted it to continue. William Leach, of the Bradford ILP, and Norman Angell, the famous international pacifist who addressed several meetings in the Bradford and Leeds areas, were inclined to submerge the ILP into the Labour Party. Yet the majority wished to remain independent. Indeed, the Yorkshire ILP Federation held a conference at Leeds where 'It proposed to open a discussion on the subject of Party policy, including such topics as "Direct Action" and the Relationship of the ILP to the Labour Party. Every branch of the Federation is being urged to send delegates.'[91] The meeting strongly favoured the continuation of the ILP as a separate political organisation and a further meeting of the Yorkshire branches, in February 1920, projected a mood of determination to continue and vigorously debated the issues of self-government for Ireland, old age pensions, the Third International and the decision of some members to leave parliamentary politics.[92] Similar sentiments and concerns were expressed in Glasgow and other areas of ILP strength.

Philip Snowden, having lost his Blackburn seat in the 1918 general election, was one of those who advocated the continued political independence of the ILP at the national level. His letters to Bruce Glasier are rich in ideas and enthusiasm for the task of rebuilding the party. It needed to bring in new blood: 'The NAC needs this contact with fresher minds. Benson has plans for remodelling the NAC. Think this is much needed. We should have a body with Executive powers which can meet more frequently. Unless this is done the Labour Party will submerge us.'[93] On other occasions he suggested the need for more propaganda work.[94] Such enthusiasm belied the fact that the ILP was beginning to move in directions that would drive Snowden out of effective participation in the party by 1921. The balance of the power within the ILP was beginning to move away from its traditional areas of dominance, such as the West Riding and Lancashire, and towards the expanding regions of Scotland, where the war had strengthened support for the Scottish ILP and from where John Wheatley, Jimmy Maxton and Patrick Dollan came to challenge for the leadership of the party. The Scottish ILP members were much more concerned with capturing the votes of the working class than with Snowden's ambition of drawing political support from all classes.

Snowden also became frustrated with the ILP's difficulties in establishing links with international socialists. In 1920 J. Bruce Glasier had sent a letter to Snowden, the contents of which were conveyed to the 1920 Easter conference. Glasier argued that the ILP should not be divided over the issue of joining the Second and Third Internationals: 'I had hoped that long ere now we should have been successful in bringing about a reassembly of the full International in which every nation and section, valid in its Socialist constitution, whether majority or minority, would have due representation. . . .'[95]

At the time, the ILP was divided between those who wished to join the Second International, now composed of reformist socialist parties and the Third International, or Comintern, dominated by Moscow and communist parties. Snowden was fearful that the ILP would be forced to join the Comintern but on the second day of the conference 'every speaker who rose was against the Bolsheviks. . . . It was unfortunate that so many of the delegates had come to the Conference pledged, or I am sure the vote for Moscow would have been much smaller than it was.'[96] In the end, Glasier's influence seems to have prevailed and the ILP left the Second International and joined the Vienna Union, on the 2½ International, which was committed to bringing the revolutionary and reformist socialist societies together. Unfortunately, the Vienna Union was ignored by most socialist parties and collapsed quickly.

The ILP was beginning to find a niche for itself, even though some of its previously leading figures like Snowden and MacDonald began to drift out of it. It introduced a new constitution in 1922, which rejected the 'Bradford Alternative', committing the ILP to a socialist state based upon parliamentary rule in favour of the 'Limehouse amendment' which supported those parts of the 1922 Constitution that accepted the 'organisation of the consumers' as the basis for democracy.[97] The new constitution was to be a guild socialist document. William Leach, in attacking this, stated of G.D.H. Cole that 'He is a very important person. He writes a book about every twenty-five minutes. The NAC, with whom he was in consultation, were impressed. They fell down and worshipped him. They were desperately afraid of being called fogies.' Cole's ideas were attacked as being a 'sort of alliance between the Cockneys and the Clyde', but Major Attlee seems to have preferred this for he felt that 'The Bradford conception of Socialism appeared to be a glorified municipality.'

Nevertheless the ILP, through strengthening both its working-class and middle-class roots and its organisation, expanded its membership almost three-fold to about 50,000 by 1925. It was a political party on the up, it saw itself as the intellectual godparent of the Labour Party watching over its socialist conscience and it had forty-five MPs in 1923. Yet there were two major rival groups within its ranks whose conflicts helped ensure that the ILP was going to decline in the mid and late 1920s when its membership faded away and the number of its MPs fell to thirty-seven in 1929 and five in 1931. On the one hand there were many members of the intellectual middle classes, led by Clifford Allen, and on the other the Clydesiders who dominated the parliamentary representation of the ILP after the return of the 'Clydeside' group in the 1922 general election. The Clydesiders were much more concerned to develop the interests of the working classes and prepared to advocate a speedy transition to socialism.

Clifford Allen, a conscientious objector in the First World War, an Oxford academic, treasurer of the ILP in 1921 and chairman in 1924, built up the finances of the ILP by attracting donations of about £10,000 per annum at a time when the party income from other sources rarely exceeded £4,500. He was described as 'perhaps the most talented spokesman of the younger generation of middle-class intellectuals who had joined the ILP during the war. . . .'[98] Allen's financial acumen enabled the ILP to fight more parliamentary contests, to set up a new paper the *New Leader*, under the editorship of H.N. Brailsford, and to reinvigorate the propaganda activities of the party.[99]

The Clydesiders contrasted sharply with the style and ambitions of Allen. They had established their influence within Glasgow as a result of their support for and organisation of issues connected with housing and rents and other related issues which were close to the heart of the community from which they emerged. In other words, as Joseph Melling and Alan McKinley have revealed, there was a continuity from the wartime experience and not, as Iain McLean would have it, a break between the wartime period and the successes of the 1922 general election, the latter of which were produced by the decisive shift of the local Irish community from Liberalism to Labour.[100] This influence did not immediately translate into political success because of the difficulties of introducing the new franchise arrangements in 1918. As a result the ILP only won the Govan seat in Glasgow but it continued to campaign on housing issues which served to cut across differences of 'gender, ethnicity, religions, skill and loyalty'[101] and helped it to maintain its momentum even after the Shop Stewards' movement became less effective after the abortive national strike it called in 1919.

With the parliamentary victories it gained in the November 1922 general election, when ten of the fifteen Glasgow seats went to the ILP, it is clear that the Clydesiders had become an important force within both the ILP and the PLP. They attacked the policies of governments that had resulted in poverty and unemployment. Their strategy was one of confrontation and disruption, which led to four of them, including James Maxton, being suspended from the House of Commons. As a result they came into conflict with Ramsay MacDonald, the Labour Party and the first Labour Government of 1924.[102] Therefore, the Clydesiders tended to impose strains in the relationship between the ILP and the Labour Party.

Under Allen's leadership, the ILP met the Labour Party in 1925 in an ill-tempered attempt to define roles and avoid conflict, the ILP claiming a 'special duty' to 'develop in detail the Socialist objectives of the movement'.[103] But relations deteriorated further once the ILP produced its 'Socialism in Our Time' policy and the commitment to a living wage. In his 1924 presidential address to the ILP, Clifford Allen had declared that 'a living wage must be enforced as a national policy'.[104] The economic theory behind it was Hobson's underconsumptionism: 'that higher production is in the long run unattainable or can at best be only spasmodic and temporary, unless there goes with it a parallel increase in the purchasing power of the mass consumers'.[105] The primary aim was to increase purchasing power as a way out of depression. Unemployment would only be cured by redistributing wealth and introducing a scheme of family allowances, to be paid out of taxation. Further purchasing power would be injected by imposing statutory wage minimums throughout industry, which would be paid for by printing money. Though this was inflationary it was felt that the added purchasing power of the workers would soon absorb industrial capital and lead to a rise in production. These actions would be supported by a variety of socialist controls, including the nationalisation of the Bank of England and those industries which did not introduce the minimum wage level.

The policy took time to evolve. The NAC of the ILP issued an interim report, through the *New Leader* and its regional papers, in January 1926 stating that 'The Independent Labour Party sets before itself the object of winning Socialism for this generation' and projecting the need for a 'direct attack upon poverty'.[106] 'Socialism in Our Time' was presented to the Easter Conference of the ILP in 1926 and its full *Living Wage* programme was published in September 1926.

The immediate reactions were mixed for while it offered solutions to unemployment, the preamble to the policy statement, pushed forward by the Clydesiders, who had replaced Allen with Maxton as chairman of the party, presented the view that the 'old order is breaking down' and that resolute socialist policy was needed to 'carry us through the period of transition from the old to the new civilisation'.[107] Thus, while most of the document appeared to be supporting capitalism the preamble was emphasising the need for a rapid move towards socialism.

The ILP's new policy was anathema to Philip Snowden and Ramsay MacDonald. The adoption of inflationary policies to stimulate industry was alien to Snowden's Liberal economic approach, which was based on deflationary measures to strengthen the pound, support for the gold standard and the revival of international free trade. Moreover, MacDonald's antipathy to the ILP ensured that its ideas would receive short shrift. He argued that the ILP's proposals would be a 'millstone' around the parliamentary party's neck and noted the contradictory approach to capitalism exhibited in the policy.[108] The 1927 Labour Party Conference debated the 'living wage' and referred it to the executive where MacDonald condemned it to political oblivion.

Many members of the ILP were equally unhappy with it and wanted complete nationalisation and not this halfway house between capitalism and socialism which appeared to be propping up Liberalism. When H.N. Brailsford lectured on 'Socialism in Our Time' at St George's Hall, Bradford, in September 1926 he was heckled by a small group of protesters and dubbed a Liberal.[109]

Relations between the ILP and the Labour Party were further eroded by the Cook–Maxton Manifesto of June 1928 which criticised the Labour Party and appeared to raise the prospect of establishing a new alliance of the Labour Left organised by the politically unattached Cook, the miners' leader, and Jimmy Maxton of the ILP. The thrust of it was an attack upon MacDonald's desire to create a party of all the social classes and the demand that a new socialist party should be a party of the working classes.[110] R.D. Denman, prospective Labour parliamentary candidate for Central Leeds, was particularly forthright in his criticism: 'The manifesto of Cook is regarded by many as an unpleasant bombshell. Personally I am inclined to welcome it. Not that I agree with its substance in the least. The criticism to which it was subjected by the "Daily Herald" was, I thought, entirely sound.'[111] The CPGB was equally dismissive, feeling that all that could occur was the emergence of some type of managed capitalism.

Under the leadership of Wheatley and Maxton it became increasingly likely that the ILP would secede from the Labour Party, at a time when its membership was falling nationally, from 34,000 in 1925 to 21,000 in 1929, and when it was facing financial difficulties. The Scottish-based ILP leaders themselves seemed cocooned from this reality since membership in the Glasgow area had almost doubled in the 1920s to about 5,000.[112]

Three factions emerged to decide the future of the ILP. Maxton and Wheatley, until his early death, led a group which was not willing to accept the Labour whip in parliament and threatened secession. Maxton had in fact come to the opinion that the ILP must leave the Labour Party following the defeat of the General Strike and the reaction of the Labour movement to that defeat.[113] Dr Cullen and Jack Gaster formed the Revolutionary Policy Committee, a Marxist group, which also favoured secession, though largely because it wished to see the ILP join with the Communist Party. The third group, led by Dr Salter and William Leach and supported by E.F. Wise, wanted to see the ILP remain within the Labour Party and questioned the value of the ILP's continuance as a separate political party.

Matters came to a head when the Labour Party's National Executive Committee demanded that all its candidates in the 1931 general election, including those of the ILP who were affiliated to the Labour Party, should sign a document indicating that they would accept the Standing Orders of the Labour Party. Nineteen ILP candidates refused to sign and were not endorsed by the Labour Party. All five of the ILP candidates returned as MPs (Jimmy Maxton, R.C. Wallhead, John McGovern, David Kirkwood and George Buchanan) had declined to accept the Standing Orders.[114]

The position of the ILP came under closer scrutiny at the 1931 Labour Party Conference, in the wake of the collapse of the second Labour government, when there was a strong current of feeling that 'party' discipline was needed. The Labour Party Conference was determined to stand 'no nonsense from the ILP' and to show the 'rebel left that it could make no capital out of the present crisis'.[115] Despite Fenner Brockway's protestations, Arthur Henderson 'thundered against the organised conscience of the ILP' and won a vote, by 2,117,000 to 193,000, against permitting the ILP to ignore the Standing Orders of the Labour Party.

In many areas, and particularly in Scotland (despite the hostility of P.J. Dollan who was an important figure against disaffiliation) and the West Riding of Yorkshire, there was a strong feeling that the ILP should secede from the Labour Party. The Bradford ILP was of that opinion. Fred Jowett favoured secession and found himself in conflict with William Leach, his old employer and close colleague. Leach felt that the ILP might be able to carry out its 100 per cent socialist policy free from the Labour Party but that it would be regarded as a' freak party'.[116] Others agreed with him. In Leeds, John Arnott called for the Labour Party to avoid the defection of the ILP.[117] The *Leeds Citizen* concurred, suggesting that 'If the ILP is dissatisfied with the Labour Party it will not improve it by committing suicide in a passion of indignation.'[118]

Against expectations, the 1932 Easter conference of the ILP decided, by a narrow margin, that it would remain within the Labour Party. Yet the campaign for secession continued and it was decided to hold a Special Meeting of the ILP at Jowett Hall, Bradford, on 30 July 1932. By that time, the Bradford ILP had voted to disaffiliate by 112 votes to 86 on 25 July 1932 and the *Bradford Pioneer* had published an 'Open Letter' imploring the delegates attending the Special Conference not to vote for disaffiliation: 'The ILP was born in Bradford. Have you come to bury it?'[119]

Maxton, Brockway, Jowett and the 'Suicide Squad', despite the entreaties of Leach and the *Bradford Pioneer*, won the day and the ILP disaffiliated from the Labour Party. A rather sad editorial comment in the *Bradford Pioneer* noted that this decision seemed to ensure 'the total sterility of a once great and influential party'.[120] The Leeds Labour Party agreed: 'a small section of the ILP will now reorganise itself on the basis of the "Marxian philosophy of the Class Struggle" to fight the Labour and Trade Union Movement with semi-Communist thunder.'[121]

These views were prophetic for there now appeared the hideous chimera of the ILP going into rapid decline. There was an attempt to organise an 'Anti-Disaffiliationist' group within the ILP but it was to no avail. Most ILP members joined the Labour Party although some joined the newly-formed Socialist League. The national membership of the ILP fell from 16,773 in 1931 to 4,000 in 1935. The Bradford ILP lost more than half of its 750 members within a month of secession.[122] Even in Scotland there were major losses as the Glasgow ILP disintegrated. Patrick Dollan, Tom Johnstone and David Kirkwood remained loyal to the Labour Party and Jimmy Maxton, of the main leaders, stood alone in his defence of disaffiliation.[123] Of forty-four city councillors in Glasgow, forty were ILP and only seven disaffiliated. Also, with a month of the Bradford conference, P.J. Dollan had formed the Scottish Socialist Society, which operated within the Labour Party, and he claimed that it was supported by 107 branches of the ILP and about 50 per cent of the membership. From then onwards, the ILP was concentrated in the East End of Glasgow under Jimmy Maxton and the Labour Party took control of Glasgow's Labour politics.

The Derby ILP was the exception to this trend, increasing its membership from 225 in 1931 to 270 in 1933, at which time it also had 30 members in the ILP Guild of Youth. Only ten of its members left the ILP to remain in the Labour Party after the disaffiliation conference.[124] Nevertheless, the fact is that the commitment to the development of socialist principles had led the ILP to follow a course of action which could only lead it into political obscurity.

The apportionment of blame for the decline of the ILP is, of course, a contentious issue. Keith Middlemass in *The Clydesiders* felt it to be an act of suicide during a temporary fit of insanity.[125] David Marquand has blamed James Maxton's lack of application and political ability,[126] while Bill Knox has suggested that the decline of the ILP was occurring anyway and that Maxton merely speeded up the process.[127] All three explanations are easily reconcilable since there is no doubt that the ILP could not be as powerful a political force in the 1920s and '30s as it had been before the First World War, for the Labour Party had become the mass socialist party of British politics. Nevertheless, there was a niche for it as a political force to contribute to the socialist debate which Maxton was to deny by his hasty action.

Throughout the rest of 1930s the ILP was a declining organisation whose only distinctive development was to drop its official commitment to pacifism to support the Republican side in the Spanish Civil War, from which it drew the support of George Orwell, whose experience during the Spanish Civil War made him a socialist of a humanitarian kind committed to opposing injustice. This was an event which provided the basis of some ILP and CPGB revival, even though the Labour Party remained aloof from any association with either organisation on the issue of the threat of European fascism and the Spanish Civil War.

THE CHALLENGE OF FASCISM IN THE 1930s

Throughout the 1930s the Labour Party slowly developed its more specific commitments to nationalisation and remained determined to keep free of any links with Marxist organisations. Indeed, in 1933 the Labour Party published a pamphlet entitled *The Communist Solar System*, which named the organisations that constituency parties were warned to keep clear of. Its list included the NUWM dominated by the CPGB and led by Walter Hannington, who was a leading member of the CPGB. This hostility to communism ran counter to the new mood of the CPGB.

As already indicated, it was the CPGB that attempted to unite all socialists to fight fascism. It suggested the need for a United Front on specific issues, and particularly fascism, in March 1933. This provoked a response from some trades councils, constituency labour parties and other organisations, but most obviously the ILP in 1933 and 1934, where there was a Communist presence except in Scotland.[128] After the Seventh Congress of the Comintern in 1935 the CPGB pressed for the new Moscow line of working with all anti-fascist parties in the People's, or Popular, Front policy against fascism.

The Labour Party was reluctant to support extra-parliamentary action in the form of street marches and conflict between the fascists and communists which were to occur. Indeed, the National Joint Council produced a manifesto entitled *Democracy versus Dictatorship* in 1933 which maintained that both fascism and communism were equally bad. As a result the Labour Party lengthened its list of proscribed organisations, adding to it the Relief Committee for Victims of German Fascism and the League Against Imperialism.

The CPGB made a determined attempt to develop an effective counter to fascism in Britain and Europe. As Michael Newman has noted, it maintained the viewpoint that Mosley and the British Union of Fascists (BUF) had to be fought and that violence was a legitimate tactic since fascism presented a serious threat to the British political system.[129] Consequently, the CPGB organised counter-demonstrations against the BUF's meeting at Olympia in June 1934 and on various other occasions such as the 'Battle of Cable Street' in the East End of London in October 1936. This contrasted with Labour's view that British democracy was strong, and that British Fascism offered no threat, was an irrelevance and should be ignored.

Communist influence grew with the outbreak of the Spanish Civil War in July 1936. Subsequently, the Socialist League (based largely upon ex-ILP members), the Fabian Society, the ILP, the Left Book Club and *Tribune*, established by Sir Stafford Cripps in 1937, were all determined that there should be a broad front of opposition levelled against fascism in Britain and Europe and attached themselves to the strategy of the CPGB through the 'Unity Manifesto' of January 1937. According to Michael Foot, the campaign was 'the most ambitious bid made by the British Left, throughout the whole period of the thirties to "break the stultifying rigidity of Party alignment"'.[130]

The Unity Campaign is supposed to have attracted an estimated 20 per cent of the Labour Party's 90,000 London members.[131] *Tribune's* first issue was dedicated to 'The Unity Campaign'. Previously the CPGB's application to affiliate to the Labour Party had been widely supported and 56 of the 62 constituency Labour parties in London had worked with the CPGB in the London County Council elections in 1936.[132] However, the campaign was blighted by the fact that the Socialist League was forced to disband in May 1937 and by the fact that the ILP and the CPGB began to fall out a few months later over the conflicts in Barcelona during the Spanish Civil War.[133]

As John Callaghan has stressed, the CPGB was enjoying a revival at this time. Its membership rose threefold to 17,539 between 1935 and 1939. Weekend sales of the *Daily Worker* often reached 200,000 and CPGB pamphlet sales topped one million. Communist influence was evident in the Left Book Club which quickly reached 57,000 members and an estimated average readership of a quarter of a million for each of its titles.[134] Callaghan notes that the Left Book Club was dominated by Marxist and

Popular Front thinking at this time, would never touch a book by Trotsky and rejected Orwell's *Homage to Catalonia*, since it was highly critical of the role of the Communists in Spain (he had returned from Spain, joined the ILP and criticised the Communists even though he feared that fascism would be triumphant because the Left would not unite).[135] One-third of its publications were written by Communists and the others were commissioned by two Popular Front advocates in V. Gollancz and Harold Laski. On May 1938 the Club created about a thousand local discussion groups and was able to distribute its literature through these, and produced its monthly *Left News*. It defended the Moscow show trials and condemned Bukharin, Trotsky, Zinoviev and the other defendants, suggesting that they were guilty of the charges laid against them.

There is no doubting that there was a revival in Marxist fortunes in Britain, and perhaps even a temporary lull in the decline of the ILP, but what is equally clear is that most of the British socialist movement was taking little notice. The Labour Party leadership was impervious to the appeals of the CPGB and ruthless in dealing with those who drifted towards Communist policies.

CONCLUSION

Despite all the developments in socialism during the interwar years, little advance had occurred in either a theoretical or practical sense. Admittedly, the Labour Party was more committed to planning by the late 1930s than it had been in 1918 but it remained wedded to gradual change through parliamentary action and never obtained a parliamentary majority for its policies. The Communist Party had not been able to make much of an impact in the 1920s, was unable to develop its policies and owed its limited successes in the late 1930s to the threat of European fascism and its attempt to work with official trade unionism by playing down its rank-and-file activities. The Labour Left, including Cripps, Laski and Cole, had aimed to develop socialism into more democratic, and less bureaucratic, forms but they failed in the face of the dominating influence of the trade union movement and the socialist moderates within the Labour Party. In the end, socialism in Britain during the interwar years went little further than the pragmatic policies that Ernest Bevin, the British trade union movement and the moderate Labour politicians would allow. The Labour Party and the trade unions operated in separate spheres but the rules of alliance and unity were already firmly in place to ensure that the dominant forces within the British Labour movement remained wedded to moderate and constitutional change.

BRITISH SOCIALISM: WAR, CHANGE AND CHALLENGE, 1940–51

The Second World War was a vital moment for British socialism. At one extreme, after the initial setback of the Nazi–Soviet Non-Aggression Pact of 1939, it pushed the Communist Party of Great Britain forward into the great patriotic fight against Nazi Germany, so much so that D.N. Pritt, a Labour MP and fellow-traveller, and Harry Pollitt were overwhelmed with demands to address meetings about the Soviet Union. At the other extreme, war restored the social democratic Labour Party to office as part of Churchill's coalition government from May 1940. There was clearly an overlap of interests between all shades of socialist opinion to such an extent that there was a concerted campaign in 1946 to get the Labour Party to allow the CPGB to reaffiliate. Yet Morgan Phillips, the secretary of the Labour Party between 1945 and 1964, set up a stringent managerial regime to thwart attempts to readmit the CPGB and to ensure that the Labour Left was controlled, isolated or expelled if it challenged the Labour Party and Labour government in too open a manner. This led Morgan Phillips to gather together his 'Lost Sheep' file on those who were to be expelled and to develop a monitoring system on those Labour MPs who were challenging the Labour leadership in too open a manner.[1] Despite wartime conditions, socialist unity was going to be just as elusive in the 1940s as it had been before the First World War. In fact, by 1945, as had been obvious for almost half a century, it was clear that there was no viable socialist alternative to the Labour Party. Thus, for any socialist group to have influence it had to work with the Labour Party, something that proved impossible for the CPGB and difficult for the Labour Left. The Labour Party's cautious programme of socialism was certainly at odds with that of other socialist groups and behind what some constituency parties were demanding.

Apart from the marked hostility that existed between the Labour Party and the CPGB, fuelled partly by the United and Popular Front campaigns against fascism in the 1930s, it is clear that it was foreign policy, and its consequence for domestic social policies and planning, that divided them as well as the various shades of opinion within the Labour Left, whether of the Keep Left, Tribunite or Bevanite persuasions. The fundamental problem was what relationships Britain should establish with the USSR and the USA. As Attlee's Labour government followed Ernest Bevin's policy of identifying with the United States, for financial and strategic reasons as reflected in the various American loan schemes and the Korean War, so the CPGB and the Labour Party moved further apart. The CPGB was strongly opposed to the signing of the Atlantic Treaty in 1949 and the effective creation of NATO. Some Labour MPs, such as Konni Zilliacus, held a genuine international perspective towards peace and were also hostile to the Atlantic Pact, while Ian Mikardo and the Keep Left Group favoured the development of a 'Third Force', based on Europe, to act as an independent buffer and to bring two great economic and ideological rivals together. On the other hand, from 1949 Michael Foot and *Tribune* moved towards supporting NATO and a firmer relationship with the United States because of the blatant Russian aggression in Eastern Europe, while others were far more concerned about the further development of nationalisation and economic planning. Foreign policy was going to be divisive to socialist politics in Britain.

Foreign policy was also inextricably interlinked with the domestic policy of the Attlee Labour government. The Second World War had seen Britain lose about a quarter of her wealth, which meant that nationalisation and the whole social welfare programme depended partly upon the availability of American money. This financial dependency bound Britain to the United States in both economic and foreign policy. While this link was accepted by some sections of the Labour Left it concerned others who felt that Britain would lose her independence and spend too much on maintaining a high level of defence. As a consequence, it was felt that this might lead Britain and the USA into a third world war against the Soviet Union. The Keep Left Group felt that this could only be avoided by the promotion of peace through the auspices of the 'Third Force', and the subsequent reduction in defence expenditure, the money from which could be used to raise the standard of living in the Third World and the rest of the world economy.

In the end, it was the Labour Party's brand of social democracy, tied to the USA, that prevailed as Communist Party intent and Labour Party discord were managed and controlled. Nevertheless, there were other socialist viewpoints in the late 1940s. Admittedly, the CPGB was marginalised in the late 1940s but the Labour Left re-formed and reorganised to some effect. In 1945 the 'hard' Left, small as it was, carried more influence than the 'soft' Left and the emerging Keep Left Group. By 1951 the Labour Left had unified more effectively than ever, as the Keep Left and 'soft' Left began to criticise the USSR just as much as they criticised the USA. In addition, the 'hard' Left, who had formed into the Labour Independent Group in 1949, united with the rest of the Left over the resignation of Nye Bevan, Harold Wilson and John Freeman in April 1951. The Labour Left's influence may have been limited in the late 1940s, carrying little weight among the vital trade union section of the Labour Party, and at Party conferences, but its constituency power was developing and helped it thrust forward the influence of the fifty to sixty Bevanites in the early 1950s. It is true that the Labour Left's bark was worse than its bite but it had developed remarkably between 1945 and 1951 in an attempt to offer an alternative to the Labour government's brand of social democracy.

It was the Labour Left that challenged the Labour Party leadership during the 1950s in the form of Bevanism. Yet there is little to suggest that it had developed viable policies. By 1951 the 'Third Force' idea was simply untenable and the extension of socialist ideas into the more thorough nationalisation of industry was beginning to look unrealistic. Perhaps, in the end, the main contribution of the Labour Left was to question the notion that Britain could, any longer, act the role of a big power. To assume a major defensive role, as Britain had done, was clearly draining the economy.

The main argument presented here is the point that the Labour Party offered the only realistic and viable form of socialism in Britain between 1945 and 1951, that the CPGB was effete and the Labour Left limited and divided. In fact the Labour government carried out many of the policies developed in the 1930s but it was very much a programme-based approach, restricted by Britain's economic difficulties and working through the existing structure of political power. There was to be no fundamental change in seeking to implement socialism. Also, while some historians have made much of the revolt of the Labour Left, the fact is that it carried little real influence within Labour ranks until the general election of 1950 and even then its influence in the party constituency organisation may exaggerate its overall power within the party. However, its legacy was that it gave shape to the troublesome Bevanite revolt of the early 1950s.

THE COMMUNIST PARTY, 1940–51

The non-aggression pact signed between the Soviet Union and Germany on 21 August 1939, which committed the Soviets to 'benevolent neutrality', was a shock to communists and socialists alike whose attitudes in the mid and late 1930s had been based upon outright opposition to the rising threat of fascism in Europe.[2] This decision came like a thunderclap to Harry Pollitt and many members of the CPGB. There had been no warning signals by Moscow and Pollitt felt uneasy about this change of events, so much so that on 2–3 October he was one of only two members of the Central Committee of the CPGB to reject the new anti-war stance. In the face of the support given by R. Palme Dutt, Pollitt was replaced as secretary of the CPGB and Pollitt's pamphlet *How to Win the War* was criticised strongly.[3] As Kevin Morgan has indicated, this produced much rancour within the CPGB, and between Pollitt and Dutt, which meant that Pollitt did not re-emerge to control the CPGB again until 1941 when the Soviet Union joined the Allies in the war effort.[4]

This change of direction has provoked a modest debate among historians of Communist Party history. Noreen Branson has suggested that there was strong reaction against the war by the Communist Party membership, and even Kevin Morgan accepts that the pacifist strand was influential within the party.[5] However, Nina Fishman disagrees and sees these views as part of the mythology which has attributed treachery to the CPGB at the moment of Britain's finest hour.[6] Fishman's argument is that many sections of the CPGB supported the war against Germany and fascism and that a substantial proportion of the members, and even the leaders, attempted to play down the significance of the anti-war approach. She offers a wide variety of evidence for her views.

In particular, she stresses that Harry Pollitt, Jimmy Campbell, and other CPGB leaders, continued to 'dilute' the new Comintern-inspired line and focused upon industrial matters in order to minimise the unpopularity of the CPGB in 1939 and 1940.[7] It appears further that the relationship between the trade unions and the CPGB remained as it was before 1939: 'British trade union leaders did not exploit the opportunity presented by the Party's anti-war position to instigate a general inquisition against Party activists.'[8] Only the Amalgamated Engineering Union and the Miners' Federation of Great Britain (MFGB) appear to have tested the relationship between Communist anti-war sentiments and the official trade union movement with its more pro-war sentiments, but even here they agreed to differ. Even Arthur Horner, a member of the CPGB and president of the MFGB was vague about his anti-war opinions and the CPGB attempted to play down the rank-and-file activities within both unions as it had done in the immediate pre-war years.[9] The development of a National People's Convention movement from January 1941, aimed at developing the people's democratic and trade union rights and at uniting both anti-war and pro-war Communist and Labour Party supporters, was even allowed to fade away for fear of challenging the trade union movement, although the German invasion of Russia in 1941 brought it to a speedy end.[10] In other words, Fishman feels that there were significant differences about the new anti-war line within the CPGB and that the CPGB, after playing appropriate lip-service to Moscow, attempted to ignore the issue of war.

Notwithstanding Fishman's challenge to the 'mythology' that the CPGB was anti-war from October 1939 and treacherous in its activities, it seems that there remains much evidence that the CPGB membership generally followed the Comintern line. Equivocation there may have been but when asked to fall into line Pollitt, Campbell, Horner, and many others who doubted the wisdom of the anti-war line, did so in their need to defend the Soviet Union. Indeed, there was much posturing by the CPGB, making the best of a difficult situation. Both the *Daily Worker* and *Tribune*, edited at that time by E.Y. Hartshorn who was something of a fellow-traveller, attempted to cast the events in terms of the failure of capitalism, to which might be added the inability of democratic socialist forces to transform British society and undermine imperialism. It was maintained that the Second World War was a capitalist war and that the Labour Party had sided with a capitalist government in prosecuting the conflict. The *Daily Worker* and *Tribune* had more difficulty defending both the Russian invasion of Poland on 17 September 1939 and the Soviet attack upon Finland in November 1939. A smokescreen of defensive reactionism could not sweep away the impression that the CPGB was defending a Soviet foreign policy which had more to do with the national interests of the Soviet Union than internationalism. Indeed, Dutt admitted that the defence of Russia was more important than anything else.[11]

Dutt informed his audiences that it was the British government that had declared war and that the extension of conflict into Scandinavia was a crime.[12] But it soon became clear that many British socialists could no longer stomach these twists and turns by a CPGB wishing to justify Soviet actions. Victor Gollancz felt that the war was more about democracy against fascism than imperial powers in conflict. John Strachey, after some initial hesitation, came to criticise the Communist moves to undermine the French resistance to fascism.[13] Nevertheless, the CPGB continued to emphasise the imperialist character of the war and called for a People's

Convention for 12 January 1941, which brought together 2,234 delegates claiming to represent more than a million people.[14]

The Labour Party was less generous towards the CPGB and the Soviet Union. It criticised the Soviet system and Hugh Dalton labelled the Soviets as 'double-crossers by nature'.[15] But all this was forgotten when details of Operation Barbarossa and the Nazi invasion of Russia reached Britain on 22 June 1941. Immediately the CPGB changed line as the Russians entered the war on the side of the Allied Powers and from now on the CPGB was as patriotic as any organisation in the war effort, although it also still focused upon the need to deal with shopfloor grievances that could hinder the British war effort and throw it into conflict with the British government, the Labour Party and the TUC. Its membership rose quickly, reaching more than 59,000 in June 1942 before falling to 45,000 in 1944, and Pollitt was recognised as one of the great campaigners against German Nazism.[16] Kevin Morgan has recorded this revival in the fortunes of the CPGB and Pollitt in immense detail. He has noted that in July 1942 a Mass Observation recorded that Pollitt gained 80 per cent applause on finishing a speech compared to about a third for D.N. Pritt, Haden-Guest and Wilf Roberts, the Labour MPs, at a Second Front demonstration in Trafalgar Square, although it has to be admitted that the audiences were normally very left wing.[17] Michael Foot, Aneurin Bevan and a number of other Labour MPs joined these meetings demanding that the British government should provide resources and support for Russia in her battle against Germany by opening the Second Front. Indeed, Bevan, having just taken over as acting editor of *Tribune* from Raymond Postgate, threw his full weight behind the new-found commitment of the Soviets and the CPGB to the war effort.[18]

Denis Noel Pritt, KC and Labour MP for Hammersmith North between 1935 and 1960, was particularly active in encouraging the new attitude of cooperation between the Labour Party, the CPGB and Soviet Russia. His diary notes, typed on small scraps of paper, reflect his constant concern to nurture the belief that the future of socialism in Britain had to be through some form of alliance and friendship with the CPGB and the Soviet Union. His main activities consisted of lecturing on behalf of the CPGB, explaining the Soviet system and temporarily promoting Stafford Cripps as a possible new Labour leader or prime minister. He attended a recruiting meeting for the Communist Party at the Palace Theatre, Reading, in March 1942, along with William Rust, one of the 'Young Turks' of the CPGB. The meeting led to a 'collection of £114 and 60 new members. I spoke to the bourgeoisie on the lines that they ought to understand the Communist Party and what it stands for, and judge it impartially. They now know they had been fooled over the Soviet Union. . . .'[19] He was also in constant touch with 'Johnny' (Ivan Maisky, a member of the Russian Embassy staff), who reflected that the Soviets preferred Churchill as British Prime Minister since 'Neither Eden nor Cripps sufficiently big . . . and everybody else just unthinkable.'[20] This followed upon the military failures and concerns of Britain earlier in the year when it appeared, for a time, that Duff Cooper and Cripps were possible alternatives to Churchill. At that time Cripps was seen as the man who helped bring Russia into the war. Pritt had hopes of forming part of a wartime government: 'An important consideration in connection with joining the Labour Party is the question whether I would be more or less likely to be invited into a government if I were an independent rather than a member of the Labour Party. This again could only be judged later on.'[21]

The Pritt diary entries convey the sense of excitement and expectation in the months immediately following the USSR joining the Allied war effort, even if there is an air of unreality about them. They also convey the sense of concern of the Soviet Union's representatives about what would happen to Germany once the war was won. At the end of 1941, Pritt had a meeting with 'Johnny' whose main concern was that 'the young and old in Germany are so completely pervaded by Nazism, that it is difficult to believe that a country containing many such people can properly behave itself.' 'Johnny's' view was that only a strong (Marxist) government, and not a pseudo-socialist government, could ensure that the Germans behaved properly in the future and that the Soviet Union would not be able to risk any possibility of there not being such a government.[22]

This was a high point of the CPGB. With the Soviet Union's entry into the war the CPGB membership rose quickly, especially as the party began to extend its influence within both British industry and the trade union movement. The party encouraged war production to help to defend the Soviet 'Fatherland', attempted to keep the rank and file from striking and encouraged the development of joint production committees (JPCs) between management and the trade unions in many engineering factories. Indeed, the CPGB seems to have built up some industrial strongholds. Napier's aero-engine works at Acton Vale, West London, became a centre of party activists under the leadership of Fred Arter, Walter Swanson and Fred Elms.[23] Les Ambrose built up CPGB strength within the shop stewards committee at Austin Aero, and numerous other Communist shop stewards and activists built up their strength in other plants and factories.[24] Also JPCs emerged in many engineering firms. However, not all was success. For instance, it was difficult to establish JPCs in the Glasgow engineering plants, particularly in Beardmore's where a works ballot rejected the formation of a JPC, partly on the basis that it might constrict industrial action.[25] War weariness also seems to have occurred in the last two years of conflict and the CPGB lost some of its membership when it became clear that they were doing little other than stimulating war production.

Other parties and groupings of the broad left also did well at the time. In particular, the Common Wealth party, an obscure but inspirational organisation, offered a number of socialist, radical Liberal and Marxist policies which appealed to the middle classes. Formed by Richard Acland, a former Liberal who became a Labour MP in 1947 and was active in Keep Left, its secretary and chairman was R.W.G. Mackay, who became Labour MP for Hull in 1945, and who also joined Keep Left. Tom Driberg was another member of this group. Its main desire was to create mass socialism. Nye Bevan, acting as an independent guardian of the socialist conscience, was also able to push forward his advanced views in *Tribune*.

Yet it is clear that it was the Labour Party that began to benefit from the popular radicalism of the time. The ideas of William Beveridge and John Maynard Keynes began to gather support and although the Labour Party began to see them as the first stages of socialism, the Labour Left and the Communists were not so certain. In April 1942, Harold Laski complained that 'in return for a handful of social reforms, some of them fundamental in character, we are inviting the vested interests of this country to strengthen their hold upon state-power . . . I suggest that on all fundamental matters we do the giving and the Tories do the taking.'[26]

The CPGB was determined to try to change this situation. When the Comintern was dissolved in 1943 there was a campaign for CPGB affiliation to the Labour Party which was lost by 1,951,000 to 712,000 votes at the Labour Party conference in 1943.[27] At this stage, Labour leaders were inclined to draw a distinction between British Communists and the far more responsible Communist Party of the Soviet Union. By the same token the Labour Left, including Fenner Brockway, Konni Zilliacus, Emrys Hughes (editor of the *Glasgow Forward*) and G.D.H. Cole, were far more critical of the capitalistic United States, an 'expanding Imperial power', than of Soviet Russia. They even acknowledged that the USSR may need political reassurance. As Nye Bevan wrote:

> It is quite natural and inevitable that Russia should influence preponderantly the life of nations immediately on her borders and that she should seek to prevent them from combinations that may be aimed at her. That is the price we have to pay for the bitter recent past.[28]

Such impressions about communism and capitalism were nurtured by the intervention of British forces in Greece in December 1944, in order to prevent a communist coup. It was felt that the pressure exerted by the United States on an old imperial power could be seen behind these actions.

None the less, the CPGB still wished to affiliate to the Labour Party, especially after its landslide general election victory of 1945, in which only two Communist MPs, Willie Gallacher (West Fife) and Phil Piratin (Mile End), were returned. The Labour Party archives reveal the immense pressure that it was placed under in 1945 and 1946 to force it to re-affiliate the Communist Party. Howdenshire Labour Party called for 'working-class unity in the country by allowing the Common Wealth, the ILP and the Communist Parties to affiliate with the National Labour Party'.[29] Many other district Labour parties and trade unions followed suit.

Yet there was never a realistic prospect that the Labour Party would allow the CPGB to affiliate. Morgan Phillips was determined to oppose any such moves and replied in discouraging terms to the advocates of the affiliation of the CPGB and prepared detailed reports on how to counter the Communist campaign. The arguments presented were almost a mirror image of those put forward in the interwar years and focused upon the differences between the Labour Party and the CPGB. Phillips argued that while the Labour Party stood for democratic socialism and wished to use the full powers of parliament and local government, 'The aims of the Communist Party are different. They aim at what they call the "Dictatorship of the Proletariat". This in practice does not mean the Dictatorship of the Proletariat at all. It means a Dictatorship over the Proletariat, exercised by the Communist Party bureaucracy.' The stark contrast was posed between democracy and tyranny and it was further maintained that the British people had voted against communist tyranny at the general election, and in any case it was operated by Moscow and had no independence of action. Phillips maintained that 'If the Communist affiliation was foolishly granted the position would be intolerable. There would be within our Party another highly organised Party working for its own supremacy. Every local Labour Party would become a battle ground for democratic socialism versus communism.'[30]

Rejected by the Labour Party Executive and conference, the CPGB was, none the less, concerned to work with the forces of socialism within Britain. In 1947 Harry Pollitt published *Looking Ahead*, which suggested that the October Revolution was not necessarily the model for social revolution and that the path to social transition may vary from country to country. This became the basis of *The British Road to Socialism* in 1951. The CPGB had clearly come to accept that it was necessary to form some type of Popular or United Front among socialists, even if socialist unity was impossible. But this objective carried no political influence within the Labour Party which objected to any arrangement with the CPGB. The Soviet rejection of Marshall Aid on 2 August 1947 and the creation of communist puppet states in Eastern Europe also drove many of the Labour Left to align more clearly with the Labour Party and even, in some cases, the pro-Western-Union foreign policy of Ernest Bevin. In the meantime the CPGB was becoming more critical of the Labour government's support for measures to intervene in Greece and to topple left-wing governments in Italy and France.

The CPGB lost even more support as a result of events in Czechoslovakia. The Labour Left felt morally obliged to defend Czechoslovakian democracy as a result of the events of 1938–9 and Harold Laski noted that its post-war democratic socialism was successful: 'If ever I saw a really democratic commonwealth I saw it in Czechoslovakia. . . . The mixed Government of Socialists, Social Democrats and National Democrats works together surprisingly well.'[31] Unfortunately, this broke down in February 1948 as non-communists resigned from the cabinet and the Communists continued to rule, suppressing many civil liberties with the support and approval of the Soviet Union. *Tribune* and many within the Labour Left were appalled at the Communist assumption of power and edged towards the foreign policy of a 'Western Union' being advocated by Ernest Bevin from 22 January 1948.

As for the CPGB, it became increasingly isolated, despite its broader approach to socialism to Britain. This became even more marked when the Comintern, which was wound up in 1943, was replaced in September 1947 by the much less representative Communist Information Bureau or Cominform, which had no British representatives.[32] By the end of the year the CPGB, following the Moscow line, was entrenched in its belief in the gathering conflict between East and West. From now onwards the CPGB was anti-American and anti-colonial, defended the East against the imperialism of the West and was ecstatic at the Communist victory in China in 1949. Its pro-Soviet attitudes began to isolate it from working-class institutions, apart from a few trade unions, and it fragmented as the quashing of the Hungarian Rebellion in 1956, and other similar if less dramatic events, began to undermine what little support it held. One of its key figures, R.P. Dutt, became to the British press the prototype of the Communist robots inhabiting Cold War propaganda. He was discovered to be 'the real power in the Communist Party' when the passionate Pollitt 'goes off the Party line', one article began, 'it is the quietly spoken Dutt who gently puts the Communist leader back in place again'.[33]

Socialism in Britain was thus, in any viable sense, left in the hands of both the Labour Party and the Labour Left – Labour's Conscience, as Jonathan Schneer has observed.[34]

THE LABOUR PARTY, 1940–51

It was the Labour Party, whose political position improved substantially in the 1940s, that was to be the major representative of socialism in Britain – even if its brand of, and commitment to, socialism was often subject to intense scrutiny. Indeed, the circumstances of the Second World War had revived Labour's political fortunes. Its creation of the social security system of the modern welfare state, the formation of the National Health Service and the nationalisation of several major industries and services in the mid and late 1940s are in fact the only tangible impact that socialism has exerted in Britain and did not amount to a fundamental change in British society.

The Labour Party firmly supported Neville Chamberlain's declaration of war on Germany on 3 September 1939, and agreed to an 'Electoral Truce', though it initially refused to join the Chamberlain government in the prosecution of the war. It did not enter the coalition government until May 1940, when Winston Churchill replaced Neville Chamberlain as prime minister. Labour did well out of the allocation of offices in the new government and benefited politically at the end of the war. But was Labour's revival and success in the 1945 general election primarily a result of the wartime experience?

There was certainly much evidence that Labour was reviving in the 1930s, after the political fiasco of 1931. In addition, it is possible, as Richard Titmuss suggested in *Problems of Social Policy* (1951), that there was a new popular radicalism emerging in Britain.[35] The bombing and evacuation had exposed social problems which had hitherto remained hidden from public view and generated a sense of commitment by central government to the strategic necessity of having a contented and healthy civilian population. In contrast, recent writers on the Second World War have been far more cautious and ambivalent. Paul Addison argues that the war helped to establish a new political consensus and that the leftward shift in popular attitudes began as early as 1940 with the appointment of sixteen Labour ministers to Churchill's wartime government, the emphasis having been placed upon establishing a fairer society and the organisation of wartime evacuations. However, the crucial factor in the change appears to have been the military catastrophe at Dunkirk, which seems to have forced the wartime government, faced with the need to restore calm and instil unity into the war effort, to offer welfare provisions for all. In the wake of Dunkirk, William Beveridge and many of the Whitehall mandarins began to organise the war effort and, according to Addison, 'The home front organised for war was becoming a model, and an inspiration, for the reorganisation of the peace.'[36] Nevertheless, Addison believes that the atmosphere of optimistic solidarity was by no means as universal as Titmuss had supposed. That Labour benefited from those social changes for the new consensus represented a 'dilution of Conservative rather than Labour politics'.[37] Indeed, it appears that the mood of the nation was changing rapidly between 1940 and 1942 and that the Labour Party benefited from its barrage of activity and propaganda.

Addison's views have been broadly supported by a wide range of historians, including Angus Calder, Henry Pelling, Arthur Marwick, Ralph Miliband and H.L. Smith.[38] Whatever their individual views on the nature of the impact of war, they are clear that the Labour Party was the great beneficiary of the growth of wartime radicalism. Even Correlli Barnett and Max Beloff, who have criticised the whole episode whereby wartime radicalism imposed upon Britain a commitment to a post-war welfare state, admit the impetus this gave to the political popularity of the Labour Party.[39]

There seems little doubt that Labour was the party that benefited most from the wartime radicalism and the new political consensus that emerged. The only significant difference of opinion seems to be the timing of this changed political mood. Addison suggests that there was a leftward swing in political opinion in 1940 while Henry Pelling suggests that this occurred in 1942. Certainly, by 1942 there was evidence of rising political support for Labour in the Gallup polls and, in December 1942, Mass Observation estimated that about two people out of five had changed their political outlook since the beginning of the war.[40] The new wartime radicalism may not have been a 'formed socialist ideology', but it was a form from which the Labour Party was well equipped to benefit.[41]

The Labour Party was well prepared to deal with the war, in contrast to its experiences in 1914. From the beginning it was looking to the future. It produced *Labour War Aims* in October 1939 and *Labour, the War and Peace* and *Labour's Home Policy* in 1940. In these statements, the Labour Party outlined the way in which a strengthened League of Nations could be used to maintain the peace 'once the rule of law' had brought about peace. But of more immediate importance was Labour's belief that 'for the Labour Party a Socialist Britain is not some far-out Utopia, but an ideal that can be realised within our time.'[42]

The Labour Party was also just beginning to develop its wartime policies. On 23 May 1941 the NEC decided to form a special Committee on Post-war Economic and Social Reconstruction.[43] This spawned thirteen sub-committees including the Central Committee on Reconstruction Problems, chaired by Emmanuel Shinwell, with Harold Laski as its secretary. Controlled by a few prominent individuals, and particularly by Herbert Morrison, this committee and its sub-committees presented their views to the Labour Party conferences and eventually in Labour's *Let Us Face the Future*, the general election manifesto of 1945.

These policies and expectations were given a boost by the fact that Clem Attlee was, effectively, Deputy Prime Minister throughout the period of the Churchill coalition government. It fell to Attlee and Ernest Bevin to provide what became known as 'War Socialism'. Health and housing provision emerged, cheap school meals were made available for all schoolchildren and the war economy was regulated. Ernest Bevin, Minister of Labour, took powers to control the movement of labour through the Essential Works Order (March 1941). Under this legislation, workers could be prevented from leaving jobs. Bevin was given the powers to direct labour, and trade union recognition and collective bargaining were encouraged.

In many respects these were simply piecemeal responses to the wartime situation, a fact which was revealed in the debate over the Beveridge Report of 1942, *Social Insurance and Allied Services*.[44] This was a comprehensive scheme that gave systematic shape to the ideas on social security, which was to be reorganised to provide a national minimum income, although it was to be dependent upon a national health service, family allowances and full employment. Churchill was suspicious about where such demands might lead but Attlee saw the Beveridge Report as an opportunity for socialism.

Attlee emphasised the point when he said that 'Socialism does not admit to an alternative, Social Security to us can only mean Socialism.'[45] To Attlee, and his supporters, it was essential that the Beveridge Report should be quickly accepted as an essential commitment by the government. Yet it was quite clear that Churchill intended to delay its publication, and Attlee even felt that it might be saved until the end of the war to form part of the Conservative programme. Attlee was also hostile to the Churchill memorandum sent round government circles in which it was suggested that the economics of life might be such as to force a choice 'between social insurance and other urgent claims on limited resources'. Attlee sent in a counter-memorandum to the government urging that 'decisions must be taken and implemented in the field of post-war reconstruction *before* the end of the war.'[46] Churchill relented, the government accepted most of the report but gave the impression that it was committed to nothing. A Labour resolution that the government should support the Beveridge Report and implement it was defeated by 335 votes to 119, but 97 Labour MPs had voted against the government, 30 had abstained and only 23 had voted with the government, 22 of these being government ministers.

It is obvious that the Beveridge Report was a sensitive document, especially after the midsummer Gallup polls in 1943 when Labour registered a lead of 11 per cent over the Conservatives.[47] In the end the government was forced to set up a Reconstruction Committee towards the end of 1943, which developed the scheme that became the 1944 Education Act.[48] In 1944 the Reconstruction Committee put forward a scheme, which gained White Paper status, for guaranteeing 'Full Employment' through state action on Keynesian lines once large-scale unemployment occurred. Ernest Bevin moved its adoption by parliament in June 1944 and found himself opposed by Aneurin Bevan who felt that it was simply a device for propping up capitalism and that socialism alone was the cure for unemployment.[49] Hugh Dalton was barely less critical, constantly referring in his diary to the vanity of Beveridge and the 'Beveridge muddle'.[50]

By 1945 the Labour Party was demonstrably the party most likely to introduce the social reforms that were essential if Britain was to avoid the economic and social mistakes of the interwar years. It won the general election in July 1945, called within two months of the end of the European war, by a substantial majority: 393 seats to the Conservatives' 213. The Liberals gained only 12 seats.

There have been three major questions raised about the Attlee Labour governments. First, to what extent was the welfare state it developed a product of the social blueprint laid down during the Second World War? Secondly, and more vital, how far was the Labour leadership committed to introducing socialism? Thirdly, how far could Britain have operated independently of the USA, given the extent of her economic dependence upon American money?

The first of these questions is not central to this book and it is sufficient to suggest that while the Beveridge Report of 1942 may have shaped the pattern of social security one must not forget that *Labour's*

Immediate Programme, written by Hugh Dalton in 1937, did advance schemes for social welfare and the creation of full employment. In essence it was the programme that was presented to the electorate in the Labour Party's *Let Us Face the Future* in 1945. Additionally, one must reflect that the Labour Party was part of the government which commissioned the Beveridge Report of 1942 and that the National Health Service owed little to Beveridge and almost everything to the ideas and socialist commitment of Aneurin Bevan. Beveridge would have organised the patients through a contributory scheme whereas Bevan effectively nationalised the hospitals, GPs, dentists and opticians and ensured that almost all the money came from the state and was non-contributory. Indeed, the NHS was paid almost entirely out of taxation.

Bevan's NHS was developed despite the opposition of some Labour politicians, most notably Herbert Morrison, who stressed that the nationalisation of hospitals was not part of Labour's manifesto commitments or Labour's *National Service for Health* (1943) policy. The fact is that the NHS Bill put forward by Bevan in 1946 went much further than the wartime blueprints had proposed and it is just not good enough for James Hinton to suggest that 'the scheme did not go significantly beyond what had been accepted in principle during the war'.[51]

The introduction of the NHS was by no means smooth, since Bevan was also faced with the strong opposition of the GPs who did not wish to become public servants. But even after the NHS was introduced in July 1948, Bevan had to battle against Herbert Morrison and Hugh Gaitskell who were insistent that the economic expenditure it involved would be controlled. However, Bevan was determined that the NHS was 'not going to be touched' by expenditure cuts.[52] Morrison, Jane Lidderdale and E.M. Nicholson rejected this notion, set a ceiling for health expenditure and raised the financial crisis of 1931 as evidence of the need for financial control.[53] In the end a decision was made by Hugh Gaitskell, Chancellor of the Exchequer, to impose charges on some areas of the health service and Bevan, who had been moved to the Ministry of Labour, resigned on 22 April 1951.

If Labour's welfare policies owed much to the pre-war socialist commitment of the Labour Party, how socialist was the party? It is this second question that forms the basis of an examination of the Attlee governments' socialist record.

The experience of war certainly provided the platform on which *Let Us Face the Future*, the Labour Party programme, was able to build. This stressed the need to avoid the failures of the 1930s and to introduce domestic legislation which would include the nationalisation of industries, full employment and improved social services. Yet, once in power, the Labour government had to deliver the programme. This has raised the question: how genuine were the attempts of Labour leaders to introduce socialism? Some Marxist and left-wing historians have tended to suggest that the Labour government appeared vague and uncommitted to anything more than the nationalisation of industries and services to which there was little public hostility. There was, apparently, no intention by Attlee, Morrison and Labour's other leaders to use public ownership as an effective weapon to control the economy. According to Miliband:

> In regard to nationalisation, there is no ambiguity at all. From the beginning, the nationalisation proposals of the Government were designed to achieve the sole purpose of improving the efficiency of the capitalist economy, not as marking the beginning of its wholesale transformation, and this was an aim to which Tories, whatever they might say in the House of Commons, were easily reconciled.[54]

James Hinton and David Howell make similar points.[55] Yet these views are hardly surprising, coming as they do from historians who perceive the parliamentary system to be an inefficient and ineffective method of achieving socialism. They contrast sharply with those of Kenneth Morgan who has emphasised the achievements of the Attlee governments, even if they evaded rather than resolved the 'beguiling vision of socialism in our time'.[56] Morgan's point is that the Labour government fell short of the ideal but that this was due to the difficult circumstances in which it operated rather from a lack of will. Apparently, Attlee's administration was not faltering and opportunistic but had a clear vision of the socialist society it was aiming to create. However, the reality of government intervention was always likely to be less attractive than the utopian vision of socialism which drove it forward. Even though the nationalisation programme lost its impetus and direction, the Attlee governments had taken a vital step towards displacing the old order of government attitudes.

These rival interpretations differ in many respects. Marxist and quasi-Marxists writers tend to see Labour policies on national insurance, health, housing and food subsidies as leaving a great deal to be desired. They also decry Labour's efforts at nationalisation, emphasising that it was the Labour Left which had to force a reluctant Labour government to nationalise iron and steel in the face of stiff opposition from the employers. They criticised Labour's foreign policy which saw Bevin become a leading architect of NATO and Britain become a military appendage to the United States in its dealings with the USSR. Morgan is far more generous, and suggests that it is to the overall success of the work of the Attlee governments that one must look, rather than their specific problems and failures. Nationalisation had its successes as well as its failures; social welfare was greatly improved and the achievement of Indian independence was a significant development in the emergence of the new Commonwealth.

Miliband and Hinton have also criticised the almost slavish loyalty of the Attlee governments to the USA in its attitude to the USSR, the Korean War and other issues. This contrasts sharply with the interpretation presented by Morgan, who stresses that despite the crippling financial difficulties which Attlee's governments faced, which thrust them on the financial mercy of the USA, they exercised a remarkable degree of independence on such issues as the atomic bomb and Palestine.

The two interpretations appear irreconcilable but both have points going for them. Morgan is right about the level of political independence that the Labour government could exercise. Nevertheless, it is clear that Britain had developed a close relationship with the USA. It has been implied by Milband and Hinton, and specifically argued by John Callaghan, that this was due to Britain's concern to preserve her political and economic position in the world. It has been maintained that Churchill's Fulton Speech of March 1946 was a fair reflection of the Labour government's political ambition which was to persuade the USA to assist Britain and Western Europe, through loans. This came to fruition with the Truman Doctrine of March 1947 and the introduction of the Marshall Aid Plan. Yet Britain needed to go further in order to defend the British Empire or Commonwealth, which was considered to be essential to Britain's future economic prosperity. As Fieldhouse suggested, the Labour government seemed to perceive that 'the Empire and Commonwealth seemed essential to the survival of Britain and to her position as a world power.'[57] In order to do this it was, apparently, necessary for Britain to gain American support by identifying communism as a worldwide threat.[58] However, this British conspiracy approach to the 'Cold War' seems somewhat exaggerated given that there were American fears of communism which needed no nurturing by the Labour government.

On balance, the Labour government did remarkably well to achieve what it did given the immediate post-war difficulties. Indeed, within a day of Labour's victory, Hugh Dalton, the new Chancellor of the Exchequer, called an informal meeting of some of the young but aspiring members of the Labour Party, including Harold Wilson, Hugh

Gaitskell, Richard Crossman, George Brown and John Freeman. Its purpose was to discuss the 'future policy and problems' of the Labour government. One of those present expressed the view that 'too many people had voted Labour in the hope that it meant more pay and less work.'[59] Another spoke of the major problems of food, homes and fuel which would be 'extraordinarily difficult to handle at any rate in the first two years. It was, therefore, necessary that there should be first-class publicity to make it clear that these difficulties were inevitable and inherited by the Labour government.'[60] Such fears were well founded, for the new Labour government faced huge economic difficulties.

During the Second World War British industry had been converted to war production at the cost of exports, facilitated by loans from the United States and the sale of British overseas assets. The result was that Britain's invisible earnings declined and its visible exports were down to about a third of their pre-war level. The Labour government's first priority was thus to secure financial support, which could only come from the United States, in order to buy food and raw materials while Britain was building up its export industries. The sudden end of the United States' 'lend-lease' aid in August 1945 exposed the weakness of the British economy and forced the Labour government to send J.M. Keynes to the USA in order to secure a new loan. Yet the final conditions of the loan were harsh, for Britain was expected to remove exchange controls and to make sterling freely convertible within a year of taking up the loan. In fact when Britain attempted to honour this agreement, in July 1947, the economy was still too weak to withstand such a change of policy, and the government was soon forced to reintroduce exchange controls. The continued fragility of the economy was further revealed by the balance of payments crisis in 1949, which forced devaluation. And matters were not helped by the severe winter of 1946–7, which led to coal shortages, the closure of factories and the temporary increase of unemployment to two million. Given the weakness of the British economy it was, as Alec Cairncross has suggested, vital that Britain obtained the American Loan.[61] Indeed, it appears that Keynes had already anticipated that there would be an 'overriding need to look to the United States for the finance necessary to cover Britain's post-war deficits', even before the war had ended.[62] The later reliance upon the Marshall Aid programme tightened that link with the United States. Inevitably, there were political consequences.

Attlee and Bevin have been criticised frequently for their almost slavish acceptance of the alliance with the United States and against the Soviet

Union. This was most certainly evident in Bevin's contribution to the Washington Treaty of 1949 and the creation of NATO. But given the circumstances at the time it is clear that the majority of the Labour Party and the Labour Left accepted this policy – though often for different reasons.

None the less, the most serious doubts about the Labour government's commitment to socialism arise from its plan for the 'socialisation of industry'. Although it moved quickly to nationalise some services and industries, it showed little compunction to go much further after the initial burst of activity and the public ownership programme slowed down from 1948 onwards. Indeed, the hesitancy of the Labour government in nationalising the iron and steel industry seems to have confirmed the worst fears of Bevan and the Labour Left that the government lacked a firmly-rooted commitment to socialist planning and control. Herbert Morrison's nationalisation list in *Let Us Face the Future*, and his belief that the nationalised industries should be managed by independent corporate central bodies, were in effect the only plans on offer. There was evidently no commitment to link the nationalised industries and services into some overall grand strategy for an assault on the bastions of capitalism, despite the numerous committees and sub-committees which Morrison set up through the office of the Privy Council, which he used to coordinate domestic policy and expenditure during the Attlee years.

The Bank of England, civil aviation, Cable & Wireless and coal were nationalised in 1946; railways, transport and electricity in 1947; gas in 1948 and the early measures for iron and steel were produced in 1948 and 1949. But there was no clear grand strategy and a reluctance to nationalise iron and steel. Indeed, it had only been Ian Mikardo's intervention in the 1944 Labour Party conference that had driven the issue forward, much against Morrison's wishes. A pusillanimous Labour cabinet faced hostile steel manufacturers, a determined Official Opposition and an obdurate House of Lords. Yet in the end, the industry was formally nationalised in 1950.

Apart from the creation of the welfare state, nationalisation was the driving force of Attlee's post-war Labour governments. If they lost their way and had no clear comprehension of how to use what was, to the Labour Party, its symbol of socialism, that did not make the effort less worthwhile. They did at least attempt to take the country in a socialist direction in domestic affairs. However, their efforts were not always appreciated by the Labour Left who were particularly critical of the Labour government's foreign policy, especially about its three-year commitment to spend £4,700 million on defence during the Korean War and the consequences in terms of Britain's domestic situation.

'The Salutary Gadfly' and the 'Lost Sheep':
Keep Left and the Labour Left, 1940–51

The Labour Party's landslide victory in the 1945 general election had paved the way for the introduction of the modern welfare state and a specific and restricted programme of nationalisation. To some writers, such as Kenneth Morgan, this was the apogee of the Labour Party's political existence and the Attlee governments were 'without doubt the most effective of any British Government since the passage of the 1832 Reform Act'.[63] Nevertheless, there was a rather amorphous body of opinion emerging in these years which is associated with the Labour Left. It emerged as a very fragmented body of opinion which was supported by several small political groupings who were often in conflict with one another. The moderate or 'soft' Left tended to accrete to the Keep Left Group, which later became the Bevanites and Tribunites, or associated with *Tribune* or Aneurin Bevan. The 'hard' Labour Left was composed of small and equally divided groups whose unity began to diminish from 1947 onwards. It included MPs such as Konni Zilliacus (MP for Gateshead, later Gateshead East), Geoffrey Bing (Hornchurch), J.F. Platts Mills (Finsbury), Lesley Solley (Thurrock) and Lester Hutchinson (Manchester, Rusholme). Most of these were expelled from the Labour Party and in 1949, with D.N. Pritt, they formed the Labour Independent Group. From time to time, those of the 'hard' and 'soft' Left found themselves in other socialist groupings such as Victory for Socialism, the Europe Group (formed by eighty MPs in 1947) and numerous small and temporary associations that developed within the Labour Party. Although it is true that the big conflict between the Labour Party and the Labour Left did not begin in earnest until the early 1950s, with the Bevanite revolt, the history of the years 1945 to 1951 is far from Eric Shaw's assessment that 'the years of the post-war Labour Government were, until the resignation of Bevan in 1951, relatively strife free.'[64] The fact is that there were deep divisions between the Labour Left and the Labour government and that the moderate Labour Left grew slowly while the 'hard' Left became almost totally ineffective.

As they emerged these Labour Left groups, ten in number by 1952, tended to adopt rather different attitudes towards the Labour Party, particularly with regard to foreign policy and the domestic economic situation. The Keep Left Group of MPs, organised by Ian Mikardo (affectionately known as Mik), Richard Crossman, Richard Acland, Leslie Hale, Benn Levy and others, tended to accept the view that a third world war could only be avoided by the creation of a 'Third Force' based upon an alliance between Britain and France and wider European support, which would encourage disarmament and the use of the money saved to develop the economies of the Third World, and thus the prosperity, through trading, of the industrial world.[65] This view contrasted sharply with that put forward by *Tribune*, and was evident when Mikardo left the editorial board of that paper in May 1949. Prompted by Mikardo's departure, Michael Foot provided a highly reasoned article justifying the House of Commons' endorsement of the Atlantic Pact and explaining why the democratically orientated USA was more to be trusted than the far more totalitarian USSR. He wrote that:

Whatever follies have been committed by American policy since 1945 (and they are manifold) the major purpose and the major result has been to provide aid without which recovery from the war would have been infinitely more arduous. The major purpose of Soviet policy has been the complete subjugation of as many countries as possible to Soviet will. . . . There is a difference worth noting between the offer of dollars to Governments, including Socialist ones, by the United States and the provision of concentration camps and execution squads for the victims, including Soviet victims, of Soviet Communism.[66]

He suggested to Ian Mikardo that it was highly unlikely that, had Britain adopted a more socialist policy, or the 'Third Force' policy, Stalin would have taken any notice at all and allowed democratic elections in Poland. Indeed, 'The Czech Socialists and all the Czech parties had taken precisely those actions of seeking accommodation with the Russians which Ian Mikardo seems to prescribe. None of them were sufficient to save them from annihilation. Neither they nor Marshal Tito were to be allowed the exercise of any scope of independence.'

When Nye Bevan resigned from the Labour government in April 1951, over the introduction of prescription charges and Britain's involvement in the Korean War which was forcing cuts in social expenditure, it is clear that he, Harold Wilson and John Freeman associated with Keep Left and other Labour Left groups in shaping a left-wing criticism of Labour which, while it did associate itself with the criticism of the development of the hydrogen bomb in April 1954, was focused much more on the need to extend the welfare state and public control of industry and services.[67] In addition, there were many individual MPs, most obviously Konni Zilliacus, who were committed to peace and therefore associated with all moves in that direction, whether sponsored by social democratic organisations or communists.

Eric Shaw has suggested that this diversity of Left groupings was somehow galvanised and unified in April 1951 when Nye Bevan, Harold Wilson and John Freeman resigned from the Labour government over prescription charges and the funding of rearmament, and joined the Keep Left ginger group, which was 'promptly rechristened "the Bevanites"'.[68] The basic facts are true but the implication of some type of unity seems exaggerated, especially in light of the deep divisions that existed between the various Left groupings. They could be brought together on issues such as armaments and eventually on the nuclear disarmament issue, but terms like Keep Left and Bevanism are too sweeping and hide the divisions within the Left after 1951.

During the Second World War there was a small Labour Left which did not always follow Labour Party policies. D.N. Pritt and Sir Stafford Cripps were the main figures. Pritt attached himself to the Communist Party and Cripps, who had proved difficult in the late 1930s, was expelled in 1939. He emerged as the leader of the Labour Left until he was sent as Ambassador to Moscow in 1940. He returned in 1942, with the reputation of having brought Russia into the war. He was eventually admitted into the wartime cabinet, where he ceased to make an impact.

The most constant Labour Left critic at this time was Aneurin Bevan. He and George Strauss had been expelled from the Labour Party in April 1939 only to be readmitted at the end of the year.[69] Throughout the Second World War 'He emerged as the foremost parliamentary critic of Churchill and the wartime Coalition, acquiring in the country at large the status of a national bogy man.'[70] He took over the editorship of *Tribune* in 1942, in the wake of the Communist-supporting H.J. Hartshorn and the, by now, less Communist-inclined Raymond Postgate. Bevan had previously been on the editorial board with George Strauss and Victor Gollancz and remained as editor until the end of the Second World War, criticising the failures of Churchill's blunders in Norway, North Africa, Greece and Malaya.[71] Bevan also highlighted the reluctance of Churchill to mount a Second Front to help Russia fight Hitler and was adamant that the war was against fascism and not the German people and that, with the sole exception of the Alamein campaign, 'the Government's military handling of the war has been one grievous blunder after another. . . . Had our position depended upon our own military disposition alone and been unassisted by the totally unexpected victories of the Red Army, we should have been in a very dire position.'[72]

None the less, Bevan joined the Labour government in 1945 as Minister of Health, and then as Minister of Labour, until his politically damaging resignation of April 1951. His leadership of the Labour Left was thus stifled and it was a small group of Labour Left figures who began to form the basis of a growing and significant Labour Left in the late 1940s. The most prominent of these groups, though by no means the most extreme, was the Keep Left Group. They grew rapidly, kept broadly within the bounds of Labour Party policy, and were, by and large, less subject to the pressures that were placed on the 'hard' Left.

Keep Left began as a small group of friends, all MPs, who began to nurture a particular and distinctive political outlook. There were about fifteen of them and they met on a regular but informal basis. The leading figures were Richard Crossman, Ian Mikardo and Michael Foot and they were joined by the likes of Fred Lee (a trade unionist), Richard Acland, George Wigg, R.W.G. Mackay, Leslie Hale, Geoffrey Bing, Donald Bruce, Benn Levy, J.P.W. Mallalieu, Stephen Swingler and Harold Davies. Others floated in and out of this group of friends. They all had distinguished left-wing credentials; Mikardo had presented the motion which committed the next Labour government to nationalisation at the Labour Party Conference in 1944; Acland and Mackay had a grounding in the Common Wealth party, the party which offered a blend of socialist, Liberal and Marxist policies that appealed to some of the middle classes. Crossman had also been troublesome to the Labour government, producing the amendment to the King's Speech in December 1946, which demanded that the Labour government should

> so renew and recast its conduct of international affairs as to affirm the utmost encouragement to and collaboration with all nations striving to secure full Socialist planning and control of the world's resources, and thus provide a democratic and constructive Socialist alternative to an otherwise inevitable conflict between American capitalism and Soviet Communism in which all hope of world Government would be destroyed.[73]

This amendment reflected some of the later views of the Keep Left Group but was defeated easily. Yet it followed upon other Labour Left protests, most obviously against the Anglo-American loan in December 1945 and the Open Letter to Attlee in October 1946. The October letter attacked the government for giving the impression that it was 'infected by the anti-Red virus which is cultivated in the United States', and was signed by twenty-one Labour MPs including Crossman, Foot, Woodrow Wyatt and Sydney Silverman.[74] The Labour Left was determinedly opposed to the Labour government's close association with the United States.

The Keep Left Group met, on an informal basis, regularly during the bad winter of 1947 and, in May, produced a 47-page pamphlet, *Keep Left*, mainly written by Michael Foot, Ian Mikardo and Richard Crossman. It congratulated the Labour government on its domestic achievements but suggested that it needed to extend nationalisation and plan the development of the economy more effectively through the creation of a Ministry of Economic Affairs and joint production committees to win the 'Battle for Production'. Yet it felt that such domestic planning and growth could not be achieved without a balanced foreign policy. Crossman, who wrote the foreign policy section, suggested that the USA and the USSR were equally responsible for the development of two hostile blocs, and that a socialist Britain could not prosper without the gradual creation of some type of unity between European nations, the great majority of whom were planning their economy on socialist lines. Crossman stressed that Britain should start by developing economic and military relations with France and that 'We should try to expand the Anglo-French Alliance into a European security pact' and renounce atomic armaments and war.[75] Emphasis was placed upon the creation of a 'regional European Security System' that would effectively act as a 'Third Force', independent of the USA and the USSR but designed to bring the two superpowers closer together.[76] There was also the implication, though not fully spelled out at this stage, that the British armed forces, and those of other nations, would be reduced and that the African colonies could be economically developed to help Britain maintain her economic independence from the United States.[77]

This pamphlet was the basis of the Keep Left approach. Subsequently, Crossman and Mikardo developed the 'Third Force' idea into the big idea and nurtured the belief that this collective arrangement in Europe would reduce the size of the armed forces and release the economic burden upon Britain, and other nations, and some of the savings could be used to stimulate the economies of the undeveloped or Third World. These subsidiary ideas can be seen partly in Fenner Brockway's report on his 40-minute meeting with Pandit Nehru on 20 September 1950, when he proposed 'that an offer should be made by one or more of the Western Powers to direct expenditure on armaments to a World Plan for lifting the standards of life of the people . . .'.[78] Brockway also discussed the need to keep open negotiations with China. Nehru felt that the 'World Power proposal is important but should be put forward at a more suitable psychological moment than at the present' and that the Labour Left ought to pressure the British government to restrain the USA and keep the door open for negotiations with China, at a time when the Korean War was being waged.

One must also reflect that *Keep Left* was produced at a vital moment in the life of the first Attlee government. Within three months of its appearance the Labour government had announced large expenditure cuts at a time when the American Loan was ending. This provoked nineteen Labour MPs, including the fifteen who had signed *Keep Left* and James Callaghan (Cardiff South) to send a letter to the *Daily Herald*, indicating the need for alternative acts and new strategies. They suggested that the armed forces needed to be cut further, that there needed to be equality of sacrifice, that Britain should develop its trading links further and that socialist planning was needed to 'secure mass production'.[79] The subsequent debate suggested that cuts of £225 million were not enough and that an expansion of production was necessary.[80] *Keep Left*, with its fight for production and socialist planning, seemed very appropriate at this time, even though it had admitted that much had been achieved in increasing output, particularly on coal and housing. This admission, conditioned as it was, contrasts with the recently expressed view that the Attlee governments never understood how to increase industrial output.[81]

Despite all the efforts of Keep Left, including its reaction against the Czechoslovakian crisis which saw the death of its beloved example of democratic socialism, one must recognise that it was a small group of a dozen to twenty MPs. There were divisions which often reduced their support, most particularly when Michael Foot was detached from the Keep Left activities in May 1949 and Ian Mikardo left the editorial board of *Tribune* at the same time due to their different attitudes towards the Atlantic Pact.[82] It was in the wake of these changes in attitude by some of its members that the Group decided to come into official existence.

Keep Left was formed officially on 25 July 1949, in order to examine the international peace situation and to put forward its views to the Labour Party.[83] There were thirteen members present at the first meeting – Dick Acland, Barbara Castle, Dick Crossman, Harold Davies, Leslie Hale, Tom Horabin, Marcus Lupton, Ian Mikardo, Stephen Swingler, George Thomas, George Wigg, Tom Williams, and Hugh Delargy who had to leave before it ended. Mikardo was made *pro tem* secretary and Leslie Hale was acting chairman. They invited economic advisers to the Group, including David Worswick and Tom Balogh, Professor of Economics at Oxford, and, rather hopefully given their previous track record, decided to remain secret for a few months and that 'just before the resumption of the House the Group should make its existence publicly known by the issue of a statement'.[84]

The Keep Left Group was anxious to develop policies and to 'rewrite *Labour Believes in Britain* in terms of an extension of Keep Left'.[85] It re-emphasised that Britain's approach to the Americans should be 'a European rather than a narrowly British line',[86] and there was considerable discussion of the Keep Left policies already outlined. The Group raised the possibility of establishing national minimum wage levels, supporting the Schuman Plan for European Unity, the reunification of Germany and the dangers of rearming Germany. Yet four issues began to dominate its debates from the beginning of 1950 – the Korean Crisis, the dissemination of socialist ideas, the survival of the Group and the resignation of Aneurin Bevan.

Ironically, the North Korean invasion of South Korea on 25 June 1950, when they marched across the 38th parallel, united the Labour Left and the Keep Left Group behind the government. Their dominating view was that the North Korean action was wrong and that the UN had the right to take 'police action' to drive them back to the 38th parallel. However, Keep Left was opposed to widening the war against mainland China and particularly condemned General MacArthur's invasion of North Korea in November 1950, and opposed the British government sending land forces to Korea.[87] While it was clear that Stalin was unwilling to mediate unless Communist China was admitted to the United Nations Security Council, Barbara Castle, seeking a compromise, suggested that America should stop backing the Nationalist Chinese in return for the Russians forcing the North Koreans to the 38th parallel.[88]

The issue of Korea and the position of Communist China continued to dominate the Keep Left Group meetings for the next six or seven months, the line of argument being that China should be admitted to the Security Council of the United Nations, that Formosa should be returned to China and that the 38th parallel should be preserved as the border between North and South Korea.[89] There was also the wider concern that Britain had decided, under American pressure, to increase its defence budget to £4,700 million over three years (not the £700 million or 7.5 per cent of national income agreed for 1950–1).[90] This decision, provoked by the Korean War, had wider implications for the British economy since it meant that British domestic expenditure would have to be reduced.

Such protest was of limited impact coming as it did from such a very small left-wing group. There was a need for Keep Left to increase its influence and Stephen Swingler had written to Mikardo in September 1949 suggesting that 'I think the major job of the Group is to produce as soon as possible on the last section of KEEP LEFT, i.e. Twenty (or Twelve) things to Do in 1950 in crisp and clear language (the language of priorities) with explanatory notes.'[91] He added that 'from a socialist standpoint, we want to know what is wrong with the Nationalised Industries and with the National Health Service and what can we do about it.' There seems to have been a genuine concern by Group members that the Labour government was ailing. The devaluation of the pound and the worsening economic situation led some Group members to feel that Britain was threatened 'with the threat of a totalitarian regime'. There was also the fear that Sir Stafford Cripps might resign and form a coalition government with himself as prime minister.[92] Such fears drove the Group to extend *Keep Left* into *Keeping Left*, now written by Acland, D. Bruce and others, and to produce Group Papers and organise the left-wing Brains Trust throughout the country in order to heighten the awareness of socialist ideas. *Keeping Left* sold more than 30,000 copies in a few months,[93] and Mikardo, who was mainly responsible for the Brains Trust scheme, was involved in voluminous correspondence when organising the meetings.[94] The Brains Trust movement, in particular, caught on and became associated with the Tribune Group in the 1950s. Indeed, Crossman referred to an NEC meeting in 1953 when he recalled how it was said that 'the next logical thing to do is to examine the Tribune Brains Trust and see if they are a party within a party.' Edith Summerskill, looking at Mikardo, 'who I think is the most hated Bevanite', suggested that suspected fellow-travellers should be expelled.[95]

The Group Papers, which rose to more than forty in number by mid-1952, were an attempt to give the Group some further cohesion, which was much required among such a disparate array of talents, who quite clearly behaved badly towards each other and required a return to a better standard of 'good behaviour, tolerance, friendliness and good comradeship'.[96] There were Group Papers on draft conference resolutions, the outline views of Keep Left, the Buscot Conferences on Anglo-American relations, economic matters, the consequences of doing without Dollar Aid, and many other related matters.[97]

Many of these papers emerged from the Buscot Conferences, so-named because they were conferences of the left and right of the Labour Party held at Lord Farringdon's country home of Buscot. Schneer suggests that the first conference was held on 15–17 July 1949 and the last on 14–15 October 1950, and these led to the publication of the *New Fabian Essays*.[98] In fact there were more meetings, for Richard Acland presented his 'Internal Policy for Living without Dollar Aid' to the third session of the Buscot Conference in December 1951.

On foreign policy, the Group Papers supported the demand for political and economic independence from the USA, and the need for a 'Third Force', already outlined, with adjustments as the changing political climate demanded. The only significant addition was the rising concern that German rearmament should not occur. The thrust of most of the other Group Papers was concern about the economy. In May 1951, Tom Balogh criticised the Budget on the basis that it was unbalanced in favour of defence, would create inflation and threatened internal stability. Instead, he wanted to see the revaluation of sterling, dividend limitations on the Stock Exchange, a readjustment of benefits in the social security system and a renegotiated wages policy. There was also a concern to tackle the financial problems that would arise from the *One Way Only* policy (issued by *Tribune* in July 1951) of the Keep Left Group which, among other things, suggested the desirability of disarmament since the Russian threat was exaggerated, the abandonment of the idea of American atomic bases in Britain, and greater financial independence from the USA.[99] There was certainly no hiding the potential social and economic costs of 'living without dollar aid' which would go beyond the savings from cuts in defence expenditure. It was suggested that capitalistic luxuries should be taxed, family allowances should be raised, land should be nationalised, waste eradicated, and proper planning be developed in order to control wages, extend education and introduce elements of compulsion.

There is no doubting that the Keep Left Group was developing ideas, but without numbers and influence they were never going to be of more than marginal importance. Indeed, the Group became increasingly concerned about its own preservation in 1950 and 1951, when the slim Labour majority gained at the 1950 general election raised the imminent prospect of another general election. There was also the concern that the membership of the Group seemed to be changing constantly. Marcus Lupton, an early Keep Left member, rejoined the Group and new members were brought in, but there was concern that some members were resigning. There were still only twelve Group members at the end of 1949 and early 1950.[100] Thereafter, the Group gradually expanded, with Brockway and Mackay joining the Group in March 1950.[101] This expansion was offset by resignations, most notably those of George Wigg, who left in January 1951, and Tom Williams and Stephen Swingler who seemed to have lapsed.[102] Donald Bruce also resigned on 22 April 1951, largely because of Crossman's criticism of Bevan:

I have a very high regard for Dick's intellectual powers and he has always been most kind to me personally but when I see Gaitskell described as a 'first rate administrator' and a 'tough politician' coupled with reference to Nye's 'flamboyant' method, 'erratic brilliance' and 'Celtic Leftism', I find it difficult to deal temperamentally towards a man who has always, at any rate in Nye's periods of considerable popularity, protested his fervent support for him.[103]

By early 1951, the Group became more self-conscious about its own position. There were two reasons for this. First, the resignation of Aneurin Bevan, Harold Wilson and John Freeman from the Labour government had, despite Bruce's departure, quickly increased its membership. All three had joined the Group within three days of their resignations and stimulated others to do so.[104] By the end of 1951 there were at least forty-seven Group members and four others were considered attached.[105] Secondly, it was obvious that the Labour government's small parliamentary majority, in the face of a left-wing rebellion, was going to produce a general election. Accordingly, throughout 1951, the Group developed the idea of a 'Mutual Aid Scheme', whereby those Keep Left MPs in vulnerable seats were assisted in their campaign by other Keep Left MPs in safe seats.[106] This meant that Bevan spoke in Brecon, Monmouth and Pembroke, Crossman in Leeds, Donnelly and Watkin in Monmouth and Delargy in a number of constituencies including Malden, Hornchurch and Brixton.

The general election of 1951 made relatively minor inroads into Keep Left but it was clear that it brought about the end of the Group in the old form. A 'Memorandum' made it clear that Keep Left had to widen its influence:

The result of the General Election and of the voting at Scarborough [Labour Party Conference] must involve a completely new view of the functions of 'Keep Left' inside the Labour Party. Both these events have shown that we no longer represent minority opinion, save in the Trade Union oligarchy and possibly in the Parliamentary Party. It would be folly, therefore, to continue an exclusiveness which in fact gives the appearance of a minority clique.[107]

According to Schneer, this was a fair assessment of the strength of the Labour Left for there was widespread criticism, evident at the conference and in the files of Morgan Phillips, that a very large proportion of Labour Party constituencies was hostile to many of the actions of the Labour government. Indeed, the Labour Left had become strong in the constituency Labour parties well before the famous 1952 annual conference, when it astonished Britain by electing six out of seven Bevanites to the constituencies section of the NEC.[108]

The message to Keep Left was clear, for it now had to abandon 'its old functions of salutary gad-fly and think in realistic terms of acquiring power'.[109] It was suggested 'that the Group should no longer be small, hand-picked and self-appointed, black-balling its potential friends on this score or on that like a snob West End club and turning them if not into enemies, at least into critics'. It was hoped that it would be increased to at least a hundred members and that all members should bring in new ones with an argument along the lines of

Listen, duckie, Keep Left has been during the last five or six years a small, haphazard Group, self-appointed on no particular principle, as always happens in these cases. We kept small for the practical reason that it was always hard for a large group to function. However, we would like you to join forces with us, as we suspect you to be socialistically inclined! So will you come along on such and such a date?

It was argued that the widened Group would then form an Executive Committee of about twenty, probably drawn largely from the existing members, and that all its adherents would be formed into small functional bodies of about ten or twelve members who would produce Group Papers on 'New Thinking on the Nationalised Industries. A Revised Relationship with America. A Policy for the Middle East. A Socialist Attitude towards Private Industry. Trade Unions in the New Society, etc.' The main point was that the new widened Group would be active in developing its influence, to go beyond having a permanent minority status and ensure that 'the majority we command among the rank and file is reflected inside the Parliamentary Party'.

The activities of the Keep Left Group go well beyond the confines of this study but what it did was to encourage the development of the Bevanites in the early 1950s, although it was but one strand of that movement. The fierce internal strife within the Labour Party, which lasted from the major backbench revolt over rearmament in March 1952, when fifty-seven Labour MPs defied the Labour whip and voted against the Conservative government's first Defence White Paper, until the eve of the 1955 general election, owed much to this reshaped and extended Labour Left grouping. The Bevanite Brains Trust, or Tribune Brains Trust, which toured the country pressing forward the left-wing cause, first emerged in the ranks of Keep Left. In addition, the petition of left-wing MPs of April 1954, which criticised the Conservative government for not meeting with the United States and USSR to control and reduce the spread of the hydrogen bomb, owed its origins to Keep Left.[110]

Nevertheless, this outright opposition that Bevan presented in the mid-1950s went some way beyond what Keep Left was prepared to contemplate in the late 1940s. The moderate Labour Left always kept its distance from the 'hard' Left – the subject of Morgan Phillips' 'Lost Sheep' file – whereas Bevan was prepared to challenge the Labour Party much more directly and was almost expelled as a result.[111]

Only a small rump of MPs, who could be regarded as the 'hard' Left, challenged the Labour leadership in the late 1940s as Bevan was to challenge it in the 1950s. They were quickly isolated by the Labour Party and were detached from the Keep Left Group. This small rump seems to have emerged on 27 March 1946, when Ernest Bevin demanded a vote of confidence from his party with regard to his foreign policy. Six Labour MPs voted against him. These were Konni Zilliacus, Elizabeth (Bessie) Braddock, Emrys Hughes, Julius Silverman, W. Warbey and Lyall Wilkes. Some of them, particularly Braddock, Hughes and Silverman, gravitated to the 'soft' Left position as events unfolded and others on the fringe, like Tom Driberg, never quite maintained their 'hard' Left credentials. Indeed, in the end it was Zilliacus plus Leslie Solley and John Platts Mills, both of whom had not been involved in the vote, who became the martyrs of the 'hard' Left.[112]

These Labour MPs, and a small coterie of other Labour MPs who varied from time to time, began to present pro-Communist attitudes. On 20 March 1946, twenty-eight Labour MPs sent a telegram to the German Social Democratic Party wishing it 'success in bringing about the political unity of the German workers on terms fair and just to both Social Democrats and Communists'.[113] A second similar telegram was sent in December 1947 when the German Socialist Unity Party in the Soviet section of Berlin convened a Unity People's Congress. They also demanded the withdrawal of British troops from Greece.[114] Inexorably, they were cutting themselves off from the Labour Party, which noted the pro-Communist nature of some of the organisations they supported and their opposition to American aid. At the same time, their pro-Communist attitudes began to offend many of the 'soft' Labour Left who were less enamoured of communist expansionism in Eastern Europe. In March 1946, Michael Foot put forward a motion, seconded by Jennie Lee, criticising the message sent in support of the fusion conference in Berlin and attempting to confine the actions of the Labour MPs to the proper PLP procedures.[115]

By early 1948 the Labour Party began to make its moves against its 'hard' Left critics. On 8 March 1948, the Labour Party Liaison Committee convened a special meeting to discuss the speeches and activities of some Labour MPs. On 15 March Attlee announced to the House of Commons the decision that communist civil servants would no longer be allowed to handle sensitive documents. On 13 April 1948, Attlee, Morrison, Dalton, Shinwell and Morgan Phillips met to discuss statements by John Platts Mills and Konni Zilliacus that were considered to be subversive to the Labour Party. This was almost at the same moment as the 'hard' Left, in a mood of general support, wrote and signed a document, a third pro-fusion telegram, addressed to Pietro Nenni and his followers in the Italian Socialist Party. Here was the pretext that allowed the Labour Party to take action.[116]

At this time the British government believed that there was going to be a communist insurrection in Italy at a time when elections were about to take place. In fact nothing of the sort occurred and the Nenni telegram had no impact except upon British Labour politics. It was a simple statement of support that had been drawn up by Geoffrey Bing, although the inspiration behind it came from Zilliacus, and it was signed by about forty Labour MPs. The Labour NEC and Morgan Phillips acted quickly to single out John Platts Mills, who appeared before the leading figures of the NEC, and the other signatories were asked to withdraw, although twenty-one refused to do so. The 'Nenni goats', as they were called by the press to separate them from 'Attlee's sheep', responded to the various threats from Morgan Phillips, in their own style.

The twenty-one MPs who did not recant met on 26 April 1948 to produce a joint response which pledged loyalty to the Labour government and which noted that they were not aware that the NEC had withdrawn recognition from the Nenni socialists. But the Party leaders did not respond sympathetically. They expelled John Platts Mills and sent out further threats to those MPs who had not recanted. Zilliacus orchestrated the response along the lines of the preservation of freedom of speech within the Labour Party. Under his guidance they produced the formulae that 'I have never belonged, do not belong and will not belong to any group in organised opposition to Party policy' and 'I will not in future take part in any such action as that now declared by the NEC to be contrary to the constitution and rules of the Party.' This seemed to satisfy the NEC, and the PLP meeting on 5 May 1948 simply laid the matter to rest.

By expelling Platts Mills, a New Zealander who was not the most popular of MPs, the Labour Party had brought a sense of unity within its own ranks and fired a warning shot across the bows of political mavericks such as Crossman, Foot and those members of Keep Left who had signed the Nenni telegram. Above all, it had established that the Labour Party was not as willing to cooperate with communists as had seemed possible in 1945. Having expelled one member of the 'hard' Left the machinery was set in motion to expel three others, Konni Zilliacus, Leslie Solley and Lester Hutchinson.

Before Zilliacus became the Labour MP for Gateshead in 1945 he had already had a remarkable career. He had attended Yale University before the First World War, joined the anti-war Union of Democratic Control, been an intelligence officer with the post-war British Mission to Siberia and joined the Labour Party in 1919. During the interwar years he was a member of the Information Section of the League of Nations Secretariat in Geneva, helped Arthur Henderson to draft the Geneva Protocol in 1924 and provided similar guidance in the 1930s. He also wrote the foreign policy section of the Labour Party's 1934 policy statement, *For Socialism and Peace*. His abiding interest was international peace and he felt that there had to be Anglo-Soviet relationships to obtain that objective. Naturally, he supported the CPGB attempt to affiliate with the Labour Party and was seen to be a fellow-traveller. He was one of the six PLP members who voted against Bevin's foreign policy on 26 March 1946 and was deeply involved in the Nenni telegram affair. Dubbed 'Silly Zilly' by the press, he quickly assumed a role somewhat akin to that of Dutt in the eyes of the British press and the Labour Party leadership. In reality, however, Zilliacus always trod his own path. He was never a communist and was excluded from the Keep Left Group, who he felt were too willing to accept American dollars. As a result, he found that he had no obvious outlet for his views, since both *Tribune* and Kingsley Martin's *New Statesman* refused to take his articles.

After the expulsion of John Platts Mills, Konni Zilliacus was a marked man. By November 1948 Morgan Phillips was taking action against him. His reselection by the national and local parties did not deter Phillips and Zilliacus's attendance at the communist-supported World Conference of Peace in Paris added to the evidence against him, and the nine-member Election Sub-Committee of the NEC expelled him from the Labour Party in early 1949. Subsequently, he appealed to the annual conference of the Labour Party but found his case opposed by the representatives of the National Union of Mineworkers, even though Geoffrey Bing, Benn Levy and others spoke up in his favour.[117] The 1949 conference rejected the motion to refer back the expulsion to the NEC. Leslie Solley of Thurrock also had his exclusion from the Labour Party confirmed at this conference. Zilliacus was eventually readmitted to the Labour Party and became an MP for one of the Manchester seats. He applied for readmission because 'the Labour Party is worth belonging to only because I believe the future is with those in the Party who are real socialists and prepared to have the courage of their convictions in foreign as well as home affairs.'[118]

The 'hard' Left was gradually excluded from the Labour Party to an extent that they were forced to form the Labour Independent Group in 1949, with Konni Zilliacus, John Platts Mills, D.N. Pritt and Lester Hutchinson being the chief figures. They continued to press forward with the idea of working with the communists and were particularly caught up with the idea of Eurocommunism once Yugoslavia, under Tito, revealed its independence from Moscow in 1949. The Labour Independent Group also associated with the ill-fated Socialist Fellowship, which promoted international socialism, and the Victory for Socialism group, which had first emerged in 1934 but failed constantly to gain significant support. The expelled Labour MPs found their influence much diminished and it is obvious, given that they posed little threat to the Labour Party leadership, that they were expelled as a warning to the 'soft' Left not to step too far out of line.

Despite these constraints the Labour Left, and particularly Keep Left, had made its contribution to the debate about the future of socialism in Britain. It offered loftier ideals than those set by the Labour Party. Indeed, of Keep Left, Ian Mikardo concluded:

> Unlike its successors, the Keep Left Group was concerned with the long term rather than the immediate. The agendas of the later Bevanite and Tribune Group meetings were and are dominated by the week's business in the House and other current or imminent issues, but in Keep Left the greater part of our discussions was about the basic philosophy of the Party and the sort of broad economic and social order we should be seeking to create. Between 1947 and 1950 we concentrated on the production of a wide-ranging programme for the next Labour government. . . .[119]

CONCLUSION

The Labour Party, with its gradualist policy of extending public ownership and providing a social security system, was the dominant socialist force in British society during the 1940s. Its success in these directions owed much to Labour's policies before 1939 but undoubtedly benefited from the wartime radicalism. Yet one should not assume that it was Beveridge who called the tune, for the Attlee governments did add a distinctive socialist contribution to the new society that emerged, most obviously with the creation of the NHS. In contrast, the CPGB carried little political influence before 1945 and practically none thereafter. The 'hard' Left was ineffective between 1945 and 1951 and even the 'soft' Left and the Keep Left Group exerted little influence since they were divided by the issues of American money, the 'Third Force' and Soviet expansionism in Eastern Europe. Even after its decision to expand its membership in the summer of 1951, Keep Left mustered barely fifty MPs. This group, as Bevanites, was able to exert some considerable influence upon Labour politics in the wake of Labour's general election defeat in 1951 and to use its influence within the constituency Labour parties to challenge the Labour Party leadership and the right-wing revisionists who were moving towards the dropping of public ownership as the coping stone of Labour's socialism. However, before 1951 their influence was limited and any real challenge to the Labour leadership was thwarted by Morgan Phillips's management of the 'Lost Sheep' . In the final analysis the Labour Left was divided and posed less of a threat to the policies of Attlee's Labour governments than is often supposed, although they created more political turbulence than Eric Shaw would accept.[120] The history of the Labour Party from 1945 to 1951 was far from being 'strife free' as it continued to reform capitalism rather than bring a socialist state into being.

CONCLUSION

Socialism in Britain developed mainly in a social democratic form through the Labour Party in the period between 1881 and 1951. It was gradualist, parliamentary, and failed to challenge the capitalist system in any fundamental way. Indeed, David Howell is right to suggest that even in 1951 social democracy had not reached its apogee even though the Labour Party may have felt that by then 'its mission had been accomplished'.[1] He may even be right to argue that the next quarter of a century saw the 'exhaustion of British social democracy'.[2] His pessimism at the prospects for social democracy in 1976, and the lack of widely accepted alternatives, seems well founded. Indeed, the prospect of achieving socialism in Britain now appears even more remote than ever for two obvious reasons. First, there is now no Marxist alternative in play. Secondly, future public ownership has been practically disowned by Tony Blair and the Labour Party, and replaced by vague concepts of justice and equity. Nevertheless, social democracy has been the only form of mass socialism to emerge in Britain because it was the only form that tapped into the working classes, through the medium of the trade union movement, and because it did so through established and recognisable political forms.

The most obvious problem British socialist organisations have had to face is that of defining their relationship with British trade unionism. The SDF struggled with Hyndman's antipathy towards trade unions. The CPGB actively sought trade union support in order to win mass party status, although it could never achieve even the limited support it obtained without sacrificing the interests of the rank and file to those of the official trade union movement.[3] Other socialist societies have made their bid for trade union support. Yet it was only the Labour Party that was able to capture significant trade union membership. With this came the political approval of the majority of the British working classes, even if that has diminished since 1951, due partly to changes in the social structure and politics of British society.

If trade unionism determined the relative success of the socialist organisations, and ensured that the Labour Party became the most successful social democratic party in Britain, there was a price to pay. One charge was that British socialism would only progress at a rate of which the trade unions approved. Once the Labour Party accepted Clause Four in 1918 it was clear that its implementation was dependent upon the trade-union majority on the NEC and the attitude of the conservative and moderate-minded trade union leaders. This is not to say that the trade-union leaders necessarily blocked developments for, as Lewis Minkin has indicated, the trade unions and the Labour Party recognised the need to keep to separate spheres of activity conditioned by ground rules which were evolving particularly during the interwar years.[4] In addition, there was a period in the early 1930s when socialist planning did develop under the leadership of Dalton and others. Yet that socialist planning operated within the context of a concordat between the moderates in the Labour Party leadership and the conservative and moderate trade union leaders. The more radical and democratic proposals of Laski and Cole were quickly marginalised.

A second cost of the trade union alliance is that there was little prospect that Socialist Unity being achieved. In other words, a viable alternative to the social democracy of the ILP, up to 1922, and the Labour Party became impossible well before the First World War. Once the LRC/Labour Party was formed, with the support of the trade unions, the ILP, which was affiliated to the LRC, was not going to sacrifice its trade union support for the doubtful advantage of securing fusion with quasi-Marxist and other socialist groups whose vision of socialism and reform was different and whose leadership had been traditionally hostile to it. There was no conflicting choice for the ILP if the alternative was between gaining the support of trade unions or the support of H.M. Hyndman and the SDF. The only tangible attempt to achieve Socialist Unity broke down between 1912 and 1914 because the BSP failed to achieve widespread support, from socialists and trade unionists alike, and because Hyndman and his supporters were at loggerheads with the supporters of industrial unionism. The BSP persistently rejected trade unionism and alienated many of the socialist trade unionists it had attracted.

Being more specific, what has arisen from this book is that socialism emerged, or re-emerged, in the 1880s but was fragmented and failed to make a major political impact. The main weakness of the various socialist societies is that they lacked political support and, by and large, shunned that of the trade union movement. From the 1890s onwards, however, the ILP grew to become the largest socialist society in Britain because it sought support from the trade unionism which many of its members considered to be the reverse side of the socialist political coin, although one should not forget that there was also a strong input from more individualistic socialists whose background was often influenced by nonconformity. The ILP reflected the political mood of the time, focusing upon local and parliamentary political successes to extend its influence. It helped to form the LRC/Labour Party and pushed forward with its commitment to state socialism, despite the criticism of Marxists and those who were hoping to create a party of Socialist Unity. In the light of the evidence the idea that Socialist Unity could have been achieved appears a marvellous myth for there was clearly not one policy that could have united state socialist with syndicalist, parliamentary socialist and Marxist.

Yet, in order to make socialism a significant movement in Britain, there was still the need to make the Labour Party socialist. This occurred in the formal sense during the First World War with the acceptance of Clause Four into the 1918 Labour Constitution, with its commitment to public ownership. In reality it was a very vague commitment to socialism which enabled many moderate socialists of various beliefs to harbour under its political umbrella while at the same time it permitted the Labour Party to continue to work through the existing political institutions. The Fabian approach of Clause Four fitted the Labour Party and the wartime situation much more readily than did either the guild socialist or educational socialist alternatives. Above all, it proved an acceptable alternative to the revolutionary Marxism that emerged after the Bolshevik Revolution of 1917.

Despite Labour's acceptance of Clause Four there was little theoretical or practical understanding of what this meant in terms of policy for either the party or the Labour governments. Lacking a serious challenge from the CPGB, which was almost devoid of members and trade-union support, and the ILP, which faced internal conflict and decline from the mid-1920s, the Labour Party simply remained wedded to gradual change through the parliamentary route. However, there were some modest advances. The move towards planning in the early 1930s paved the way for the Labour Party to be more precise about which industries and services might be taken into public ownership and represented some improvement on the 'doctrineless socialism' which was boasted of in *Labour and the Nation*

(1928). Nevertheless, the Labour Party did withdraw from its vital commitment to taking the joint-stock banks into public ownership, accepted at the 1932 conference, by the late 1930s, although it kept the commitment to the public control of the Bank of England.

Labour's planning exercise, and particularly *Labour's Immediate Programme* (1937) did provide the blueprint for the Attlee governments' public ownership and welfare state provisions in the late 1940s, along with the wartime radicalism. Attlee's socialist measures, however, represented no fundamental change in the basis of the British economy, four-fifths of which remained in private hands. There was much criticism of the failure of the Attlee governments to apply socialism more effectively, and to detach themselves from the influence of the United States, but neither the CPGB, whose political influence diminished with the Cold War, nor the Labour Left offered a sufficient challenge to deflect them from their course or to force them to consider the further extension of socialist policies.

In the final analysis, it is clear that the Labour Party was incapable of breaking away from political orthodoxy and becoming truly innovative. In many ways it simply strengthened capitalism by managing it more effectively and alleviating some of its worst features. Yet given the fragility of the socialist alternatives this is, perhaps, not surprising.

NOTES

INTRODUCTION

1. G. Stedman Jones, *Language of Class: Studies in English Working Class History 1832–1982* (Cambridge, Cambridge University Press, 1983); P. Joyce, 'The imaginary discontents of social history: a note in response to Mayfield and Thorne, and Lawrence and Taylor', *Social History*, XVIII, 1 (January 1993); P. Joyce, *Visions of the People: Industrial England and the Question of Class 1848–1914* (Cambridge, Cambridge University Press, 1991). Also look at D. Mayfield and S. Thorne, 'Social history and its discontents: Gareth Stedman Jones and the politics of language', *Social History*, XVIII, 1 (January 1993); J. Lawrence and M. Taylor, 'The poverty of protest: Gareth Stedman Jones and the politics of language', *Social History*, XVII, 2 (May 1992); N. Kirk, 'History, language, ideas and post-modernism: a materialist view', *Social History*, XIX, 2 (May 1994).
2. Jones, *Language of Class*, p. 21.
3. Joyce, *Visions of the People*, p. 3.
4. K. Jenkins, *Rethinking History* (London, Routledge, 1991), p. 69.
5. P. Joyce (ed.), *Class* (Oxford, Oxford University Press, 1995).
6. Eugenio F. Biagini, *Liberty, Retrenchment and Reform: Popular Liberalism in the Age of Gladstone, 1860–1880* (Cambridge, Cambridge University Press, 1992); Eugenio F. Biagini and Alistair J. Reid (eds), *Currents of Radicalism: Popular Radicalism, Organized Labour and Party Politics in Britain 1850–1914* (Cambridge, Cambridge University Press, 1991).
7. Biagini and Reid, *Currents*, pp. 18–19.
8. *Ibid.*, p. 1.
9. *Ibid.*, p. 5.
10. It is surprising that E.P. Thompson should be criticised in this way given that he accepts the idea of 'social process over time'. See E.P. Thompson, 'Eighteenth-century English Society: Class Struggle without Class', *Social History*, III, 2 (May 1978), p. 147.
11. M. Savage, *The Dynamics of Working-class Politics: The Labour Movement in Preston 1880–1940* (Cambridge, Cambridge University Press, 1987); D. Tanner, *Political Change and the Labour Party 1900–1918* (Cambridge, Cambridge University Press, 1990).
12. Biagini and Reid, *Currents*, pp. 18–19.

13. David E. Martin, '"The Instrument of the People"?: the Parliamentary Labour Party in 1906', in David E. Martin and David Rubinstein (eds), *Ideology and the Labour Movement* (London, Croom Helm, 1979), pp. 125–46.

14. Pat Thane, 'Labour and local politics, radicalism, democracy and social reform, 1880–1914', in Biagini and Reid (eds), *Currents*.

15. Duncan Tanner, 'Ideological debate in Edwardian labour politics: radicalism, revisionism and socialism', in Biagini and Reid (eds), *Currents*.

16. Thane, 'Labour and local politics', pp. 261–7.

17. L. Minkin, *The Contentious Alliance: Trade Unions and the Labour Party* (Edinburgh, Edinburgh University Press, 1991).

18. R. Miliband, *Parliamentary Socialism* (London, Merlin, 1972 edn), p. 288.

19. J. Callaghan, *Socialism in Britain* (Oxford, Blackwell, 1990), p. 168.

20. *Ibid.*, p. 161.

21. K.O. Morgan, *Labour in Power 1945–51* (Oxford, Oxford University Press, 1985), p. 503.

22. The *Guardian*, 20 July 1987.

23. Miliband, *Parliamentary Socialism*, p. 331.

24. J.E. Cronin, *Labour and Society in Britain 1918–1979* (London, Batsford Academic and Education, 1984), chapter nine; B. Pimlott (ed.), *Fabian Essays in Socialist Thought* (London, Heinemann Educational, 1984).

25. D. Howell, *British Workers and the Independent Labour Party 1881–1906* (Manchester, Manchester University Press, 1983).

26. Howell, 'Was the Labour Party Inevitable?', *Bulletin of the North-West Labour History Society* (1984), pp. 1–8.

27. S. Yeo, 'A New Life: The Religion of Socialism in Britain, 1883–1896', *History Workshop Journal*, IV (Autumn 1977), pp. 5–56.

28. J. Hinton, *Labour and Socialism: A History of the British Labour Movement 1867–1974* (Brighton, Wheatsheaf Harvester, 1983).

29. M. Bevir, 'The British Social Democratic Federation 1880–1885', *International Review of Social History*, XXXVII (1992), pp. 207–29.

30. *Ibid.*, p. 217.

31. N. Fishman, *The British Communist Party and the Trade Unions, 1933–45* (Aldershot, Scolar Press, 1995); R. Stevens, 'Trades Councils in the East Midlands, 1929–1951: Trade Unionism and Politics in a "Traditionally Moderate Area"' (University of Nottingham, unpublished PhD, 1995).

32. Callaghan, *Socialism in Britain*; L.J. MacFarlane, *The Communist Party of Great Britain 1920–1929* (London, MacGibbon & Kee, 1966); W. Kendall, *Revolutionary Movements 1900–1921* (London, Weidenfeld & Nicolson, 1969); Fishman, *British Communist Party and the Trade Unions*; Frances Beckett, *Enemy Within: The Rise and Fall of the British Communist Party* (London, John Murray, 1995).

33. D. Childs, ' The Cold War and the "British Road", 1946–53', *Journal of Contemporary History* (1988).

34. Thane, 'Labour and local politics'.

35. P. Snowden, *The Individual Under Socialism* (Keighley, Keighley ILP, 1903 and 1905).

36. P. Snowden, 'The Two Salvations', *Labour Prophet*, April 1898.

37. G. Eastwood, *Harold Laski* (Oxford, Mowbray, 1977).

38. H. Laski, *Grammar and Politics* (London, 1925).

39. R.P. Arnot, *William Morris: A Vindication* (London, 1934); H. Collins, 'The Marxism of the SDF' in A. Briggs and J. Saville (eds), *Essays in Labour History,*

vol. 2 (London, Macmillan, 1971); E.J. Hobsbawm, *Labouring Men* (London, Weidenfeld & Nicolson, 1971).

40. M. Bevir, 'H. M. Hyndman: A Rereading and a Reassessment', *History of Political Thought*, XII, 1 (Spring 1991); Bevir, 'British Social Democratic Federation 1880–1885'; M. Crick, *The History of the Social Democratic Federation* (Keele, Ryburn Publishing, Keele University Press, 1994).

41. J. Hill, 'Manchester and Salford Politics and the Early Development of the Independent Labour Party', *International Review of Social History*, XXVI (1981); K. Laybourn and J. Reynolds, *Liberalism and the Rise of Labour 1890–1918* (London, Croom Helm, 1984); K. Laybourn, ' "One of the Little Breezes Blowing Across Bradford": The Bradford Independent Labour Party and Trade Unionism', in K. Laybourn and D. James (eds), *The Rising Sun of Socialism* (Wakefield, West Yorkshire Archives, 1991); K. Laybourn, 'The Bradford ILP and Trade Unionism', in D. James, T. Jowitt and K. Laybourn (eds), *The Centennial History of the Independent Labour Party* (Halifax, Ryburn Press, now Keele University Press, 1992), which also contains relevant articles by P. Dawson and R.W. Perks; D. Clark, *Colne Valley; Radicalism to Socialism* (London, Longman, 1981); D. James, 'Local Politics and the Independent Labour Party in Keighley', in Laybourn and James (eds), *The Rising Sun of Socialism*.

42. D. Tanner, *Political Change and the Labour Party* (Cambridge, Cambridge University Press, 1990); M.G. Sheppard and J.L. Halstead, 'Labour's Municipal Election Performance in Provincial England and Wales, 1901–13', *Bulletin of the Society for the Study of Labour History*, 39 (Autumn 1979).

43. Howell, *British Workers and the Independent Labour Party*.

44. Those arguing that Labour only emerged as a result of the Liberal split in the First World War include P.F. Clarke, *Lancashire and the New Liberalism* (Cambridge, Cambridge University Press, 1971); T. Wilson, *The Downfall of the Liberal Party 1914–1935* (London, 1966); M. Bentley, *The Liberal Mind, 1914–1929* (Cambridge, Cambridge University Press, 1977). Those who suggest that Labour was emerging before the First World War due to its capture of the vote of the working class include R.I. McKibbin, *The Evolution of the Labour Party 1910–1924* (Oxford, Oxford University Press, 1974); K. Laybourn, *The Rise of Labour: The British Labour Party 1890–1979* (London, Edward Arnold, 1988); Sheppard and Halstead, 'Labour's Municipal Election Performance'.

45. Howell, *British Workers and the Independent Labour Party*, pp. 389–97; Yeo, 'A New Life', pp. 5–56; M. Crick, ' "A Call to Arms"; The Struggle for Socialist Unity in Britain, 1883–1914', in James, Jowitt and Laybourn (eds), *Centennial History of the Independent Labour Party*, pp. 181–204; Crick, *Social Democratic Federation*, pp. 83–92, 238–60.

46. K. Laybourn, 'The failure of Socialist Unity in Britain c. 1893–1914', *Transactions of the Royal Historical Society*, sixth series, IV (1994), pp. 153–75; K. Laybourn, ' "A Story of Buried Talents and Wasted Opportunities": The Failure of the Socialist Unity Movement in Yorkshire 1911–14', *The Journal of Regional and Local Studies*, vol. 7, no. 2 (Autumn 1987), pp. 15–31.

47. T. Jowitt and K. Laybourn, 'War and Socialism: the experience of the Bradford ILP 1914–18', in James, Jowitt, Laybourn (eds), *Centennial History of the Independent Labour Party*, pp. 163–78.

48. McKibbin, *Evolution*, pp. 91, 195–6; J.M. Winter, *Socialism and the Challenge of War: Ideas and Politics in Britain, 1912–1918* (London, Routledge & Kegan Paul, 1974).

49. R. Harrison, 'The War Emergency Workers' National Committee, 1914–1920', in A. Briggs and J. Saville (eds), *Essays in Labour History* (London, Macmillan, 1971), pp. 211–59.

50. Fishman, *British Communist Party and the Trade Unions*, particularly the conclusion. Also, Stevens, 'Trades Councils in the East Midlands, 1929–1951'.

51. Pamela M. Graves, *Labour Women: Women in British Working-class Politics 1918–1939* (Cambridge, Cambridge University Press, 1994).

52. Hinton, *Labour and Socialism*, pp. 171–2; Miliband, *Parliamentary Socialism*, p. 288.

53. Nick Tiratsoo (ed.), *The Attlee Years* (New York, Columbia University Press, 1991).

54. Morgan, *Labour in Power*, p. 503.

55. E. Shaw, *Discipline and Discord in the Labour Party* (Manchester, Manchester University Press, 1988), p. 30; Miliband, *Parliamentary Socialism*.

56. J. Schneer, *Labour's Conscience: The Labour Left 1945–51* (London, Unwin Hyman, 1988).

57. D. Howell, *British Social Democracy* (London, Croom Helm, 1976), preface and acknowledgements.

CHAPTER 1

1. S. Shipley, *Club Life and Socialism in Mid-Victorian London* (Oxford, History Workshop Pamphlet, 5, 1971).

2. R. Harrison, *Before the Socialists: Studies in Labour and Politics 1861–1881* (London, Routledge & Kegan Paul, 1965).

3. K. Marx and F. Engels, *Marx – Engels Selected Correspondence* (Moscow, Progress, third edn, 1975), pp. 295, 300–1.

4. P.A. Watmough, 'The Membership of the Social Democratic Federation, 1885–1902', *Bulletin of the Society for the Study of Labour History*, no. 34 (1977), pp. 35–40.

5. Bevir, 'British Social Democratic Federation'.

6. S. Pierson, *Marxism and the Origins of British Socialism* (London, Cornell University Press, 1973); and, particularly, S. Pierson, *British Socialists: The Journey from Fantasy to Politics* (London, Cornell University Press, 1979).

7. Max Beer, *History of British Socialism*, Vol. II (London, Bell, 1929), p. 238.

8. A document on the 'Proposed Democratic federation' located in a small archive on the Democratic Federation and the Social Democratic Federation in the British Library of Economic and Social Sciences, London School of Economics.

9. Democratic Federation, 'Socialism Made Plain', in H. Pelling (ed.), *The Challenge of Socialism* (London, Black, 1954), p. 131.

10. H.W. Lee and E. Archbold, *Social Democracy in Britain, The Social-Democratic Federation* (London, 1935).

11. Kendall, *Revolutionary Movements*; C. Tsuzuki, *H. M. Hyndman and British Socialism* (London, Heinemann and Oxford University Press, 1961).

12. Crick, *Social Democratic Federation*.

13. Arnot, *William Morris*, p. 6.

14. Tsuzuki, *Hyndman*.

15. Hobsbawm, *Labouring Men*, pp. 234, 237–8.

16. Collins, 'The Marxism of the SDF', p. 67.

17. Pierson, *Marxism*, pp. 61, 273.

18. W. Wolfe, *From Radicalism to Socialism* (New Haven, Yale University Press, 1975), pp. 96, 99, 105.
19. Bevir, 'H. M. Hyndman'; Bevir, 'British Social Democratic Federation'.
20. *Justice*, 19 January 1884.
21. Bevir, 'British Social Democratic Federation', pp. 225–6.
22. *Ibid.*, p. 227.
23. Crick, *Social Democratic Federation*, p. 296.
24. Y. Kapp, *Eleanor Marx*, vol. II (London, Virago, 1979).
25. *Ibid.*, p. 59.
26. In a letter from Hyndman to Marx, 29 October 1881, in the Marx Correspondence and quoted in S. Pierson, *Marxism and the Origins of British Socialism. The Struggle for a New Consciousness* (London, Cornell University Press, 1973), p. 67.
27. H.M. Hyndman, *Historical Basis*, quoted in Tsuzuki, *Hyndman*, pp. 55–6.
28. Bevir, 'British Social Democratic Federation', p. 228.
29. Letter from F. Engels to Laura Lafargue, 4 May 1891, quoted in Kapp, *Eleanor Marx*, p. 475.
30. T. Mann, *Memoirs* (London, Labour Publishing Company, 1923), p. 41.
31. *SDF Annual Conference Report, 1894*, pp. 28–31.
32. P. Thompson, *Socialists, Liberals and Labour: The Struggle for London 1885–1914* (London, Routledge & Kegan Paul, 1967), p. 122.
33. Tsuzuki, *Hyndman*, pp. 70–1.
34. Lee and Archbold, *Social Democracy in Britain*, p. 109.
35. E.P. Thompson, *William Morris: Romantic to Revolutionary* (London, Merlin Press, 1977 edn).
36. *Ibid.*, pp. 125–6.
37. R.P. Arnot, *William Morris: the Man and the Myth* (London, Lawrence & Wishart, 1964), p. 15, effectively a reprint of Arnot, *William Morris*.
38. F. MacCarthy, *William Morris: A Life of Our Time* (London, Faber & Faber, 1994), p. xii.
39. *Ibid.*, p. 64.
40. Kapp, *Eleanor Marx*, p. 61.
41. *Ibid.*, p. 63.
42. William Morris, *News from Nowhere*, ed. by G.D.H. Cole, p. 131.
43. W. Morris, 'How I Became a Socialist', *Justice*, 16 June 1894.
44. Extract from *Commonweal*, 19 May and 17 August 1889, and quoted in Thompson, *William Morris*, p. 550. For another examination of the ideas of Morris regarding parliamentary activities and anarchists look at F. Boos (ed.), *William Morris's Socialist Diary* (London, Journeyman Press, 1985).
45. William Morris's statement on why he and his colleagues left the SDF, 13 January 1885, Morris correspondence, International Institute of Social History, Amsterdam.
46. A letter from William Morris to the Revd John Glasse, 23 May 1887, Morris correspondence.
47. Letter from William Morris to J.L. Mahon, 17 May 1887, Morris correspondence.
48. Report of the Delegates of the Leeds Branch of the SDF, 8 February 1885 by J.L. Mahon, Socialist League Correspondence, p. 598. Also look at *Commonweal*, March 1885.
49. Yeo, 'A New Life', pp. 5–56; *Manifesto* of the Socialist League.
50. *Ibid.*, p. 25.

51. *Ibid.*, p. 31.
52. L. Barrow, 'Socialism in Eternity: Plebeian Spiritualism 1853–1913', *History Workshop*, 9 (Spring 1980), pp. 37–69, argues that plebeian (working and lower-middle class) interests were evident from the early and mid-nineteenth century until the beginning of the twentieth and developed in a zig-zag manner to connect Owenism with the socialism of the late nineteenth century. Spiritualism, with its attack upon Christianity, attempted to unite (unsuccessfully) with the secularists against Christianity. Spiritualism was evident in the ILP just as much as it was evident in the early activities of the Fabians.
53. Pierson, *British Socialists*, p. 9. The roots of this development can be seen in L. Barrow, 'Socialism in Eternity', pp. 37–69. Plebeian is used to refer to the working and lower-middle classes in Barrow's articles and one major theme is that spiritualism carried forward aspects of Owenism.
54. Pierson, *Marxism*, p. 113.
55. *Ibid.*, p. 116.
56. G.B. Shaw, *A Manifesto*, Fabian Tract, 2 (London, 1884).
57. G.B. Shaw, *The Radical Programme*, Fabian Tract, 6 (London, 1887).
58. S. Webb, *Facts for Socialists*, Fabian Tract, 5 (London, 1887).
59. *Fabian Essays in Socialism* (London, Fabian Society, 1889).
60. Hobsbawm, *Labouring Men*, pp. 250, 268.
61. *Ibid.*, p. 268.
62. Crick, *Social Democratic Federation*, p. 61.
63. E.P. Thompson, 'Homage to Tom Maguire', in A. Briggs and J. Saville (eds) *Essays in Labour History* (London, Macmillan, 1960).

CHAPTER 2

1. L. Minkin, *The Contentious Alliance: Trade Unions and the Labour Party* (Edinburgh, Edinburgh University Press, 1991).
2. H. Pelling, *Origins of the Labour Party* (Oxford, Oxford University Press, 1965 edn), p. 54.
3. J. Shepherd, 'Labour and parliament: the Lib.-Labs. as the first working-class MPs. 1885–1906', in Biagini and Reid (eds), *Currents*, pp. 187–213.
4. Samuel Shaftoe, secretary of the Bradford Trades Council throughout the 1880s and up to 1892, was the leading advocate of LEA ideas in Bradford and was strongly supported by Walter Sugden, an insurance agent, and a small band of supporters.
5. T.R. Threlfall, 'The political future of Labour', *Nineteenth Century*, 35 (February 1894), pp. 213–14; also quoted in Shepherd, 'Labour and parliament', p. 195.
6. Dona Torr, *Tom Mann and his Times* (London, 1956), pp. 273–5.
7. F. Reid, 'Keir Hardie's conversion to socialism', in A. Briggs and J. Saville (eds), *Essays in Labour History*, 2, *1886–1923* (London, Macmillan, 1971).
8. James J. Smyth, 'The ILP in Glasgow 1888–1906: the struggle for identity', in Alan McKinlay and R.J. Morris (eds), *The ILP on the Clydeside 1893–1932: from foundation to disintegration* (Manchester, Manchester University Press, 1991), p. 21.
9. Joan Smith, 'Taking the leadership of the labour movement: the ILP in Glasgow, 1906–1914', in McKinlay and Morris (eds), *The ILP on Clydeside*, p. 56.
10. E.J. Hobsbawm, 'General labour unions in Britain 1889–1914', in Hobsbawm, *Labouring Men*.

11. Thompson, 'Homage to Tom Maguire'.
12. Bill Lancaster, *Radicalism, Cooperation and Socialism: Leicester working-class politics 1860–1906* (Leicester, Leicester University Press, 1987), pp. 85–93.
13. Apart from Thompson's article mentioned above, the details of the Manningham Mills strike can be found in C. Pearce, *The Manningham Mills Strike in Bradford December 1890–April 1891* (University of Hull Occasional Papers in Economic and Social History, 7, Hull, 1975) and K. Laybourn, 'The Manningham Mills Strike December 1890 to April 1891', in James, Jowitt and Laybourn, *Centennial History of the Independent Labour Party*, pp. 117–36. Also look at Laybourn and Reynolds, *Liberalism and the Rise of Labour 1890–1918*, pp. 40–2.
14. *The Labour Journal*, 7 October 1892.
15. *Bradford Observer Budget*, April 1891.
16. The Bradford Labour Union was formed in Bradford on 21 May 1891, after a preliminary meeting that was held at the end of April 1891.
17. *Workman's Times*, 18 June 1892.
18. *Yorkshire Factory Times*, 29 May and 25 September 1891; Colne Valley Labour Union, Minutes, 21 July 1891; *Keighley News*, 8 October 1892 and Laybourn and Reynolds, *Liberalism and the Rise of Labour 1890–1918*, pp. 42–3.
19. Laybourn and Reynolds, *Liberalism and the Rise of Labour 1890–1918*, p. 45.
20. Lancaster, *Radicalism, Cooperation and Socialism*, pp. 121–33; Howell, *British Workers and the Independent Labour Party*, p. 280.
21. This is deposited in the West Yorkshire Archives collection, Bradford branch.
22. Pelling, *Origins*, pp. 121–31.
23. *Labour Leader*, 2 April 1914.
24. Laybourn and Reynolds, *Liberalism and the Rise of Labour 1890–1918*, pp. 60–3; *ILP News*, May, June 1898, March 1899; R.B. Perks, ' "The Rising Sun of Socialism": Trade Unionism and the Emergence of the Independent Labour Party in Huddersfield', in Laybourn and James (eds), *The Rising Sun of Socialism*, p. 84; J. Reynolds and K. Laybourn, 'The Emergence of the Independent Labour Party in Bradford', *International Review of Social History*, XX, 3 (1975).
25. Hill, 'Manchester and Salford Politics', p. 189.
26. Smyth, 'ILP in Glasgow', p. 31.
27. Pelling, *Origins*, p. 243.
28. *Bradford Labour Echo*, 1 January 1898.
29. *Ibid.*, 27 April 1895.
30. *Ibid.*, 15 August 1896.
31. *Ibid.*, 9 November 1895. Also look at K. Laybourn, 'Trade Unions and the Independent Labour Party: The Manningham Experience', in J.A. Jowitt and R.K.S. Taylor, *Bradford 1890–1914: The Cradle of the Independent Labour Party* (Bradford, Bradford Centre Occasional Papers 2, 1980), pp. 34–40.
32. L. Smith, 'John Trevor and the Labour Church Movement' (Huddersfield Polytechnic, MA dissertation, 1986).
33. *Bradford Labour Echo*, 20 March 1897.
34. L. Smith, *Religion and the Rise of Labour: Nonconformity and the Independent Labour Movement in Lancashire and the West Riding 1880–1914* (Keele, Ryburn Publishing, Keele University Press, 1993). He argues that the links between Nonconformity and Labour were incidental, in contrast with the view expressed by T. Jowitt, 'Religion and the Independent Labour Party', in Laybourn and James (eds), *The Rising Sun of Socialism*, pp. 121–34. Jowitt maintains that the ILP was very much dominated by the religious impulse of Nonconformity.

35. Yeo, 'A New Life', pp. 5–56.

36. Clark, *Colne Valley*.

37. M. Crick, 'To "Work and Wait and Wait Working", The Life and Times of Edward Robertshaw Hartley, Pioneer Socialist', *The Journal of Regional and Local Studies*, 14, 2 (Winter 1994), pp. 13–30.

38. Stockport ILP Minute Book, 6 December 1896; Howell, *British Workers and the Independent Labour Party*, p. 335.

39. *Labour Leader*, 3 June 1894.

40. Glasier Diaries, 4 June 1896, University of Liverpool Library.

41. *Ibid.*, 7 October 1900.

42. J. Hannam, *Isabella Ford, 1855–1924* (Oxford, Blackwell, 1989).

43. J. Clayton, *The Rise and Decline of Socialism in Great Britain, 1884–1924* (London, Faber & Gwyer, 1926) pp. 84–5.

44. J. Hannam, 'Women and the ILP, 1890–1914', in James, Jowitt and Laybourn (eds), *Centennial History of the Independent Labour Party*, pp. 205–19.

45. P. Hollis, *Ladies Elect: Women in English Local Government 1865–1914* (Oxford, Oxford University Press, 1987), pp. 65–6.

46. *Ibid.*, pp. 135–6.

47. K. Laybourn, 'The Defence of Bottom Dog: The ILP in Local Politics', in D.G. Wright and T. Jowitt (eds), *Victorian Bradford* (Bradford, Bradford Metro, 1982).

48. Laybourn, 'One of the Little Breezes Blowing across Bradford', pp. 15–21; K. Laybourn, 'The Bradford ILP and Trade Unionism', in James, Jowitt and Laybourn (eds), *Centennial History of the Independent Labour Party*, pp. 148–53.

49. Articles by P. Dawson, K. Laybourn and R. Perks in Laybourn and James (eds), *The Rising Sun of Socialism*; Hill, 'Manchester and Salford Politics'; Lancaster, *Radicalism, Cooperation and Socialism*.

50. Clark, *Colne Valley*; D. James, 'Local Politics and the Independent Labour Party in Keighley', in Laybourn and James (eds), *Rising Sun of Socialism*, pp. 111–12; D. James, 'The Keighley Independent Labour Party 1892–1900', in Jowitt and Taylor, *Bradford 1890–1912*; D. James, *Class and Politics in a Northern Industrial Town, Keighley 1880–1914* (Keele, Keele University Press, 1995).

51. K. Laybourn, *Philip Snowden: a biography* (Aldershot, Temple Smith/Gower, 1988), pp. 167–71.

52. Snowden, 'The Two Salvations', and also quoted in Laybourn, *Snowden*, p. 34.

53. Tanner, *Political Change and the Labour Party*, p. 317.

54. K. Laybourn, 'Recent Writing on the History of the ILP, 1893–1932', in James, Jowitt and Laybourn (eds), *Centennial History of the Independent Labour Party*, pp. 327–9.

55. K. Laybourn and J. Reynolds, *Liberalism and the Rise of Labour* (London, Croom Helm, 1984).

56. Sheppard and Halstead, 'Labour's Municipal Election Performance', pp. 39–62.

57. Smyth, 'ILP in Glasgow', p. 79.

58. D. Tanner, 'Elections, Statistics and the Rise of the Labour Party, 1906–1931', *Historical Journal*, 34, 4 (1991), pp. 893–908.

59. For Labour and local politics also look at M. Savage, 'The Rise of the Labour Party in local perspective', *Journal of Regional and Local Studies*, 10 (Summer 1990).

60. Clarke, *Lancashire and the New Liberalism*, p. 139.

61. J.R. MacDonald, *Ramsay MacDonald's Political Writings*, edited with an introduction by Bernard Barker (London, Allen Lane, Penguin Press, 1972).

62. J.R. MacDonald, *Socialism* (London, Social Problems Series, T.C. & E.C. Jack, 1907), p. 122.

63. C. Wrigley, 'Labour and the Trade Unions', in K.D. Brown (ed.), *The First Labour Party 1906–1914* (London, Croom Helm, 1985). Not all parts of Britain followed this trend as suggested by Sam Davies, *Liverpool Labour: Social and Political Influences on the Development of the Labour Party in Liverpool, 1900–1939* (Keele, Keele University Press, 1996).

64. *Ibid.*, p. 142.

65. *Ibid.*, p. 152.

66. *Ibid.*, p. 151.

67. Sheppard and Halstead, 'Labour's Municipal Election Performance', p. 42; Laybourn and Reynolds, *Liberalism and the Rise of Labour*, pp. 109, 149.

68. J. Liddington and J. Norris, *One Hand Tied behind Us* (London, Virago, 1984); A. Phillips, *Divided Loyalties* (Virago, 1987); S. Holton, *Feminism and Democracy* (Cambridge, Cambridge University Press, 1988).

69. C. Colette, *For Labour and for Women* (Manchester, Manchester University Press, 1989), p. 35.

70. Graves, *Labour Women*.

71. Report of the Annual Conference of the Women's Labour League, in *League Leaflet*, March 1913, quoted in Graves, *Labour Women*, p. 9.

72. Colette, *For Labour and for Women*, p. 37.

73. Crick, *Social Democratic Federation*, p. 198.

74. Watmough, 'Membership of the Social Democratic Federation 1885–1902', p. 38; R. Barltrop, *The Monument: The Story of the Socialist Party of Great Britain* (London, Pluto Press, 1975); R. Challinor, *The Origins of British Bolshevism* (London, Croom Helm, 1977).

75. Crick, *Social Democratic Federation*, pp. 104, 168.

76. Lee and Archbold, *Social Democracy in Britain*, pp. 158–60; Crick, *Social Democratic Federation*, pp. 94–5.

77. *Justice*, 12 August 1893, 20 January 1894.

78. A.J. Kidd, 'The Social Democratic Federation and Popular Agitation amongst the Unemployed of Edwardian Manchester', *International Review of Social History*, 37 (1992), p. 336.

79. Francis Johnstone Collection, 1901/45, Rochdale, a letter from Shallard to J.K. Hardie, July 1901.

80. Crick, *Social Democratic Federation*, p. 330.

81. T.A. Jackson, *Solo Trumpet* (London, Lawrence & Wishart, 1953), p. 66.

82. *Justice*, 30 August 1902 and also quoted in Crick, *Social Democratic Federation*, p. 165.

83. M. Cole, *The Story of Fabian Socialism* (London, Mercury, 1963); M. Cole (ed.), *The Webbs and their Work* (London, Muller, 1949).

84. A. McBriar, *Fabian Socialism and English Politics, 1884–1918* (Cambridge, Cambridge University Press, 1962).

85. Howell, *British Workers and the Independent Labour Party*, pp. 389–97; Yeo, 'A New Life', pp. 5–56; M. Crick, '"A Call to Arms"; the Struggle for Socialist Unity in Britain, 1883–1914', in James, Jowitt and Laybourn (eds), *Centennial History of the Independent Labour Party*, pp. 181–204; Crick, *Social Democratic Federation*, pp. 83–92, 238–60; K. Laybourn, 'The Failure of Socialist Unity in Britain c 1893–1914', *Transactions of the Royal Historical Society*, sixth series, IV (London, 1994), pp. 153–75.

86. Howell, *British Workers and the Independent Labour Party*, p. 389.

87. R. Moore, *The Labour Party 1880–1924* (London, Hodder & Stoughton, 1978), p. 53 quoting Beatrice Webb's Diary, 10 July 1895.

88. Howell, *British Workers and the Independent Labour Party*, pp. 393–7.
89. J. Hill, 'Social Democracy and the Labour Movement: the Social Democratic Federation in Lancashire', *Bulletin of the North-West Labour History Society*, 8 (1982–3).
90. *Clarion*, 4 August 1911.
91. *Ibid.*, 11 August 1911.
92. *Ibid.*, 6 October 1911.
93. *Justice*, 7 August 1897.
94. *ILP News*, August 1897.
95. *ILP Annual Conference Report*, 1898.
96. *Justice*, 27 August 1898.
97. *Clarion*, 3 December 1898.
98. J. Hill, 'The ILP in Lancashire', in James, Jowitt and Laybourn (eds), *Centennial History of the Independent Labour Party*, p. 50.
99. *ILP News*, March, September and October 1898.
100. *Bradford Labour Echo*, 11 April 1896.
101. Hill, 'Social Democracy', p. 53.
102. Lee and Archbold, *Social Democracy in Britain*, p. 159.
103. D. Howell, 'Was the Labour Party Inevitable?', *Bulletin of the North-West Labour History Society* (1984), p. 17.
104. *Clarion*, 7 February 1902.
105. J.M. McLachlan and E. Hartley, *Should Socialists Join the Labour Party – a verbatim report of the debate* (1909).
106. *Clarion*, 7 July 1911.
107. *Ibid.*, 13 October 1911.
108. K. Laybourn, ' "A Story of Buried Talents and Wasted Opportunities": The Failure of the Socialist Unity Movement in Yorkshire 1911–1914', *The Journal of Regional and Local Studies*, 7, 2 (1987), pp. 15–31; D. Morris, 'The Origins of the British Socialist Party', *Bulletin of the North-West Labour History Society*, 8 (1982–3), pp. 34–5.
109. Crick, *Social Democratic Federation*, p. 198.
110. *Conference BSP, 1912*, p. 8.
111. Laybourn, 'A Story of Buried Talents and Wasted Opportunities', p. 25; A. Gardiner, Scrap Book.
112. BSP Papers 1910–14 (Birmingham) in the British Library of Political and Economic Science, Coll. Misc. 155, M228, collected by H.B. Williams, particularly item 48/49/5, and item 46, the letter from Wintringham to Williams.
113. Look at Zelda Kahan article 'Peace and its Perils' in *British Socialists*, I, 1912, pp. 56–68.
114. *Justice*, 8 February 1913; *Clarion*, 21 June 1913.
115. *Ibid.*, 28 May 1914.
116. Yeo, 'Religion of Socialism', p. 31.
117. H. Pelling, *A History of British Trade Unionism* (London, Penguin, 4th edn, 1987), p. 130, and J. Hinton, *The First Shop Stewards' Movement* (London, George Allen & Unwin, 1973), p. 278.
118. B. Holton, *British Syndicalism 1900–1914: Myths and Realities* (London, Pluto Press, 1976).
119. *Ibid.*, p. 119.
120. G. Haupt, *Socialism and the Great War: The Collapse of the Second International* (Oxford, Oxford University Press, 1972), chapter 10, pp. 195–215.
121. Laybourn, *Snowden*, p. 64; Crick, *Social Democratic Federation*, pp. 261–83.

CHAPTER 3

1. A. Marwick, *The Deluge* (London, Macmillan, 1975 edn); P. Abrams. 'The Failure of Social Reform, 1918–1920', *Past and Present*, 24 (1963); Miliband, *Parliamentary Socialism*; McKibbin, *Evolution*; Winter, *Socialism and the Challenge of War*.
2. Thirteen of the twenty-three NEC members were directly elected by trade unionists.
3. McKibbin, *Labour Party*, pp. 105–6.
4. J. Winter, *The Great War and the British People* (London, Macmillan, 1986, reprinted 1987), pp. 103–4.
5. McKibbin, *Labour Party*, p. 91.
6. Miliband, *Parliamentary Socialism*; Harrison, 'The War Emergency Committee', pp. 211–59.
7. Winter, *Socialism and the Challenge of War*, p. 184.
8. *Ibid.*, pp. 187–8.
9. Harrison, 'War Emergency Committee', pp. 236–7.
10. Winter, *Socialism and the Challenge of War*, pp. 214–15.
11. *Ibid.*, p. 215.
12. Harrison, 'War Emergency Committee', p. 256.
13. McKibbin, *Labour Party*, p. 97.
14. B. Barker, 'The Anatomy of Reform: The Social and Political Ideas of the Labour Leadership in Yorkshire', *International Review of Social History*, XVIII (1973), pp. 1–27.
15. McKibbin, *Labour Party*, p. 97.
16. Harrison, 'War Emergency Committee', p. 259.
17. Laybourn and Reynolds, *Liberalism and the Rise of Labour*, chapter 7.
18. D. Powell, 'The New Liberalism and the Rise of Labour, 1886–1906', *Historical Journal*, 29, 2 (1986); H.C. Matthew, R.I. McKibbin and J.A. Kay. 'The Franchise Factor in the rise of the Labour Party', *English Historical Review*, XCI (1976); D. Tanner, 'The Parliamentary Electoral System, the "Fourth Reform Act" and the Rise of Labour in England and Wales', *Bulletin of the Institute of Historical Research*, LVI (1983); Clarke, *Lancashire and the New Liberalism*.
19. Laybourn and Reynolds, *Liberalism and the Rise of Labour*; Thompson, *Socialists, Liberals and Labour*, p. 170; Lancaster, *Radicalism, Cooperation and Socialism*; and others, examine some areas of Labour's rapid growth. The following articles suggest that New Liberalism was not particularly strong in some areas or could not break the control of the Old Liberals: K.O. Morgan, 'The New Liberalism and the Challenge of Labour: The Welsh Experience, 1885–1929', in K.D. Brown, *Essays in Anti-Labour History* (London, Macmillan, 1974); A.W. Purdue, 'The Liberal Party and the Labour Party in North East Politics', *International Review of Social History*, I (1981).
20. Sheppard and Halstead, 'Labour's Municipal Election Performance', p. 16.
21. Clarke, *Lancashire and the New Liberalism*; Wilson, *The Downfall of the Liberal Party*; K.D. Brown, *The English Labour Movement* (London, Gill and Macmillan, 1982); K. Burgess, *The Challenge of Labour* (London, Croom Helm, 1980); R. Douglas, 'Labour in Decline 1910–1914', in Brown (ed.), *Essays in Anti-Labour History* (London, Macmillan, 1974).
22. Wilson, *Downfall*, p. 23.
23. M. Bentley, *The Climax of Liberal Politics: British Liberalism in Theory and Practice 1868–1918* (London, Edward Arnold, 1987), p. 152.

24. Clarke, *Lancashire*, pp. 1–14.
25. Douglas, 'Decline', pp. 116–19.
26. C. Cross, *Philip Snowden* (London, Benn, 1966).
27. *Bradford Pioneer*, 8 November 1915, refers to the Executive and General Council of the Union of Democratic Control, many of whom were Liberals who later moved over to the Labour Party.
28. *Bradford Pioneer*, 22 October 1915.
29. *Ibid.*, 9 April 1915.
30. *Ibid.*, 2 June 1916.
31. F. Brockway, *Socialism over Sixty Years: The Life of Jowett of Bradford 1864–1944* (London, 1946), p. 152.
32. *Bradford Pioneer*, 2 June 1916.
33. *Ibid.*, 13 April and 2 June 1916.
34. Republished, from the *Merthyr Pioneer*, in the *Bradford Pioneer*, 21 April 1916.
35. *Bradford Pioneer*, 2 June 1916.
36. *Ibid.*, 28 April 1916.
37. *Ibid.*, 21 May 1915.
38. *Ibid.*, 25 February 1916.
39. *Ibid.*, 1 March 1918.
40. Joseph Melling, 'Work, culture and politics on "Red Clydeside": The ILP during the First World War', in McKinley and Morris (eds), *The ILP on Clydeside*, p. 114.
41. *Ibid.*
42. *Ibid.*, p. 115.
43. *Ibid.*
44. Quoted in C. Wrigley, 'Trade Unions and Politics in the First World War', in B. Pimlott and C. Cook (eds), *Trade Unions in British Politics* (London, Longman, 1982), p. 79.
45. J. Hinton, *The First Shop Stewards' Movement* (London, George Allen & Unwin, 1973), p. 278.
46. A. Reid, 'Dilution, Trade Unionism and the State', in S. Tolliday and J. Zeitlin (eds), *Shop Floor Bargaining and the State* (Cambridge, Cambridge University Press, 1985), pp. 46–74.
47. J. Melling, ' "Whatever happened to Red Clydeside?": Industrial Conflict and the Politics of Skill in the First World War', and J. Foster, 'Strike Action and Working-class Politics on Clydeside 1914–1919', in *International Review of Social History*, XXXV (1990), pp. 3–32, 33–70.
48. K. Laybourn, *A History of British Trade Unionism* c. 1770–1990 (Stroud, Alan Sutton, 1992), pp. 109–19.
49. Crick, *Social Democratic Federation*, pp. 268–9.
50. Tsuzuki, *Hyndman*, p. 243.
51. *Ibid.*, p. 277.
52. *Labour Leader*, 7 June 1917; Laybourn, *Snowden*, pp. 78–9.
53. S. White, 'Soviets in Britain: The Leeds Convention of 1917', *International Review of Social History*, XIX (1974), p. 192.
54. *Yorkshire Factory Times*, 14 July 1917.
55. White, 'Soviets in Britain', p. 191.

CHAPTER 4

1. Fishman, *British Communist Party and the Trade Unions*; R. Stevens, 'Trades Councils in the East Midlands'.

2. L. Minkin, *The Contentious Alliance*.

3. R. McKibbin, 'Why was there no Marxism in Great Britain?', *English Historical Review*, April (1984), pp. 297–331.

4. Howell, *British Social Democracy*, p. 12.

5. *Labour Party Conference Report, 1935* (London, Labour Party, 1935), p. 179.

6. A. Booth, *British Economic Policy 1931–1949: Was there a Keynesian Revolution* (London, Harvester Wheatsheaf, 1989); S. Glynn and A. Booth, *The Road to Full Employment* (London, Allen & Unwin, London, 1987).

7. Minkin, *Contentious Alliance*, p. 1.

8. TUC, *Congress Report, 1925*, pp. 363–4.

9. Amalgamated Engineering Union, *Monthly Journal*, 24 November 1924, quoted in H.A. Clegg, *A History of British Trade Unions since 1889: Volume II, 1911–1933* (Oxford, Oxford University Press, 1985), p. 378.

10. W.M. Citrine, *The Trade Unions in the General Election* (London, TUC, 1931), p. 5.

11. TGWU *Record*, June 1931, p. 327, quoted in R. Shackleton, 'Trade Unions and the Slump', in B. Pimlott and C. Cook (eds), *Trade Unions in British Politics* (London, Longman, 1982), p. 123.

12. Clegg, *British Trade Unions, 1910–1933*, p. 356.

13. The Council of Action, *Report of the Special Conference on Labour and the Russian-Polish War, 13 August 1920, Central Hall, Westminster* (London, Labour Party, 1920), p. 3.

14. R. Palme Dutt, 'Notes of the Month', *Labour Monthly*, 6, 5, May 1924, 264.

15. R. Skidelsky, *Oswald Mosley* (London, Macmillan, 1975), p. 248.

16. *General Council Minutes*, 20–1 August 1931.

17. *Labour Party Conference Report, 1920* (London, 1920), pp. 181–3.

18. *Labour Party Conference Report, 1922* (London, 1922), pp. 222–3.

19. *Labour and the Nation* (London, Labour Party, 1928), p. 6.

20. *Labour Party Conference Report, 1928* (London, 1928), pp. 200–3, 212–15.

21. H. Laski, *The Crisis and the Constitution: 1931 and After* (London, Hogarth Press, 1931).

22. H. Laski, *Democracy in Crisis* (London, Allen & Unwin, 1933); Callaghan, *Socialism in Britain*, pp. 121–2.

23. G. Eastwood, *Harold Laski* (Oxford, A. R. Mowbray, 1977), p. 55; B. Pimlott, *Labour and the Left in the 1930s* (Cambridge, Cambridge University Press, 1977), p. 95.

24. G.D.H. Cole, *The Next Ten Years in British Social and Economic Policy* (London, Macmillan, 1929).

25. R.H. Tawney, *The Choice before the Labour Party* (London, Socialist League, 1933); Sir S. Cripps, *Problems of a Socialist Government* (London, Gollancz, 1933).

26. Minkin, *Contentious Alliance*, pp. 30–4.

27. E. Durbin, *The Politics of Democratic Socialism* (London, 1940).

28. Pimlott, *Labour and the Left in the 1930s*.

29. B. Pimlott, *Hugh Dalton* (London, Macmillan, 1985), p. 206.

30. *Ibid.*, p. 213.

31. Howell, *British Social Democracy*, p. 72.

32. *Ibid.*, pp. 217–18.

33. *Labour Party Conference Report, 1935*, p. 23; *Labour Party Conference Report, 1936*, p. 250.

34. Pimlott, *Dalton*, pp. 237–8.

35. NEC of the Labour Party, Minutes, 2 September 1924, outlines the whole issue from 1922 to 1924.
36. *Ibid.*, 23 September 1924.
37. *Ibid.*
38. Fishman, *British Communist Party and the Trade Unions*, p. 34.
39. *Class against Class* (London, CPGB, 1929).
40. *Ibid.*
41. D. Blaazer, *The Popular Front and the Progressive Tradition: Socialists, Liberals, and the Quest for Unity, 1884–1939* (Cambridge, Cambridge University Press, 1992).
42. T. Buchanan, *The Spanish Civil War and the British Labour Movement* (Cambridge, Cambridge University Press, 1991), p. 3.
43. *Daily Worker*, 4 February 1937.
44. Buchanan, *Spanish Civil War and the British Labour Movement*, chapters 5 and 6.
45. J. Reynolds and K. Laybourn, *Labour Heartland: A history of the Labour Party in West Yorkshire during the inter-war years 1918–1939* (Bradford, Bradford University Press, 1987); W. Gallacher, *Revolt on the Clyde* (London, Lawrence & Wishart, London, 1979 edn), chapter xi.
46. Blaazer, *Popular Front*, pp. 148–54; Pimlott, *Labour and the Left in the 1930s.*
47. K. Morgan, *Against Fascism and War: Rupture and Constitution in British Communist Politics, 1935–1941* (Manchester, Manchester University Press, 1989), pp. 36, 131–3.
48. *Leeds Citizen*, 3 February 1939; Huddersfield Labour Party, Minutes, 21 February 1939; Halifax Labour Party, Minutes, 25 May 1939.
49. City of Leeds Labour Party, File 72/6, circular of Militant Labour League, Leeds branch, 24 September 1938, 28 December 1938, 8 May 1939.
50. Graves, *Labour Women*, p. 1.
51. *Ibid.*, p. 85.
52. Marion Phillips, 'Birth Control – A Plea for Careful Consideration', *Labour Women*, March 1924, 34; Graves, *Labour Women*, p. 86.
53. *Labour Party Conference Report 1925* (London, 1925) p. 44.
54. Graves, *Labour Women*, p. 99.
55. S. Macintyre, *A Proletarian Science: Marxism in Britain 1917–33* (Cambridge, Cambridge University Press, 1980); S. Macintyre, *Little Moscows: Communism and Working-class Militancy in Inter-war Britain* (Croom Helm, London, 1980).
56. *South Wales News*, 25 May 1926, quoted in Macintyre, *Little Moscows*, pp. 44–5.
57. R. Challinor, *The Origins of British Bolshevism* (London, Croom Helm, 1977); W. Kendall, *The Revolutionary Movement in Britain 1900–1921* (London, Weidenfeld & Nicolson, 1969).
58. Morgan, *Against Fascism and War.*
59. J. Callaghan, *Rajani Palme Dutt: A Study in British Stalinism* (London, Lawrence & Wishart, 1993), pp. 47–8.
60. R. Martin, *Communism and British Trade Unionism 1924–1933* (Oxford, Clarendon Press, 1969), pp. 37–8.
61. *Report of the National Minority Movement Conference*, 1924, p. 20.
62. *Ibid.*
63. Trades Union Congress, *Report*, 1927, p. 320.
64. Reynolds and Laybourn, *Labour Heartland*, p. 76.
65. N. Branson, *History of the Communist Party of Great Britain 1927–41* (London, Lawrence & Wishart, 1985), p. 14.

66. J. Callaghan, *Socialism in Britain* (Oxford, Basil Blackwell, 1990), p. 102.
67. *Workers' Bulletin*, 13 May 1926.
68. TUC General Council, *Report of Proceedings at a Special Conference of Trade Unions*, 20–1 January (London, TUC, 1927).
69. M. Jacques, 'Consequences of the General Strike', in J. Skelley (ed.), *The General Strike 1926* (London, Lawrence & Wishart, 1976), p. 375.
70. C. Wrigley (ed.), *A History of British Industrial Relations, Vol. II, 1914–1939* (Brighton, Harvester Press, 1987).
71. K. Morgan and R. Duncan, 'Loitering on the party line: The unpublished memoirs of J. T. Walton Newbold', *Labour History Review*, vol. 60, part 1, 1995, pp. 35–51. This article is based upon the surviving records and papers on Newbold which are to be found in the John Rylands University Library of Manchester.
72. *Workers' Weekly*, 12 September 1924; Morgan and Duncan, 'Loitering on the party line', p. 49.
73. Phil Piratin, the CPGB's only other MP, was returned for Mile End, London, at the 1945 general election but was defeated at the 1950 general election, when Gallacher also lost his parliamentary seat. Born 15 May 1907, Piratin rose to fame when he joined the CPGB following the Olympia Demonstration against fascism at which he was one of the protesters. He died 10 December 1995.
74. Callaghan, *Dutt*, chapter four. Callaghan particularly refers to J.T. Murphy's article, 'Socialism By Kind Permission', *Communist International*, 3, 2, 15 October 1926, p. 18; *Class against Class*, pp. 9, 14, 17.
75. Fishman, *British Communist Party and Trade Unions*, pp. 31–7.
76. *Ibid.*, p. 37.
77. Central Committee Minutes of the CPGB, 17 February 1933.
78. *Ibid.*, 18 February 1933.
79. *Ibid.*, 20 February 1933.
80. *Daily Worker*, 19 March 1933, quoting from *Pravda*, and further quoted in the Central Committee Minutes of the CPGB, 24 March 1933.
81. Central Committee Minutes of the CPGB, 9 March 1933.
82. Morgan, *Against Fascism and War*, p. 419.
83. Stevens, 'Trades Councils in the East Midlands', R. Stevens, ' "Disruptive element?": The influence of the Communist Party in Nottingham and District Trades Council, 1929–1951', *Labour History Review*, 58, 3 (1993), pp. 22–37.
84. Stevens, 'Trades Councils in the East Midlands', p. 93.
85. *Ibid.*, p. 100, quoting from the Nottingham Trades Council Minutes, 3 and 17 April 1935.
86. Stevens, 'Trades Councils in the East Midlands', pp. 415–16.
87. Fishman, *British Communist Party and the Trade Unions*, p. 154.
88. *Ibid.*, p. 154.
89. *Ibid.*, p. 4; *The Daily Worker*, 2 January 1937.
90. *Ibid.*, p. 154.
91. Francis Johnson Collection, ILP Archive, letter from F.J., which could be F. Johnson or Fred Jowett, dated 9 September 1919.
92. *Leeds Citizen*, 13 February 1920.
93. Glasier Papers (deposited in University of Liverpool Library), 1/1919/99; letter from Snowden to Glasier, 26 January 1919.
94. *Ibid.*, 1/1919/100; letter dated 28 January 1919.
95. *Ibid.*, 1/1920/95; letter dated 2 April 1920.
96. *Ibid.*, 1/1920/97; letter dated 2 April 1920.

97. *Bradford Pioneer*, 21 April 1922.
98. D. Marquand, *Ramsay MacDonald* (London, Cape, 1977), p. 277.
99. R.E. Dowse, *Left in the Centre* (1966); F. Brockway, *Inside the Left* (1943).
100. Joseph Melling, 'Work, culture and politics'; McLean, *The Legend of Red Clydeside*; Alan McKinlay, 'Doubtful wisdom and uncertain promise: strategy, ideology and organisation, 1918–22', in McKinlay and Morris (eds), *The ILP on the Clydeside*, pp. 123–53.
101. McKinlay, 'Doubtful wisdom', p. 140.
102. W. Knox, 'Ours is not an ordinary Parliamentary movement: 1922–1926', in McKinlay and Morris (eds), *The ILP on Clydeside*, pp. 154–76.
103. NEC Minutes of the Labour Party, Labour Party Archive, 23 May 1925: Joint Meeting of the NEC of the Labour Party and the NEC of the ILP.
104. A. Marwick, *Clifford Allen. The Open Conspirator* (Edinburgh and London, Oliver & Boyd, 1964), p. 102.
105. ILP, *The Living Wage* (London, ILP, 1926), p. 9.
106. *Bradford Pioneer*, 1 January 1926.
107. *Ibid.*
108. *Socialist Review*, March 1926.
109. *Bradford Pioneer*, 1 October 1926.
110. R.K. Middlemass, *The Clydesiders: A Left Wing Struggle for Parliamentary Power* (London, Hutchinson, 1965), p. 216.
111. *Leeds Citizen*, 29 June 1928.
112. Alan McKinlay and James J. Smyth, 'The end of "the agitator workman" 1926–1932', in McKinlay and Morris (eds), *The ILP on Clydeside*, p. 180.
113. W. Knox, *James Maxton* (Manchester, Manchester University Press, 1987), chapters 5 and 7.
114. K. Laybourn, ' "Suicide During a Fit of Insanity" or The Defence of Socialism? The secession of the Independent Labour Party from the Labour Party at the special conference at Bradford, July 1932', *The Bradford Antiquary*, Third Series, Number 5 (1991), pp. 41–53.
115. *Bradford Pioneer*, 9 October 1931.
116. *Ibid.*, 19 February 1932.
117. *Leeds Citizen*, 11 December 1931.
118. *Ibid.*, 29 January and 1 April 1932.
119. *Bradford Pioneer*, 29 July 1932.
120. *Ibid.*, 5 August 1932.
121. *Leeds Citizen*, 5 August 1932.
122. *Bradford Pioneer*, 26 August 1932.
123. McKinlay and Smyth, 'The end of the agitator', p. 98.
124. The statistics are drawn from the Derby Labour Party *Annual Reports*, 1932–37, and quoted in Stevens, 'Trades Councils in the East Midlands', p. 152.
125. Middlemass, *The Clydesiders*, chapter 12.
126. Marquand, *MacDonald*.
127. Knox, *Maxton*, p. 106.
128. Central Committee of CPGB, Minutes, 18 February 1933.
129. M. Newman, 'Democracy versus Dictatorship', *History Workshop* (Spring 1978).
130. Pimlott, *Labour and the Left in the 1930s*, p. 77.
131. J. Jupp, 'The Left in Britain 1931–41' (University of London, unpublished MSc dissertation, 1956), p. 182.
132. J. Wood, 'The Labour Left and the Constituency Labour parties 1931–1951' (University of Warwick, unpublished PhD thesis, 1982), p. 67.

133. *Tribune*, 21 May 1937.
134. Callaghan, *Socialism in Britain*, p. 134; Pimlott, *Labour and the Left in the 1930s*, chapter 16.
135. A. Zwerdling, *Orwell and the Left* (London, Yale University Press, 1974), pp. 76–9.

CHAPTER 5

1. 'The 'Lost Sheep Files', Labour Party Archives, General Secretary's Papers, Box 4; Communist Party CS/COM/HR series and GS/COM/36ii.
2. K. Feiling, *The Life of Neville Chamberlain* (London, Macmillan, 1946), p. 414.
3. Callaghan, *Socialism in Britain*, p. 198.
4. Morgan, *Pollitt*, pp. 107–16.
5. Branson, *Communist Party of Great Britain, 1927–41*, pp. 270–3; Morgan, *Against Fascism and War*, pp. 92–5.
6. Fishman, *British Communist Party and the Trade Unions*, p. 251.
7. *Ibid.*, p. 259.
8. *Ibid.*, p. 261.
9. *Ibid.*, pp. 261–9.
10. *Ibid.*, pp. 271–2.
11. Callaghan, *Socialism in Britain*, p. 182.
12. V. Gollancz, *Russia and Ourselves* (London, Gollancz, 1941), p. 97.
13. J. Strachey, 'The Communist party line now', *Left News*, July 1940.
14. Callaghan, *Socialism in Britain*, p. 194.
15. J. Jones, *The Russia Complex* (Manchester, Manchester University Press, 1977), p. 35.
16. Fishman, *British Communist Party and the Trade Unions*, p. 345.
17. Morgan, *Pollitt*, p. 131, quoting M/TC 8/5.
18. J. Campbell, *Nye Bevan and the Mirage of British Socialism* (London, Weidenfeld & Nicolson, 1987), pp. 106–7.
19. D.N. Pritt Papers, British Library of Political and Economic Science, 1/3, diary date 15 March 1942.
20. *Ibid.*, diary 17 February 1942.
21. *Ibid.*, diary 15 January 1942.
22. *Ibid.*, diary 29 November 1941.
23. Fishman, *British Communist Party and the Trade Unions*, pp. 294–5.
24. *Ibid.*, p. 296.
25. *Ibid.*, pp. 310–11.
26. H.J. Laski, 'The Party and the Future', 4 April 1942, Laski Papers, Labour Party Archives, Princess Street, Manchester.
27. *Labour Party Conference Report*, 1943.
28. *Tribune*, 7 April 1944.
29. Labour Party Archives, General Secretary's Papers, Box 4, Communist Party, GS/COM/HR. There were other similar resolutions from the Melton Mowbray Labour Party, GS/Com/45, the Cirencester & Tewkesbury DLP, GS/Com/54 and many others, all of which received replies from Morgan Phillips.
30. *Ibid.*, GS/Com/36ii.
31. *Forward*, 10 May 1947.
32. Morgan, *Pollitt*, p. 155, quoting from the CPGB archive, Points for report to Executive Committee; 11.10.47 (HP); report to CP EC 13.12.47.
33. Callaghan, *Dutt*, p. 231, quoting from the *Observer*, 17 October 1948.

34. Schneer, *Labour's Conscience*.
35. R.M. Titmuss, *Problems of Social Policy* (London, HMSO, Longman Green, 1951), p. 508.
36. P. Addison, *The Road to 1945: British Politics and the Second World War* (London, Jonathan Cape, 1975), p. 118.
37. *Ibid.*, p. 271.
38. A. Calder, *The People's War* (London, Jonathan Cape, 1965); H. Pelling, *Britain and the Second World War* (London, Fontana, 1970); A. Marwick, *Britain in the Century of Total War* (London, Bodley Head, 1965); Miliband, *Parliamentary Socialism*; H.L. Smith (ed.), *War and Social Change: British Society and the Second World War* (Manchester, Manchester University Press, 1986).
39. C. Barnett, *The Audit of War: The Illusion and Reality of Britain as a Great Nation* (London, Macmillan, 1986); M. Beloff, *Wars and Welfare* (London, Edward Arnold, 1982).
40. Addison, *The Road to 1945*, p. 126.
41. Miliband, *Parliamentary Socialism*, p. 274.
42. G.D.H. Cole, *A History of the Labour Party since 1914* (London, Allen & Unwin, 1948), p. 380.
43. Labour Party, Policy Committee Minutes, 23 May 1941.
44. *Social Insurance and Allied Services*, report by Sir William Beveridge (London, HMSO, 1942); J. Harris, 'Some Aspects of Social Policy in Britain during the Second World War', in W.J. Mommsen (ed.), *The Emergence of the Welfare State in Britain and Germany* (London, Croom Helm, 1981).
45. K. Harris, *Attlee* (London, Weidenfeld & Nicolson, 1982).
46. Harris, *Attlee*, p. 220.
47. *Ibid.*, p. 223.
48. *Ibid.*, pp. 227–30.
49. *Ibid.*, p. 231.
50. H. Dalton, *The Second World War Diary of Hugh Dalton 1940–45* (ed.) B. Pimlott (London, Jonathan Cape, 1986), pp. 455, 538, 564.
51. Hinton, *Labour and Socialism*, p. 170.
52. This statement was made at a Labour rally in Staffordshire on 25 September 1949, *The Times*, 26 September 1949.
53. Cab. 124, file 1188, letter dated 11 March 1950.
54. Miliband, *Parliamentary Socialism*, p. 288.
55. Hinton, *Labour and Socialism*, pp. 171–2; Howell, *British Social Democracy*, chapter 5.
56. Morgan, *Labour in Power*, p. 503.
57. D.K. Fieldhouse, 'The Labour Government and the Empire-Commonwealth 1945–51', in R. Ovendale (ed.), *The Foreign Policy of the British Labour Governments 1945–51* (Leicester, Leicester University Press, 1984), p. 88.
58. Callaghan, *Socialism in Britain*, pp. 158–66.
59. H. Gaitskell, *The Diary of Hugh Gaitskell* (ed.) P.M. Williams (London, Jonathan Cape, 1983), p. 15.
60. *Ibid.*, p. 14.
61. A. Cairncross, *Years of Recovery: British Economic Recovery: British Economic Policy 1945–51* (London, Methuen, 1985).
62. *Ibid.*, p. 90.
63. Morgan, *Labour in Power, 1945–51*, pp. 3–4.
64. Shaw, *Discipline and Discord*, p. 30.
65. Keep Left Group Minutes, 28 July 1949 to 27 February 1951, to be found in the

Jo Richardson Papers at the Labour Party Archives, Manchester, and scattered throughout the Ian Mikardo Papers, also in the Labour Party Archives, Manchester.

66. *Tribune*, 20 May 1949.

67. The Mikardo papers, in a letter and notes file, contains a five-page petition, signed by Labour MPs who wished to see Britain, the USA and USSR meet together to consider anew 'the reduction and control of armaments'.

68. Shaw, *Discipline and Discord*, p. 31.

69. Labour Party Archives, The General Secretary's Papers, 1945–64, Box 4, 'Lost Sheep' file, GS/LS/10ii.

70. M.G. Foot, *Aneurin Bevan Vol. 1 1897–1945* (London, MacGibbon & Kee, 1962, Paladin edn, 1982) p. 301.

71. *Tribune*, 1 and 8 May 1942.

72. *Hansard*, vol. 395, cols. 1615–27, 15 December 1943.

73. Schneer, *Labour's Conscience*, p. 58.

74. Copies of the letter are to be found in the Benn Levy papers, file 57 in the House of Lords Record Office, and quoted in Schneer, *Labour's Conscience*, pp. 56–7.

75. R.H.S. Crossman, M. Foot and I. Mikardo, *Keep Left* (London, New Statesman, 1947), pp. 38, 40–1. There is a copy in the Ian Mikardo Papers (partly merged with the Jo Richardson Papers) at the Labour Party Archives, 103 Princess Street, Manchester.

76. *Ibid.*, p. 40.

77. *Ibid.*, pp. 76–7.

78. Ian Mikardo Papers and Correspondence, Group Paper 75, 'Report on talk with Pandit Nehru, 20 September 1950', written by Fenner Brockway, 22 January 1951.

79. *Daily Herald*, 8 August 1947.

80. *Ibid.*, 13, 22, 29 August and 5, 12 September 1947; cuttings from Michael Foot Papers, P 3.

81. S. Fielding, P. Thompson and N. Tiratsoo, *England Arise: The Labour Party and Politics in the 1940s* (Manchester, Manchester University Press, 1995).

82. *Tribune*, 20 May 1949.

83. Jo Richardson Papers, Labour Party Archives at Manchester, Keep Left Group Minutes. The first meeting, erroneously put down as in 1948, called a meeting for 27 July 1949, which was held and inaugurated other meetings on a regular basis.

84. *Ibid.*, minute 21, 7 September 1949.

85. *Ibid.*, 31 August 1949.

86. *Ibid.*, 7 September 1949.

87. Jo Richardson Papers, Keep Left Minutes, 11 July 1950.

88. *Ibid.*, 18 July 1950, item 208.

89. *Ibid.*, 18 July, 28 November, 5 December 1950 and 31 January 1951.

90. Schneer, *Labour's Conscience*, pp. 196–8.

91. Mikardo Correspondence, letter from Swingler to Mikardo dated 4 September 1949.

92. *Ibid.*, letter (no name and details) dated 9 February 1949.

93. Jo Richardson Papers, Keep Left Minutes, 8 March 1950.

94. *Ibid.*, 6 & 7 October 1950 refer to the idea (item/res. 225) that several Brains Trusts should be held each year. The meeting of 31 October 1950 listed several such meetings. The Mikardo Correspondence is full of organisational material connected with these meetings.

95. R.H.S. Crossman, *Backbench Diaries* (London, Hamish Hamilton and Jonathan Cape, 1981), p. 196; Shaw, *Discipline and Discord*, p. 37.

96. Jo Richardson Papers, Keep Left Minutes, 14 June 1950.

97. Thomas Balogh, 'Draft Policy Statement', Group Paper 2; R.H.S. Crossman, 'Buscot Conference, session 2', Group Paper 19; R. Acland, 'Internal Policy for Living without Dollar Aid', Group Paper 21; F. Brockway, 'Copy of Article for Labour's *Northern Voice*', Group Paper 23; 'Draft Conference Resolutions', Group Paper 31; B. Castle, 'Who Was Right?', Group Paper 41; R.H.S. Crossman, 'Note on back History of German Rearmament', Group Paper 42.

98. Schneer, *Labour's Conscience*, pp. 97–9.

99. Look at Group Papers 19 and Group Paper 21.

100. Jo Richardson, Keep Left Minutes, 29 September 1949 and 1 March 1950.

101. *Ibid.*, 14 March 1950.

102. *Ibid.*, 19 January 1951 and 30 October 1951.

103. Mikardo Correspondence, letter from Donald Bruce to I. Mikardo, 22 April 1951.

104. *Ibid.*, 26 April 1951 records the presence of Bevan, Freeman and Wilson among the fifteen members present.

105. Mikardo Correspondence contains an undated listing of forty-seven names plus Lord Faringdon, Lord Silkin, Tom Balogh and Dudley Sears.

106. Mikardo Correspondence, Group Paper 14, 'Plan for Mutual Aid'. The Jo Richardson Papers also include a map of the distribution and majority of the seats of the Keep Left Group members.

107. 'Memorandum', a circular in the Jo Richardson Papers.

108. Schneer, *Labour's Conscience*, chapter 7 on 'The Labour Left and the Constituencies' and p. 188.

109. 'Memorandum'.

110. Jo Richardson and Ian Mikardo Papers, for 1952, contain the five-page petition of the MPs.

111. The General Secretary's Papers (Morgan Phillips), Box 4, 'Lost Sheep Files', GS/LS/49 to GS/LS/72 contain the accusations levelled against Bevan and the minutes of meetings.

112. Schneer, *Labour's Conscience*, chapter 5.

113. *Ibid.*, p. 105.

114. Christ Church College Library, Tom Driberg papers, L/2, Zilliacus to Driberg, 8 March 1948, refer to a meeting of some of the 'hard' Left at the Wimbledon flat of Tom Braddock in February 1948. This is also referred to in Schneer, *Labour's Conscience*, p. 108.

115. *Daily Herald*, 20 March 1946; Liaison Committee minutes, 2 May 1946; Schneer, *Labour's Conscience*, p. 106.

116. Labour Party, NEC minutes, vol. 95, p. 248, 13 April 1948.

117. Labour Party, *Annual Report, 1949* (London, Labour Party, 1949), pp. 119–26.

118. Mikardo Correspondence, 1949, contains a letter from Zilliacus to Mikardo on 28 August 1951 about going before the NEC on 26 September 1951. This file also contains a letter from Zilliacus to R. Jones, Acting Secretary of the Marylebone Labour Party, noting that between 1919 and 1949 he never belonged to any other party than Labour, and stressing that he was not the only critic of Labour's foreign policy.

119. I. Mikardo, *Ian Mikardo: Back Bencher* (London, Weidenfeld & Nicolson, 1988), pp. 118–19.

120. Shaw, *Discipline and Discord*, p. 30.

CONCLUSION

1. Howell, *British Social Democracy*, p. 176.
2. *Ibid.*, p. 301.
3. Fishman, *British Communist Party and the Trade Unions*.
4. Minkin, *Contentious Alliance*.

BIBLIOGRAPHICAL ESSAY

All the sources used in the preparation of this book, both primary and secondary, are referred to in the chapter notes. The principal purpose of this section is to indicate the main books, articles and, in some cases, document collections that are readily accessible and which might be consulted profitably on the various aspects of the history of British socialism. It is by no means exhaustive and represents less than the tip of the iceberg of what is readily available to readers. For books, only the place and date of publication have been given.

Of the broad-ranging books on British socialism, many are written from a more left-wing perspective than this one. R. Miliband's *Parliamentary Socialism* (London, 1961) is a critique of the Labour Party's failures. J. Hinton, *Labour and Socialism: A History of the British Labour Movement 1867–1974* (Brighton, 1983), is similarly dismissive of the policies and actions of the Labour Party. On the other hand both J.E. Cronin, *Labour and Society, 1918–1979* (London, 1984), and R. Price, *Labour in British Society* (London, 1986), are far more positive towards the Labour Party and suggest that Labour needs to be more in tune with the political demands of the modern age. One might also consult G.D.H. Cole's *History of the Labour Party from 1914* (London, 1948). For a more wide-ranging book, which places more emphasis upon the Marxist tradition, one should consult J. Callaghan, *Socialism in Britain* (Oxford, 1990). In addition, the best studies on socialist thought are M. Beer, *History of British Socialism* (London, 1929), and G. Foote, *The Labour Party's Political Thought* (London, 1985). For an eminently readable and concise study of British labour movements J. Saville, *The Labour Movement in Britain* (London, 1988), takes some beating. The Marxist and Trotskyist Left is dealt with in J. Callaghan, *The Far Left in British Politics* (Oxford, 1987) and, for a broad sweep of topics on British socialism, one should not forget to examine E.J. Hobsbawm's *Labouring Men* (London, 1964). The whole relationship between class and British political developments in the nineteenth century has, however, been called into question in a collection of essays edited by E. Biagini and A.J. Reid, entitled *Currents of Radicalism: Radicalism, Organised Labour and Party Politics in Britain, 1850–1914* (Cambridge, 1991). The defining theme of this volume has been the attempt to establish a common link between radicalism, Chartism, Gladstonian Liberalism and the rise of Labour. G. Stedman Jones, *Language of Class, Studies in English Working Class History 1832–1982* (Cambridge, 1983), and P. Joyce, *Vision of the People: Industrial England and the Question of Class 1848–1914* (Cambridge, 1991), also challenge traditional notions of class.

There are also many useful biographical studies available, most obviously, J. Callaghan, *Rajani Palme Dutt: A Study in British Stalinism* (London, 1993); B. Pimlott, *Harold Wilson* (London, 1992); K. Morgan, *Harry Pollitt* (Manchester, 1993); K. Laybourn, *Philip Snowden: a biography* (Aldershot, 1988); W. Knox, *James Maxton* (Manchester, 1987); J. Campbell, *Nye Bevan and the Mirage of British Socialism* (London, 1987); B. Pimlott, *Hugh Dalton* (London, 1985); M. Foot, *Aneurin Bevan, Vol. 1 1897–1945* (London, 1982 edn); M. Foot, *Aneurin Bevan, Vol. 2, 1945–1960* (London, 1982 edn); K. Harris, *Attlee* (London, 1982); D. Marquand, *Ramsay MacDonald* (London, 1977); B. Donoghue and G.W. Jones, *Herbert Morrison* (London, 1973); and A. Bullock, *The Life and Times of Ernest Bevin: Trade Union Leader* (London, 1960). P. Weiler, *Ernest Bevin* (Manchester, 1994), offers a less detailed update on Bevin's role. One should also study C. Wrigley, *Arthur Henderson* (Cardiff, 1990), for a trade union-based approach to one of the architects of the early Labour Party.

The Social Democratic Federation has not attracted much analytical literature until recently. C. Tsuzuki, *H. M. Hyndman and British Socialism* (Oxford, 1961), is a very narrative study which makes no real attempt to analyse the role and place of Marxism in Britain. However, it is more than compensated by S. Pierson, *Marxism and the Origins of British Socialism* (Cornell, 1973), and by M. Crick, *The History of the Social Democratic Federation* (Keele, 1994). M. Bevir has also produced two excellent studies on Hyndman and his thought in 'H. M. Hyndman: A Rereading and a Reassessment', *History of Political Thought*, XII, 1 (Spring 1991) and 'The British Social Democratic Federation 1880–1885', *International Review of Social History*, XXXVII (1992). Although it is now challenged because of its representation of a dominating and inflexible Hyndman, one should not ignore the article by H. Collins entitled 'The Marxism of the Social Democratic Federation', in A. Briggs and J. Saville (eds), *Essays in Labour History, 1886–1923* (London, 1971).

As a subsidiary to this topic there has been considerable debate on the related question of why Britain never saw the creation of an effective, or representative, Socialist Unity party. Apart from some of the more general books on the SDF, the ILP and the Socialist League the four main articles on this subject are M. Crick's ' "A Call to Arms": the Struggle for Socialist Unity in Britain, 1883–1914', in D. James, T. Jowitt and K. Laybourn (eds), *The Centennial History of the Independent Labour Party* (Halifax, 1992); K. Laybourn, 'The failure of Socialist Unity in Britain c 1893–1914', *Transactions of the Royal Historical Society* (Sixth Series, 4, 1994); K. Laybourn, 'A Story of Buried Talents and Wasted Opportunities: The Failure of the Socialist Unity Movement in Yorkshire 1911–1949', *The Journal of Regional and Local Studies*, 7, 2 (1987) and D. Morris, 'The Origins of the British Socialist Party', *Bulletin of the North-West Labour History Society*, 8 (1982–3).

The Communist Party of Great Britain is well served. N. Branson, *History of the Communist Party of Great Britain 1927–1941* (London, 1985) provides an excellent if narrow examination of its history. In addition one can usefully consult W. Kendall, *Revolutionary Movements 1900–1921* (London, 1969), S. Macintyre, *A Proletarian Science: Marxism in Britain 1917–1937* (Cambridge, 1980), and S. Macintyre, *Little Moscows* (London, 1980). L.J. Macfarlane, *The British Communist Party: Its Origins and Development until 1929* (London, 1966), offers a rather administrative approach to the study of the CPGB. On the communists and trade unions R. Martin, *Communism and the British Trade Unions 1924–1933* (Oxford, 1969), examines the rise and fall of the National Minority Movement and N. Fishman, *The British Communist Party and the Trade Unions* (London, 1995), takes the issue further and suggests that there was little that divided Communists and Labour by the late 1930s.

Indeed, she argues that the Communist Party was increasingly successful between 1933 and 1945 because it followed the Harry Pollitt and Jimmy Campbell approach of playing down the rank-and-file interests in favour of those of the official trade union movement. K. Morgan, *Against Fascism and War: Rupture and Constitution in British Communist Politics, 1935–1941* (Manchester, 1989), focuses upon the CPGB's attack upon fascism and the difficulties that the Russian–German pact of August 1939 created for the party, especially in the light of the fact that there appears to have been broad support for the new Comintern-inspired anti-war line. For a more wide-ranging study of the factors that made Marxism a failure, based upon the nature and structure of British society, R. McKibbin, 'Why was there no Marxism in Britain', *English Historical Review* (1984), is a valuable, innovative and decidedly non-Marxist study. Also for a critical study on the formation of the CPGB one should look at R.C. Challinor, *The Origin of British Bolshevism* (London, 1977).

The Socialist League and William Morris are well provided for through E.P. Thompson's *William Morris: Romantic to Revolutionary* (London, 1977) and F. MacCarthy, *William Morris: A Life of Our Time* (London, 1994). There must also be upwards of another one hundred books dealing with Morris, most of them worth dipping into although R.P. Arnot's reprint of a book he first wrote in the 1930s, *William Morris: the man and the myth* (London, 1964), should be examined if only because of the way in which he knocked down the idea that Morris's socialism was an aberration. S. Yeo, 'A New Life: The Religion of Socialism in Britain 1883–96', *History Workshop Journal*, no. 4 (1977), also provides an excellent, and controversial, study of the impact of William Morris's commitment to 'making socialists'. The Fabians are similarly well provided for, not least because many of them were writers, and the more than useful M. Cole, *The Story of Fabian Socialism* (London, 1963) comes with the partisan label. *Fabian Essays in Socialism* (London, 1889), which has been reprinted many times, and A.M. McBriar, *Fabian Socialism and English Politics* (London, 1966), are worth a read simply because they indicate the diversity of the Fabians' early views and their variable impact. The link between the middle classes and socialism is further evidenced in a collection of essays edited by C. Levy entitled *Socialism and the Intelligensia* (London, 1987).

The history of the Independent Labour Party has produced an even more voluminous literature. H. Pelling, *The Origins of the Labour Party* (London, 1954) is an excellent starter. E.P. Thompson, 'Homage to Tom Maguire', in A. Briggs and J. Saville (eds), *Essays in Labour History* (London, 1960), was a seminal article emphasising that the ILP was the first major socialist society to emerge outside London and in the provinces. Since then there have been numerous books and articles on the subject. D. Howell, *British Workers and the Independent Labour Party 1888–1906* (Manchester, 1983), must take pride of place but the following are also very useful: D. Clark, *Colne Valley: Radicalism to Socialism* (London, 1981); K. Laybourn and J. Reynolds, *Liberalism and the Rise of Labour 1890–1918* (London, 1984); B. Lancaster, *Radicalism, Cooperation and Socialism: Leicester working-class politics 1860–1906* (Leicester, 1987); K. Laybourn and D. James (eds), *The Rising Sun of Socialism* (Wakefield, 1991); Alan McKinley and R.J. Morris, *The ILP on Clydeside 1893–1932: from foundation to disintegration* (Manchester, 1991); and D. James, T. Jowitt and K. Laybourn (eds), *The Centennial History of the Independent Labour Party* (Halifax, 1992). Also, despite its title, L. Smith, *Religion and the Rise of Labour* (Keele, 1993) provides a detailed local study of the links between the ILP and the nonconformist denominations. For the interwar years it is also worth examining F. Brockway, *Inside the Left* (London, 1942), R.K. Middlemass, *The Clydesiders* (London, 1965) and R.E. Dowse, *Left in the Centre* (London, 1966), all of which offer the nearest thing to a study of the ILP for this period.

The Labour Party has been the subject of hundreds, if not thousands, of articles and books. Among the most useful are D. Howell, *British Social Democracy* (London, 1976); R. McKibbin, *The Evolution of the Labour Party 1910–1924* (Oxford, 1974); K. Laybourn, *The Rise of Labour* (London, 1988); B. Pimlott, *Labour and the Left in the 1930s* (Cambridge, 1977); K.O. Morgan, *Labour in Power, 1945–51* (Oxford, 1984); and R. Eatwell, *The 1945–1951 Labour Governments* (London, 1979). Some of these books focus upon the Labour Party and the trade union movement but L. Minkin, *The Contentious Alliance* (Edinburgh, 1991) is the monumental work on the history of trade union and Labour Party relations in the twentieth century. Some of the above-mentioned books also provide a corrective to the communist-inclined Labour MP, D.N. Pritt's study *The Labour Government 1945–51* (London, 1963). One should not ignore P. Addison's *The Road to 1945: British Politics and the Second World War* (London, 1975), which provides an excellent study of the context out of which the post-war Attlee Labour governments emerged. J.M. Winter, *Socialism and the Challenge of War: Ideas and Politics in Britain, 1912–1918* (London, 1974) also concentrates upon the issue of war and the way in which the Labour Party came to accept Clause Four in 1918. On this particular issue R. Harrison, 'The War Emergency Workers' National Committee 1914–1920', in A. Briggs and J. Saville (eds), *Essays in Labour History* (London, 1971), is essential reading. K.D. Brown (ed.), *The First Labour Party 1906–1914* (London, 1986) is a more than useful collection of essays half of which disagree with the editor's assumption that the Labour Party had not made a political breakthrough before 1914. D. Tanner's *Political Change and the Labour Party* (Cambridge, 1990) agrees with Brown but has been subject to much detailed criticism.

Women played an important part in the development of British socialism. This is testified to in J. Hannam, *Isabella Ford, 1855–1924* (Oxford, 1989), J. Hannam, 'Women and the ILP, 1890–1914', in D. James, T. Jowitt and K. Laybourn (eds), *The Centennial History of the Independent Labour Party* (Keele, 1992), C. Colette, *For Labour and For Women* (Manchester, 1989), J. Liddington and J. Norris, *One Hand Tied behind Us* (London, 1984) and in S. Holton, *Feminism and Democracy* (Cambridge, 1988). One of the most useful and recent additions to this list is P. Graves, *Labour Women: Women in British Working-class Politics 1918–1932* (Cambridge, 1994), which maintains that issues that particularly concerned women, such as birth control and family allowances, were at the front of Labour politics in the 1920s but became lost in the quest for political unity and revival in the 1930s.

The Labour Left, and its failures, have occupied the minds of many writers. The most impressive work in this direction has been produced by B. Pimlott in his book *Labour and the Left in the 1930s* (London, 1977). D. Blaazer, *The Popular Front and the Progressive Tradition: Socialists, Liberals, and the Quest for Unity 1884–1939* (Cambridge, 1991), also reflects upon the role of the Labour Left, the Socialist League and other socialist groups and attempts to fit them into the progressive tradition of a popular front. T. Buchanan, *The Spanish Civil War and the British Labour Movement* (Cambridge, 1991), also reflects upon the fragmentation and failure of the Labour Left, and the Left more generally, when confronted by the problem of what action to take over the Spanish Civil War. J. Schneer's *Labour's Conscience: The Labour Left 1945–51* (London, 1988) is very good on the limited impact of the 'hard' and 'soft' Labour Left in the late 1940s although there is now more primary material, which appears for the first time in this book, to supplement his discussion of the Keep Left Group. Although it is technically outside the period, E. Shaw, *Discipline and Discord in the Labour Party* (Manchester, 1988), provides a more up-to-date study of the challenge of the Labour Left through a study of the Bevanites and the study of dissension in Liverpool, Nottingham and other areas.

Finally, and obviously, in a study as broad as this there are literally thousands of original pamphlets, documents and books that could be studied – some of them accessible but many not. A. Bevan, *In Place of Fear* was produced in 1952 and reissued in London in 1978. The following document collections on William Morris are also valuable: M. Morris (ed.), *William Morris: Artist, Writer and Socialist* (Oxford, 1936); A.L. Morton (ed.), *Political Writings of William Morris* (London, 1976); F. Boos (ed.), 'William Morris's Socialist Diary', *History Workshop Journal*, 13 (1982) and F. Boos (ed.), *William Morris's Socialist Diary* (London, 1985). H. Gaitskell, *The Diary of Hugh Gaitskell*, edited by P.M. Williams (London, 1983) and H. Dalton, *The Second World War Diary of Hugh Dalton, 1940–45*, edited by B. Pimlott (London, 1986) deal with two of the most prominent Labour leaders of the 1930s and '40s. K. Laybourn, *The Labour Party 1881–1951: A Reader in History* (Gloucester, 1988), also offers a useful set of documents upon which to draw, although it is strictly confined to the Labour Party. There are also some extensive collections of documents on British socialist thought in H. Pelling, *The Challenge of Socialism* (London, 1954) and A. Wright, *British Socialism* (London, 1983).

INDEX